LOST

IN

TIME

POEMS

George Arthur Brennan

Order this book online at www.trafford.com
or email orders@trafford.com

Most Trafford titles are also available at major online book retailers.

Cover Design and picture illustration by
    Carol Lou Gibson

Edited by
    Jane Smith

Print information available on the last page.

ISBN: 978-1-4907-7711-5 (sc)
ISBN: 978-1-4907-7712-2 (e)

Library of Congress Control Number: 2016915380

Trafford rev.   10/07/2016

Trafford.
PUBLISHING®   www.trafford.com
North America & international
toll-free: 1 888 232 4444 (USA & Canada)
fax: 812 355 4082

Old One Room

School House

Picture

Here Illustration

By

Carol Lou Gibson

The books cover is of the old one room
schoolhouse where my brothers and sisters and I
went to get our education.

Being a long ago place with a hand pump for
any water supply for washing or drinking.

Beside the school was an old woodshed where
each student took turns in carrying wood to the
furnace, keeping everyone warm during the long
cold winter months.

An old oak tree, just behind the woodpile, had
names carved into it of who loved who framed
by a heart.

By Carol Brennan Gibson

Self Judgment Challenges

When love has no trust to explore, you must recline
Those ones that judge men, there's too many characters
Have been through the realms of kin folk, some rude
If my true compassion has a bad effect, that's fine
Those regrets are inscribed for a long ago place
If this man were to write history, it's not so divine
There was excess dimmed by the effect always
An all life wish to change opportunities in my space.

A rueful mystery whence made a claim for peace
Long after still comes that whisper of remembrance
Once again have been irked by kin with no effect
Will always be loyal to good friends others will cease
One thing for sure there's no need to ponder over disgrace
Well it's like men to boys, men are all grown up people
Life is like a bump in the road, once you get over it, it's smooth
Nonsense rings true when you said do not come to my place.

The old fashion saying "try my way or there's the highway"
There's a big sun shining out here, it's for both of us.
You can be an augur all day long, that's not including me
Kiss my ass I'm Irish, can sing this song every day
Shall never have personified means ever to be there jerk again
Nothing can sway my tolerance or treat me bad as before
I'm not really a bad guy there's just some bad people out there
Any matter at hand my goodness of heart will reign

INTRODUCTION

The poems in this book are based on episodes that I have actually experienced during my life. There are days of events in different parts of a year that are entirely different in every way. Many times I have sat pondering over old times wondering how one ever got through unscathed in every episode. Most of my relatives derived from the farming lot, knowing what hard times were, which made better people down through generation to generation with some regrets along the way, leaving this forever lost. So many grandchildren and great grandchildren making a whole wonderful family, sometimes whooping it up or just merely spending time together as much as possible, depending, sometimes not so lucky to do so. Knowing right well all our young one's are precious as can be, to be always welcome, always just give us a call then have them come right on over encouraging our love ones to stay for some time, sharing good times. Wanting to be around as long as possible for their sakes, sharing every happy moment for some beautiful fulfilled episodes to come, we are not meant to be here forever. Having put up with the odd bad neighbor knowing they have nothing to gain by being awful just spitting themselves with very little to gain but more to lose by not being part of decent people that have only love in their hearts. Todays youths are in the world having radical change unaware of our past hardships that had made this day of the utmost, having no back breaking labour to content with, a computer answers everything from A to Z sitting down letting their fingers do the walking. By chance there will be more corrupt people in modern times that can crate trouble because of drugs causing of dramatic change to rue this world of wonder. No one in this young generation will be able to understand them old times that sponsored hard work havens to sweat from the brow, now lost forever.

FOREWARD

The three hundred poems contained in this book tells about people, places and events from generation to generation caught up in a mode for a fast changing world.

Looking back to yesterday's world we were almost prehistoric, using a team of horses to work the land, using a mule-board one furrow plow to turn the land over, then cultivate it to plan seeds. A lot of hard back breaking work from sun up to sun set, never seeming to end. Soon came the model T Ford car that had to be started with a crank below the car's radiator. When the car started it was very noisy, putting down an old gravel road, kicking up clouds of dust across the fields.

Our phone system was called a "party line" where you had to wait for your neighbor to finish their conversation before you could use the phone which sometimes took an hour. The hand pump beside the porch was our only source of drinking water, a galvanized pail hung on the pump spout while each stroke of the pump handle finally filled the pail. My father's next car was a Plymouth that had a battery with a starter to start up the car's engine which was so much better, especially in the winter. Nothing was ever very nice with only modesties between hardship, which ruled our everyday lives where accentually were in short supply being the war years with all it's rations.

A belt or stick made us tow the line from day to day, follow the rules or else get what's coming to you, leaving marks from the lickings. If someone was given a skeleton key to enter this long ago house, as you stepped inside a stale smell from the every day smoke of scent of a wood burning cook stove lingered throughout the kitchen, never really going away. Being there forever.

Seems every year we would reemerge doing the same thing as we'd done the year before, with the belief in what we were doing was the only way, just filling the void of every days work into the problematic future. Part of me thought working hard is genuine but there must be a better way out of this doubt and discontent that would make life more worth while.

Each poem stresses moments of escape as a disciple of discovery by contributing to methods of discovery in the world beyond the old business of living in poverty.

Although reality was a long way off in those times hope brought me change for a better life. However the old times of barefoot in summer and shoes in the winter is a special mention to those hard years of the poor people times. Of a real experience one never forgets. My boyhood years had one inspiration because of no achievements what so ever, only difficulties overshadowed by complex problems created through being poor, barely getting by.

Within the official image brought about by my poems, the one that stands out is me being the second oldest. Hand-me-downs from the older one is the clothes that I wore then to be handed down again until those clothes wore out.

The poems lost in time imply hard times, while stressing this imaginative life of the forties and fifties emphasizing the outlook with the surroundings of a frame house having a cinder laneway leading out to the main road of gravel of one mile between concession roads bordered by farmer's fields.

The morning walk to a one room school house three concession roads away consisting of three miles out in the middle of nowhere. These circumstances indeed have been told in poetic verse, that obvious enough has its numerable definitions of the old life situations with the pitfall things to contend with on very little money.

Part of my poetic thought is to share my instances having separate formats in an old folk way now lost in time it seems. These happenings in olden days where not of the ordinary kind, being full of pitfalls that are of the extreme within an urban living. A whole world full of experiences vital for a livelihood motivated by logic values of a poor quality of living that implies a lot of doubt as each day went by emphasized in poems for different years.

Perhaps some did not realize the suffering of other people less fortunate than them of yesterdays knot of no contentment as every week went by, told by a poems vital statistics many times throughout the book.

It is assumed that anyone sincere enough will understand whatever was the credence implied to each poem was modeled for each different era. The specials mentioned was the extremes of the times.

POET'S IMPLANTED MEMORIES

For example in my mind of this old clap board house, at the age of four years, in the evening smelly coal oil lamps flickering up and down cause different shades of light to travel up across the ceiling coated with layers of soot.

In this dim lit room you could here the flies moving to another, more dark, spot to sleep. Seems we could never get rid of the flies that managed to get through the screen door during the daylight hours, then in the morning waking hour they would land on your neck or arms bugging you for as long as you stayed in bed.

When I would come into the kitchen someone had sprayed the whole area to kill the flies before we ate breakfast. We were unable to eat until the spray smell was gone. Our breakfast consisted of a bowl of porridge with milk and brown sugar on it as well as two eggs on top of four slices of bacon. A very hearty breakfast for nine members of our family sitting around an old oaken table with a checkered table cloth.

After breakfast the cast iron stove had to stoked up with wood again after shaking the ashes out through the grates with an aftermath of dust floating across the kitchen, later collecting on every surface around.

My Sunday job after all was said and done was churning butter in a daisy churn over and over all day long so that the family would have enough butter for the week.

The old cook stove was very hot making the paint on the wall behind it to blister giving off a bad smell from the lead paint along with a scorched wood smell that lingered all winter long making my stomach queasy, seemingly it was better to stay out in the cold the put up with that awful air in the kitchen.

During the week days we walked three miles to school in the bitter cold over high drifts of snow along with howling winds some days arriving at a one room school in the middle of nowhere.

Nobody plowed the roads in them days, everyone got around by horse and cutter to go shopping for food or going to the doctor ten miles or so away.

Before the winter was over there was snow banks as high as high as the hydro poles, with buildings deep in snow having to dig your way out most of the winter.

When summer came it was either bring in hay for our cows or helping a neighbor bring his hay to feed the livestock through the next winter. All summer hauled wood piling it close to the house for to keep warm through the next long cold winter. There was also that chore of weeding a big garden all summer long. A real back-breaking job after school and on the weekends along with picking apples as well as fruits to can or store for the long cold days ahead faced with every year.

At chore time at night and in the morning the collie dog, Ted, would round up the cows for milking, he knew the exact time to fetch them to the barn every single day for as long as he lived.

Flies also pestered the cows, so there was a sprayer also full at the barn to spray every time before milking them. The night and morning milk was taken to the road in big cans for the Carnation milk factory.

It was hard work on the farm at Sparta, Ontario, but it was the only way to get by in them days.

INDEX

350.	Illingsworth Airoplane
351.	Underhills Hills
352.	Forever Crossed My Mind
353.	Pondering Times
355.	Some More Typified
356.	Took The Train
357.	Life's Evils
358.	Flabbergasted One
360.	Old Stick In The Muds
362.	United Churches Gone
363.	A Fud Time
364.	No Pride Episodes
365.	No One Prayed
366.	A Dill Pickle Crock
367.	Saturday Night Lilt
368.	Tin Lizzies
369.	Life's Folly
370.	Us Regular Folks
371.	Inspired Ecstasy
372.	Lewdness Persons
373.	A Cat Or Two
374.	An Amiable Father
375.	The Memorare Category
376.	Taunts In Life
377.	Beg Your Pardon
378.	Avid Parents
379.	Who Daddy Version
380.	Wild Onions
381.	The Bridge
382.	Wings Of Hope
383.	Without Felicity
384.	Folks Empathy Jest
385.	Puff Balls In Fall
386.	Many Respites
387.	A Seedy Reed
388.	Mature Modest Folks
389.	Wartime Food

WAITING FOR TOMORROW

Was a cloudless sky, sunshine all around
One less morning to go before summer arrives
Was a difference now with longer daylight
Warm winds sweeping across the open ground
Better days coming with growing of daylight
Hoping for wonderful happenings that will be
Looking forward to garden time again
Along with other great things of natures sight

Wanting twilight hours to hurry to another day
Most thought ready for tomorrow, much better
Every night streetlights tell it's time for bed
Asleep waiting for dawn to come my way
A hooting owl has said his peace once more
Did drift on into dreams to wake at last
Was now able to look at tomorrow it seems
Once again bright sun peered in my window
The sounds of night was heard then it past

Then comes the day's first knock on my door
Someone in such a short while, this day just began
Having heard the first steps in the hallway
These were friends of a divine day once more
Having found happiness with friends is meant to be
Everybody drops by to make this day complete
Another nighttime brings about a lonely room
All worth the living with loving the people you see

FADED PICTURES

Them times caught up in life we're aware
A wonder of it all we will sigh in ah
To recall black pictured images of old folks
Our thoughts leave faded foot steps there
Those mindful casts of away back then
Everyone now lost days hence gone forever
One's true love did pass on a very special day
These pictures in my mind, shall relive again

Most days with scenes in a wandering thought
A rave of men with fedora hats taken off in church
While most women wore the Eugenie hat style
Had seen this always in church, I never forgot
Was showing the holy respect to our almighty this way
Wore our Sunday best in the house of the Lord
Came a lonely bell sound off in the distance
Now Sunday ringing reminds me of yesterday

Came some reminding moments in a dream last night
A voice calling out upon winds of lost time
Them unanswered whiles as I searched my mind
Then a new day came to fade them from sight
Have kept old pictures with memories of love
Those lost times revived just once more
Our day will come to be lost with life
Comes the glory event of open doors up above

SOMEONE'S CULPRIT

In school stood up for brother's as well as my sisters
Then was punished by the teacher with a razor strap
No one ever is truthful, claiming to be innocent bystanders
To always stand up for my rights with the instigators
The ex wife's boyfriend tried to cut my head off one day
He had a javelin swinging it at me many times to cut me
To save my self kick him in the crotch four times or more
His head came forward, busted his nose, then he ran away

The ex wife called the police to have me charged with assault
Nobody heard my side of the story, which was the truth
All I was doing was trying to save my life any way one could
Her along with the boyfriend cooked up lies that it was my fault
At the court case they charged me then went on probation
This boyfriend had serious concession on the critical list
As for me they sent me to Napanee prison for four months
What her and him said was a two way liars bad combination

Here as a young boy a mother was beating on me every day
From childhood on up was always the culprit no peace of mind
One night company came in winter to stay over night
The blankets were all given to these people, I had nothing to
say
When the fire went out this boy pees on the Morris chair a lot
In the morning because of this accident was beat with one
cordwood
If my father had not been there our mom would beat me to
death
For being the person she called a culprit this is what I got

Had devoted my time to helping others the thank part never came
Here in these people's world being deceitful was the role they knew
Never truthful using their charm to manipulate these people
No matter who you helped the culprit part ended up the same
Here in a perplexed world of so and so's they lie their way
Always the people who cause the problem claim their innocence
So much conniving through the ignorance of an obnoxious world
Must we wait for an understanding that will come some day

WHO TO BELIEVE

Seems humble people become the commandeered one's
How strange is the world of wonder with its forbearers
Despite you integrity watch out for users of the world
Once betrayed, twice shy watch out for some more reruns
There is never sure hope to congratulate you forever
For the grace of boldness, do not confide ever, there's
intentions
A sincere heart is always used to manipulate your kindness
For who's sake do we grant some trust, my say always is never

In my hour of need no one comes around they are just to busy
Ever since Murphy's Law whatever it is there is no change
Being the narrator am trying to find decent people in the world
Forever there is nice pleasant people that are not really
trustworthy
My thoughts of only truth are for different yours of only lies
As for some people out there they are only obstacles in my way
With kindness all things can be found while choosing good
friends
The fibbers come in groups of thirteen not one soul ever denies

My anticipation is to rid the space of do-gooders when possible
Come to a pause for a little while to enjoy a days silence
Want deceit to be unfounded stricken from our everyday lives
Under oath is a crutch to hide the truth that is probable
Have found so many examples of humanity no straight shooters
The innocent are always taken because of their good humour
Looking after my affairs whole heartedly checking them twice
For a month of Fridays have had none of them household
snoopers

It's not what we do, it's how we present ourselves each day
Those that tell the truth are not always clearly understood
The truth is who ever is trusted with good advice always
For a life time have had a motor mouth with much to say
Must keep most things to your self was someone's advice
Do not let a lonely heart lead me astray, know what to do
Beware of wretches on the prowl with plans up their sleeves
Some people who want something that's why they are nice

CASTING LOVES SHADOW

Let's build our human fort where everybody can attend
Go the second mile for happiness it is well worth the time
Can we carry out with both word and deed make a pleasing
day
For sure designated friends names should be plausible to send
As a matter of fact whichever bonefide action works real good
When the starlight of justice is reveled claim who you are
With your mortal nature rendered do the very best you can
A delighting partner possessing trust we would help him all we
could

Just declare full truth then love for all will follow close behind
Our home ground with akin shall not be touched by malice foe
Use kindness it begins all good things in this great land
Been with gulosity it ruins the day, stop your dealing with this
kind
Some that are the most devoted should be presented the
honour roll
To fulfill tomorrow's needs must get in readiness tonight
Best to arbitrate them people that are most deserving an
award
There is justification indeed in the world for everyone all toll

Better to embrace gracious beings that fit and be tied by a fool
Them old fashion ways have to see as to what pleases who
One's love has purpose as well as grace to be your own contender
Hearts held in splendor are accomplishing good stature as a rule
Those pondering useless people do not amaze me, nothing gets done
According to hope it appears there might be gestures from some
The ambitions of life we are not eager to belong to charity
Some spongers humble themselves to share inhumanity stuff everyone

Many time have felt the compunction of an awful demise
The future turning into a whole lost world devastating one's heart
Was days when death occurred knowing for sure was an absolute thing
Have needed instructed days of helping just get a fellow through
How about please help me, considered merited that would be wise
Also sought eagerness as a helpful moment to clear a man's mind
Was no answers came from a silent room while a clock ticked away
Had looked outward into a lamp lite room wondering about tomorrow
Did initiated things that made a life, now there is not anything I find

RESENTFULLY TRUDGING ALONG

Had fixed everything firmly in my mind walk where I want to
Shall become to overwhelming to be recognized out there
Have set a stage to get peoples attention as never before
As for me do not believe in infinite kindness, leaving it up to you
Do not ask me any questions, have no answers of logic
anymore
It's called an ineludible time frame resisting all good times
Will wear a poppy for an everyday occasion to get attention
Need not show me any doctrines to be faithful what fore

Here's is a man's reputation, not as before, a disgrace to
honour
Want to be arrogant not capable of error, snooty as can be
With no desire for passion, cannot smile anymore be hectic
No one can demerit such a mood because it's my sad hour
Am lacking the necessary ability to be sane again
Good hospitality has gone out with the bath water, gone
forever
Better not to strive wholeheartedly best sleep half of the day
Need no offerings it will infuriate my temper to being mad

Have to become overwhelming to be recognized being upset
Walk with a scowl to animate an untrue face from the nurds
Not eloquent as things use to be, have a rotten mood to
declare
An old saying was just you wait and see this is what you get
Will not appease or conciliate sacrifices, here's a heart of stone
It's a preamble style with closed lips not even saying good day
Was resentfully trudging along a pathway avoiding who I am
No need for a feather in my cap, can do it all on my own

For these days it's an indescribable future for all concerned
There is no absolute value to people half of them are worthless
Had an unlimited mood being sarcastic as hell since morn
Can be like all the rest to not get along is a lesson learned
That parental alienation it was her who started bad vibes
They have treated me like they want to be treated now
Where has the love of folks gone when skullduggery comes around
It must be a family of discontent using lies along with bribes

LOVES DEFINITION

There is another day
Ever serene and fair
And here comes another sunshine
Then one more darkness comes there
Never mind sadness it fades away
Never mind the silent place
There is people for you that care

Here is a brighter place to find
Here among your chosen few
Being with friends some how betwixt
Hence for all this love we can bind
Among us amid splendor so true
Forever the affection holds worth
The sunshine can bring smiles anew

Be like a leaf in a stream did not return
The past is gone leaving behind tears
We have faith for tomorrow time
With conjunction of mind sometime a concern
Some days a fragile spirit in a silent place
These nighs parley causing a sad day
Was loves spirit again we come to face

AUTUMN BLISS

Here it seems a sleeping landscape has come to be
All the summer glory gone suddenly passing us by
That earthly trend of coloured leaves scattered everywhere
Has become a mode of a natures din place here to see
The bare silence now plodding life's so gracious earth
In the stillness many thoughts inspire each dawning day
Once again raveled leafy by ways awaiting winters onslaught
Must comprehend it's destiny with the aim of cold rath

The weather stands forth while waiting for winter to appear
Behold natures dues having frost embarking at morn
In the stark stillness all the leafed tree's bare again
There's the timely grace remaining not the same every year
During a lifetime such winter months are to well known
Many thoughts revived seeing floating leaves in the wind
So long ago captivated memories come back to haunt us
With all the leaves down it's like them past spirits blown

The unimagined place with summers shade now remote
For the onslaught of it all not like old time winter days
All shall proceed to a less creative phase of a lifetime
Our autumn goodbye by the songsters farewell note
Every window now frosted where the sun peeps at dawn
Soon howling wind sounds with snow covering the ground
No more preservation of calm for now till spring again
Now silent mornings most of the feathered one's gone

Without any robins each morning to greet one there
Here comes another onset to contend with as before
At winter does not wait for Christmas to come along
These sunsets are so gloomy with all of it's chilled air
Must conquer the day dawning without a sun once more
A voice calling from the north with a feeling so forlorn
Each dawn for the first of winter makes one less day
With all overcast days there must be something in store

DENFIELD DAYS

On over the crest of the village hill was our home
To travel from London here telephone poles for many miles
The entrance to the village was marked by a United Church
Here the railway tracks followed the road where rabbits did
roam
In memory have so many joyful moments to be told
Still remember those distant sounds of far off trains coming
Every roadway had wigwags for crossing the tracks always
At night a train light broke through the darkness of the village
On Sunday morning calling people to church the big bell
ringing

In winter sleigh bells ringing people traveling around
Here we were in the sleigh covered in blankets from the cold
Every roadway drifted in by snow squalls for the whole day
Our winters had forty feet of snow over the ground
Had a wonderful horse that was part of our family growing up
When Piccadilly, our horse, reach the drifts her hooves came
up high
To always remember them horses in their winter harness display
After stopping for a while would tell the horse to getty up

While the sun was downing on the horizon it was bitter cold
Here was the village of Denfield right in a snow belt
Being people of the times had to struggle in many ways
Was a challenged mission of the times the story has been told
Once in a while a reborn feeling reminiscing child times
For sure there is still good memories from good old days
Them days in winter when we had to dig to get from our homes
In winter is was a muffled sound when the church bell chimes

No buses we walked to school through the driving snow
The teacher walked the railway tracks to get to the school
Only heating was a furnace in the classroom to keep feeding
wood
Had a toilet outside called a privy if we wanted to go
Water for drinking or washing came from an outside pump
This hand pump had to be primed every time it was used
At break time everyone brought an armful of wood to burn
There was a wood rack each armful of wood we did dump

URBAN URCHINS GARB

Every day we were ridiculed by our peers for being poor
The knees and seat of our trousers were patched back then
In winter all of us wore gumboots made of rubber causing stink
Had mackinaw coats black in colour weighed a ton for sure
One of our peers mother called us the urchin children then
Could not afford dinner buckets had to use honey pails
Seems we took jam and peanut butter sandwiches every day
With a family of seven children we managed as one can

Coles school was a mile away, with having eight hour classes
Was a big belfry on the school house that rang at recess and
noon
All the summer months wore sneakers giving stinky feet
People were so cruel to not so well off people with patches
A boy named Larry Wallace said you are wearing my shirt guy
Then in rage said to him try taking it off of me Mr. Big Shot
His mother came to the school to tell the teacher what I said
The teacher strapped me giving me six on each hand that day

All the donations from the Sally Ann was for four girls now
For each school day morning hated getting up because of the
peers
Always remember our first orange in our lunch for school
When my brother Bill was given a new bike had to say wow
My bike had to earn some money to buy it while in grade six
With the youngest brother he had to buy his bike also
One award but not all was not fair it degraded us always
Having a used bike it always breaking down again to fix

Here was me the protector for my sisters and brothers then
One day Don Small almost choked my brother Bill to death
Right away pulled him off of my brother then punched his nose
When I had finished with him his nose was busted, blood
coming down
For fighting the teacher took the razor strap till my hands were
sore
Said to the teacher no one touches my family while I am
around
There was no peer ridiculing any more because they knew
better
Was so tired of people calling us urchins could not take it
anymore

PASSING MY WAY

Had recognized someone passing my way
An old friend not forgotten of years passing
Having changed so much from them times before
After recognizing him, had plenty to say
With aging not the same person to see
That youth look lost, now gone to wrinkles
Them moments in time now rendered too old
These days now we are the elders to be

There were so many thoughts that came to mind
Where our knowledge comes along with years
Had remembered friends in the work place
Only some of them were the good buddy kind
So soon those retirement days came to stay
These days want to forget as elder times
A mind wondering where yesterday went
Should this senior linger in thought any way

Am now reaching out onto streets of old
A mind plodding along unforgettable paths
Always in search of dreams of lost hope
Having now a shorter time to prosper it's told
Each future day comes, how slow our pace
So many events with pain occur each day
You're not the same person you one time were
Not ourselves today we wear a new face

BOUNDLESS LOVE

Within living moments of precious days
Each trend of loving emotion tends to unfold
There's no time to be lonely in arms of love
A heart held desire in such wonderful ways
Love welcomed home forever so gracious to be
A place with caring remains a real home forever
Having compassion creates a world a better place
Such hearts with no blue side of lonesome to see

Our dawning days beneath some new dreams
For each moment to hear good heart feelings
Somewhere on life's pathway shall find peace
There's always loves hand reaching out it seems
Be happy while waiting the dawning of the day
The wonders of hope arises along life's road
Let's keep the world on the sunny side with love
Best to keep in touch even when we're far away

All this love revives us remembering it so well
Many a birthday's come to mind sometimes
Another day to be cherished same as before
With get-togethers' there's these times to tell
Have enjoyed great memories in loves everlasting place
Remembering rejoicing sounds relives lasting hope
In a gathering of heart filled love means a lot
A home that stands out having streets of time to embrace

OPEN SHUTTERS

Every evening at the Sparta home many bats flew around
From open dormer shutters at dusk these creatures came
They made a high pitched scream as they swooped at you
There was also bigger orange coloured bats with a different sound
Seems bats were catching moths and skitters as they flew
The orange bats were attacking may beetles most of all
These creatures fly around until dawns first light
Some nights with a corn broom we had killed quite a few

Our cats did not like these night flyers they hid under the step
Ted the dog laid under our car as soon as bats came out
From the open shutters five bats flew out at one time
Here nightly sleeping birds in the pine trees did not say a peep
Them phantoms of the night made our house a spooky place to be
Such a fowl smell came as they flew by like Kerosene
The family moved from Sparta to Plainfield in summer
Was so glad when we moved from here no more bats to see

These flying creatures from open shutters have feces stuff
Have claimed bats carry rabies to other wild animals
Out of open shutters something contagious can come along
When a pet gets stricken with this virus the going is ruff
So many things in childhood days virus as well as others
A saying take care of your famous one the hell with the rest
To walk through long ago life with always a bitter feeling inside
Such was the home with that not give a damn caring mother

CHARMLESS EPISODES

Every fact assumed with some making sense
Avoiding prayers will determine our fate
There are those that sell their soul to the devil
A person guilt is remote with their hidden pretense
Hence here's servants of the devil in a place
Some one like a double edged sword of sorts
The onset is to ensue some better ways
There's always effigy people in an insane race

Have made a conscious effort to be heard
Shall find ways of caring, by being one's self
Let some humorous thoughts leak out for a laugh
All good times are remembered mark my word
Some traits are known to people of the boastful kind
Would be better to cross them bridges then bum them
Many have exerting moments related to fault finding
A strident voice makes it impossible to talk your mind

Even with closed lips secrets tend to have a short stay
To come upon many with an attitude unable to smile
There's other inopportune times causing embarrassment
When caught up in an episode one wants to get away
So many pessimist out there to drive you mad
There's many times people have an arrogant opinion
To leave the scene you will turn out to be glad

WHERE EVERYDAY BEGAN

Having walked along life's tedious road
Our past is swallowed up in a venture there
An old sun taking the same path going on forever
As for sometimes life has an ever changing episode
Comes special days to raise a banner for it all
These roles of parents played with trails throughout
We will always have religion setting the right path
For always them most difficult times we recall

Them funerals with wedding are hand in hand per year
Our house repairs follow a normal coarse of events
As for everyone's yard dandelions never cease to grow
There's death with taxes one thing that's sincere
Good luck is out there but never rears it's head
To always do our best even if we stay poor
Want to become a lotto winner fixed for a life time
While helping the poor leaves you more poor instead

The work fact pressed to the utmost force
To hold your breath to bare the grief of it all
Such a great wall of silence to rehearse it's dues
Our unbearable finds no new found source
Will have to cut expenses by doing without
Had to regroup some resources to recover once again
To over spend is not hard for one to do
Just make a monthly budget is best no doubt

UNFORGOTTEN MEMORIES

A child to not be seen at play
Many cruel scenes of life haunt my heart
Having a life full of work from morn till night
Was caught up in endless consequence every day
One's life held within the constraint of time
Must be up at five to do the chores
Then head off to school one mile away
The pay for all these years was not a single dime

To trudge on home to start milking at four
First was the feeding of livestock to do
Then the milking was separated it's cream to use
Was off to supper at six once more
A lot of whole milk I poured into heavy cans
Two heavy cans were placed on a cart at night
Another two heavy cans put with these at morn
Always counting on a mere boy that was their plans

In nineteen fifty four a farm was bought miles away
A place near Belleville close to Trenton air base
Here a house with no running water having a privy place
Was the village of Plainfield we went to stay
From here was sent to a farm to earn my pay
My parents came to gather my cheque there
They left me broke not a measly cent to bare
No money to buy clothes cried alone each day

The day I was eighteen this farmer gave me a pay
At this age the parent could not take my money anymore
Having saved each cheque for one whole year
Took the train to St. Thomas many miles away
Went to see Harvey Nicholson on a turkey ranch there

ONCE UPON A DREAM

A lost moment treads back from yesterday
To fall on deaf ears cast away no sound to wake
There's no living forever or start over again
Here on earth knowingly have one life to stay
Some tears fall among the pages of reality there
To spill out one's soul to paper dreams to come true
Have all those day's of my life been rendered to lost dreams
Only hidden thoughts in drawers of time left unaware

Here in my earthly home time has grown so old
Being unfounded lost forever, it all seemed so real
A life being locked into lost moments of an unreal dream
That wonder fact where life's dream became cold
A whole life to have waited upon, some rested hope
There's no living forever to plan all new horizons
One's dreams to be left for tomorrow in dusty drawers
All alone to be left with deep emotions to cope

In the end heaven reaps the sorrow of it all
These idol dreams fall along the way lost forever
On through the midst of it all collecting my thoughts
The old folk introduction was found we recall
To accept the things reality has bound within me
In my heart lingers strong emotions of past times
Those reality dreams with enough years of grace
Would be wonderful moment come true to really see

YEARS WHILED AWAY

A period from yesterday in mind
At our homestead so long ago
To be recalling growing up years
Those tender years left behind
Many friends lost in a time place
Did laugh or cry through it all
Have walked on life's rambling road
So much remembering which to face

We planted time watched it grow
With crowded thought in quiet rooms
One more dawn wakes us once again
The morns of yesterday we all know
That crying of babies a long ago sound
Once called Dad a Granddad now
To be glad when they all come home
Our child a parent had come around

Have pondered my thoughts every day
An oldy having reached into tomorrow
A receding brow with grey hair tones
Some remembered times seem so far away
These songs of times are not the same
When we measure ourselves not so tall
Will forever reminisce about the past
Only us with those four walls remain

OLD RAMBLING ROADS

On that gravel road comes the image of square back cars
To recall puddles after rain storm along the road way
That font of rebirth seemed every year bestowed on life
Here there is no words to enlighten a boy as summer nears
These ideas sustained in days of old where to custom always
Comes everlasting thoughts in observing the recurrence of
doubt
How mediocre it was having these eternal pastures of grazers
Was days of perpetual partakers in smelly work was the ways

For a families sake there is only this mystery of hope
Have to beg these pardons from a single lads foreshadowed
days
Had no honour on this road, days were as empty as they can
be
Each day was indescribable with it outcome in which to cope
At rest can retain my sanity with these dreams at night
Was according to purpose that things had gotten done back
then
Same kindred aims year after year nothing got any better
In a heart of a believer every portion of old never was right

Let us be convinced that merit was not part of growing up
Did have faith as well as hope, with some help from charity
Inasmuch the unity of purpose had no promise to depend on
These daily chores all through the summer was an endless trip
No need to count the deeds it was routine until darkness came
A person can sum up the words mentioned to get things done
Had walked these roadways governed by signs of the times
Our parents attentive needs conformed to life always the same

Here was a place having teachings coming from pioneer time
A farm where words followed actions daily no mercy
The intent which was there wearied each portion for us
That host of reluctance out there was unending in our prime
There is no one there from where an old life came, it's
departed
At the end of the journey of hope have claimed our reward
Must admit we upended a lot of strife on our rambling road
With all the family life that's left, to unite let's all get started

HERE IS MY WORLD

That doorpost of believers in the truth, no sure hope
With one heart and one soul must consider my integrity
This land is your land, this land is my land for ever can be
By some decree of faith loves understanding can cope
During latter days remembered being oppressed half the time
Than tomorrow comes once again to do all of our biddings
In all sincerity of unfailing goodness unity belongs forever
No one showed partiality, just bad manners in my prime

Since yesterdays journey we have seen the worse of man kind
All of life's compassion has dignity with outstretched hands
Shall accomplish that which I purpose, one must succeed
Be worthy from the beginning create well being for the mind
Here is my candles need someone to light them, you will see
Through a remedy of forgiveness comes to most hearts again
In regards to deceitful words they are for all spiteful people
Come to a welcome home a place filled with love always to
be

Have endured bad days, best be prepared for some being
worse
We come steadfast to prosper with good foundations now
For honour you will find mingling with believers in your work
To be a great family as in according to plan we must rehearse
Have to walk on together through life doing whatever we can
All things are not ours like we want them to be, better to share
The whole world has undivided joy to render every single day
That author of life has told provoking stories since time began

Someone can change many things in the world no one
changes a mind
Out of the mouth of wisdom no kindness is every being heard
A two sided story remains a burden for time to come
We can change a moment but not a whole day you will find
Better to devote some ability for activities more define
Shall we dream all our best dreams hoping some do come true
Lets all be true hearts as believers in accordance to good plans
To choose an entire house for friendship come over to mine

A SNICKERING MAMA

Was always putting me down a snickering belittling way
Mostly done in company pointing while laughing at her son
So bazaar must say egad for the confusion depressed part
Would like to genuflect my foot on someone's ass than run
away
Be best to talk to the grim reaper he would be more fun
In a hebetude household it's like an illusion taking place
Everything was one sided all for one and none for all occasions
Here was a creation o malice fiasco mollycoddling son

Best stay in Mama's peril, get along better this kind of way
For all times the oldest onset was better then the whole bunch
Such hectic ways of life in a shameful home atmosphere
All things said by the second son snickering at everything he'd
say
Must get out of this house ma got a date for sonny one day
Lets call it mesosphere of no claim game in a bastard place
Best call him Billy bayou an upright son the only one that counts
Cannot stick around might steal his gusto for his flirtago play

There was a jughead motive to contend with as always
How hectic it was to buy Brylcreem for someone else to use
The fain ransacked his brothers colognes plus other needed
stuff
Was an offset family of seven children here those days
A mother claims it's insignificant we all should share
Was all one-sided which gets me, all for one none for all
Me and my younger brother put our things under lock and key
To steal whatever the eldest wanted certainly was not fair

All the wood sawing and chopping was always done by me
Could not have the head honcho with blisters on his hands
His mom cooked up a social life, here is a some how do you do
How awkward that cuckoo block space had really come to be
Just read my lips there is a Casanova lurking in our vein
To be cute means bow legged, that's how it was for him
So strange was yesterday with no mentor in our midst
The story is not made up every line read is all true

REBOUNDS IN LIFE

The places in life, were many proposed to time
Was my first time married had five children back then
After ten years of marriage the woman was not up to par
A lady that steals money plus cigarettes that's a crime
With deviant behavior cheated when I went to work each day
Tried suicide three or four times, seems she not right to me
A filicide act of trying to smother her children came to be
Soon a divorce was on the menu that was the only thing to say

Before to long parental alienation took place in her home
When the courts gave the spouse custody was not right you
see
She made it seem to the children that Dads the bad egg
Each time of visitation ask the courts where's the kids how
come
A boyfriend of hers took an axe to my front door no police did
show
They stole all the furniture this same day when I was at work
Always worked hard trying to make ends meet no thanks for
that
After calling the police why they stayed away Lord only would
know

Soon was married again to get away from this awful dilemma
Things seem all well and good for a year or so, everyone so nice
As soon as the mother said you got a new Dad now they turned on me
The jealous part raised it's ugly head saying we love only our Mama
Doing all kinds of nasty things against me every single day
During these times their mother was diagnosed with terminal cancer
Three months later she died and they cremated her with remain
Each time they spited me maybe it's not best to stay

A couple of years later got married to another widowed woman
Then we bought a house together everything turned out fine
After five years she was cured of colon cancer no trace
Was living a good life for twenty years married to this man
Again cancer came back and in just four months she died
A lot of hard work got us to where we are leaving a sad day
Every evening sit alone wonder what a man should do
So much of a loving life together so much good times denied

SAME OLD SCENES

A disenchanted moment under a nightly sky
To become reposed within the silence of it all
Some new vision sends me down that road again
Here was unknown places an answering voice to reply
Being an observance part way through my rest
Was looking into an unreal vision this while
There's no turning back in dream's that come to be
In an unreal place our conscience did it's best

Every night there's scenes shadowing me there
Them nightly idle times wishing for better dreams
Was far beyond the limits of a searching heart
Many times that same old scene haunts me here
In sleepy time in moments of a nightly wonder place
Here comes another day, foot steps in the hallway
On the kitchen radio sad songs playing days of regret
Outside heard thunder another rainy day to face

The keeper of the stars helped me through last night
Having in mind to do yesterdays things left undone
A one track mind always thinking far back
That rain storm gone now with sunshine so bright
Had to smile joining up the day of sunshine here
Should one change scenery go to places unknown
On past the old house its out of my mind
When evening shadows fall another night to fear

TIME SLIPS AWAY

Another morn to wipe sleepers from my eyes
Should one stand idly by watching a day be born
That glowing sun starts filtering through the trees
From on the porch yawning watching sun rise
So many times have walked out or in my door
Another day of a million plans waiting again
Had many high hopes that will not amount to much
Such pretense to reality to finish work once more

Same thing as last summer flowers bloom robins sing
Here's my hand to enter them gates of time
Through my gate back down the road to yesterday
Have laid my worries to rest to leave sadness thing
If the world stalled you can picture me there
That wondering that crosses my mind is forever
Shall always remember my overalls from Sears
Had stored stones in these pockets of every pair

Once in a while my mind finds that old place
So long ago were them bib overalls for that world
To make someone chuckle like to find an old pair
These memories stay deep inside me forever
A long gone home of hard times to face
That old place once called home haunts my dreams
There is so much times with hard ships to recall
Now life is like summer roses it's fading away
An old man has to light up his own world it seems

IN AN OLD WORLD

A morning sun red on the horizon sky
All alone this day watching the old clock
Our summer has turned in autumn winds
Those hazy lazy days we will have to say goodbye
Everyday keep sitting in my world trying to win
That shadow filled room memories dwell there
Having only just one life to walk through
Being elders we live in a much different light
The passing years a choice left in wait to compare

Once in a while my heart finds memories lost in time
An old stray can be relived once in a long while
These people never last only old towns and cities
Our feeble years hang in lonely rooms, life has to recline
A hand of life is not forever for us to hold
So many things our life dreams are made of
On this weary road comes a cloud of lonesome
Every story will live once again we been told

Many unforgettable moments when youth was around
We have changed but everything else stays the same
A wish to erase those lines from my face
To pray helped when grieving times in life were found
Some dreams like castles in the sand washed away
On awakening seeing a faded picture on the wall
In the dim light an image of a passed on parent
All my collected thoughts are on that bygone day

MEMORIES IN MIND

An old stage opens up to another day
The black of night closes waiting for tomorrow
Takes so many days to turn back pages of time
To recall embers in the fireplace simmering away
So much thought revives days long ago
These moments grow late we have played our world
Must take time to retrieve thoughts of faded memories
Old folks mantel pictures all in a straight row

One's thoughts drift off to a long ago birthplace
We were not carefree children away back then
An old time thought see's many empty stages
The past on people are our shadow walking race
All we needed was love the old song everyone sings
Unlike stones we are not around forever
That wonder of it all soon one's life is gone
Only lost moments and the sadness it brings

Many a broken promises gone astray, that went unkept
To chose devotion is like heaven in a dream
Only true love can go on faithfully to the end
Even when people are old, best keep our respect
Have past remembrances of folks, that life faded
Only one life sooner or later we walk through it
Here once stood a family, now lost in time
The souls we long for and loneliness is related

JUST PASSING THROUGH

Such amends are pursued for idealizing things
There is mysteries in starting a whole new day
In need of revival from weariness, rested again
Each time of prayer so much silence it brings
Out of that earthly dwelling no goodness of heart
Crude circumstances did follow our daily lives
Was not wellbeing, no genuine good living traits
Our hopes were fooled in this life from the start

Many times would like to rejoice with others
That exemplar unharmonized needs no envy
Was no hand offered to guide us through life
In need to treat a friend as sisters or brothers
Made my use of time performing thought in hope
Them long ago days always a bad circle of events
Need peace to take root in our hearts always
Lost days resentments one must always cope

There was no real truths that's precious to life
Whole heartedly we strive prompting the future
One's honour has endless glory still in my heart
Had the loving spirit to quench us from all strife
Being poor had no values in those days
In the midst of conscience comes a diversion
Had to hold back tears seeing sad one's weeping
Without a happy world nothing matters what one says

A DISTANT WHISTLE

Some still hours leaves time to inspire a thought
Each incident imperils as precious time on rolls
There's still more roads left in stories untold
Always wandering in memories to be sought
A railroad rattling train has come to mind
That somber whistle stays in my thought forever
From away back then seems it still resounds
Such a memory recalled to those tender years
A distant whistle refrain left so far behind

A far off whistle blowing, smoke curling into the sky
Was so long ago since Dad's train past through
Them heavy iron wheels rambling down the track
Our father waving as the black freight rolled by
On the laneway waited for the trains arrival
Sometimes after nine watched it's light open the night
Was that New York Central coming down the line
Being hard times in old days for a families survival

As of now during my elder days it comes to thought
Thinking on past trains with black smoke rising high
The whistle breaking the stillness wailing away
From those childhood days only some fond moments it brought
Have recalled dispelling moments by the way side
Forever in yesterday keeps calling me once more
That one incident from long ago keeps reminding me
We were poor people back then having only our pride

SONGS TODAY

Today one's house had jarred noisily at dawn
A house hold now poised with no moments of peace
To have comprehended teenage music as a whole
No more sound of wonderful lyrics they are now gone
One's mind explodes with new raptures loud to the ears
Them old songs of easy listening for our times
Thither with this music beat enjoyed by us all
Had such wonderful music through those years

Harkened we are to noisy music now made by man
Seems a demon came down to earth to unveil this music
Could we make a silent place bring it to an end
To have beautiful melodies touch our heart is a plan
The worlds charm wishing for the best of days
Even during the harshest of hours hopes coming through
Often changes bring back old songs once again
In need of love songs vested simply in the old ways

We have left old times at dawns gate, gone so fast
Easy listening now stilled in streets of time
Old times now gone merely a shadow from a paling sky
A land we wandered through posed to peril at last
Today amble slowly, becoming dreary tired and old
The day is lost wearing late with sunset to fall
These many hills that's been climbed, left to a tranquil place
All them memories of songs will come back it's been told

OUR YOUNGSTER DAYS

Our brother sisterly love is best of all
In those bygone days with flights of many feet
To be told the sandman sprinkled our eye's at night
This heart of hope wanting a days joy be the call
Have a smile to flood our face starting a new day
Amid our drowsy sleepy time pensive dreams to be
A family of nine in all did meekly dwell here
The frailty of money was from a war time pay

Had prayers to protect us through each night
These good words spoken with empty pockets it seemed
Did pass countless years doing without ambling along
The youngster years without any reprieve in sight
To grow tired days with a worried state of mind
A childhood Christmas back then was an orange and apple
Every morning chores at five watching the dawn break
Them old hard times as a boy now left far behind

Another lost day with a red sky a setting sun to fall
That family life was so hard in a long ago place
Have cast many a stone down life's road
A youngsters vision representing on old world to recall
Here a farming lowly place now with sleeping shadows there
Had traveled down the gravel road hardly a car in sight
Old days were etched in my mind, a long lost haydays
Away back then there was nothing one today could compare

HAPLESS TIMES

Merely urging myself away from old sad memories today
An old sad heart surely is able to love again
How sweet is that chanting word called passion
In my moody silence sadness is bound to stay
Once in a while comes a happy day a pure delight
Between each of these days there's time to breathe
Then comes despair, we are some what famished for love
Awaiting days end leaving a rest time in sight

Sometimes times there's good humour with laughter here
During the down cries comes strife of life
Many other days lingering thoughts from the past
Have corralled life as a whole to be really sincere
Once in a while an awe will fall upon my heart
To be acquainted with sorrows a man knows about grief
While being forlorn had to dispel sad thoughts once more
Yesterdays tasks finished, soon another day to start

The silence brings memories as the twilight falls
Outside the window darkness will steal my time again
From beyond the fringes a night dreams close in
These ever bearing dreams come after midnight I recall
Here a mere mortal welcoming night rituals around
Them most thoughts being entwined in nightly shadows
While deep in slumber them farfetched journeys to behold
To be awaken in morn by an intent crowing sound

DARKEST NIGHT

The darkness had tented the sky above
A murk had closed off the moon and the stars
Here a motley street of dim lights flickering here
That char black sky with clouds not wanting to move
After prayers comes a silence just waiting for a dream
To slumber on through a sojourn reverie so black
Was best to pray to bless my house each night
Then finely dream times that speal off into a vigil it seems

On awakening in early morn an alarm clock ticking away
A mind setting flaunt with shadows all around
Here growing tyrannies of sunbeams in the window
Small gust of wind makes trees sway
A sun rising great day waiting for the fog to disappear
Next a morning time for flowers to start unfolding
From a far sky birds came to land in my trees

The raining darkest night brought out a terrain of green
On dripping tree branches squirrels looked at me
Could hear morning doves cooing in worlds ears
Lined along my backyard fence sparrows were seen
My one pear tree had blossoms to blow
Just behind me a drop of rain touched a rose leaf
Here morn time ventures came to a noonly scene

FRAMED IN BLACK

Those kind of people who have treated you so bad
To be well deserved them framed in black
Should curse their ways deserving no better than that
Being the way these people are it's really awfully sad
They shall be the rue of someday to sit in gloom
Such a nasty person will reach their deserving goal
To recognize them by their frowning face in a bleak world
Here these one's sit an elder home in their lonely room

Once again the feat of sorrow meets such a lonely day
These one's will reach out for love that's never there
No one comes to comfort them during their pleading times
They have made their own bed we are so sorry to say
Will leave everything to be cold it's deserving there
Had waited for your day to arrive that now came to be
An old man shall get what's coming to him in the very end
You son's have created life's moments without any care

Them unhappy roads will haunt future days to come
Each stride of life has so many goodwill parts
Best to send our prayers that's what helps a lot
To have many friends then to be dogmented by some
Put hope to the challenge with it's precious grace
Pull the bells rope ring out them best wishes to all
Wishing friends to come during every beckoning time
Let's not heed for trouble times let's give it lots of space

These meaning of love words everyone has to know
A prayers blessing will never be for those wretched souls
Those being framed in black is truly what it's all about
It's better not to attend those with a senseless bad show
Had an alienated performance from a single parent mom
They had a dire mood of respect for an all good father
The motive reeks with that ironical spouse bitterness thing
From out of it all untruthful lies for sure had to come

AN OLD WORLD WAY

Must break the silence of those by gone years
Had not been a pretty sight for this young lad
So much abuse it was real hard to learn in school
A home with so much beatings leaving a child in fears
Here with no love at home, just always a nasty place
Was a mere child being blamed for all of their mistakes
Even a neighbor boy beaten by her a total disgrace
Having a mother with a mental problem was hard to face

Nobody liked our mom, she was the wretch of the town
For all our sake to never laugh when she came around
There was a reason for all fingers pointing a beware sign
A person that never smiled she always had a frown
All of us children went to church, but parents never showed
their face
Being a poor family had one set of good clothes for church
protocol
As to why we could not be like another child in church
The boys of our home wore tams to a holy mentioned place

Again to protest that memory lane of life so insane
Always a barefoot child in summer shoes during winter
To walk on gravel roads to school torture at it's best
We were go glad for winter to wear shoes once again
Wearing patched clothes was better than no clothes at all
The pigs were part of our food line fed slop from the house
Had a garden patch for weeding all them summer's long
Was the canning of preserves always were labours of fall

Where in war time of world food rations, hope would end
We can blame Germany for all our grief back then
One meal per day in which it was for all of us
A lot of hard times all families in Canada did comprehend
Even the passing of it all still bad memories remain
The Germans are in hell a good place to claim their goal
In hopes there was no blessings to our father satins their dad
This war had no meaning even with victory to sustain

A WIFE AT DAYBREAK

The alarm clock blares out at four
To square one my wife does go
A wife up before daybreak it came to be
Was up for that two hour walk once more
She returns at daybreak for a snooze
Has a sound sleep for an hour or so
Having breakfast at six thirty each day
Maybe clean the house after was for her to choose

At Christmas she has cards to send on their way
There will be fifty or more gone afar to friends
Also cards to relatives in that Nova Scotia place
This with house work is part of her lengthy day
She cries the blues when things are not done
Always says her prayers before starting daily work
The time being watched to know her time to eat
Things to be finished up is everything under the sun

To catch a movie on TV we must have supper at five
After seven a game of Scrabble is the call
A two hour game is what we will do
Then soon after this our sleepy time will arrive
To say our prayers always comes as number one
In bed we do crossword puzzles for a little while
The lights out, time again to rest our aches and pains
Another night for dream land for us two have begun

AWAY BACK THEN

On my eighteen birthday worked on a farm far away
My parents came every month to get my cheque
Amid these trails of yesterday a hell place for me
My parents wanted my money they knew the very day
So many bad scenes on this farming sight
Not a pretty picture again with rags to wear
During summer, worked in fields of stones to pick
This farmer with no compassion worked me day and night

A house having no honesty or prayers in mind
So bad was each day with it's remorse consequences
Way back then shame was left in the shadows there
Here a dark curtain blocked the way no love to find
Such hard feats performed by a boy in his teens
No passion only grief brought sadness with tears
Was ungrateful moments always to be oppressed
So many befriended day of yelled at scenes

These overseer views the unforgettable kind
My thought taunted me what the farmer had in store
Worked in the barn all day plowed fields all night
Was not a child of eighteen no more, a new job to find
Took my cheque boarded a bus went to Sparta place
Became a hired hand for a turkey rancher there
My thoughts now no one could take the pay cheque from me
This employer would not let my parents rob me was the case

ALL OUR FRIENDS

If nobody care what happened to you
And nobody helped you along
If everyone just looked after himself
And everything was to be wrong
If nobody cared just a little for you
And nobody thought about me
If all stood alone in the battle of life
What a dull world this would be

Life is made sweet by the friends that we meet
And the things that in common we share
We want to live not because of ourselves
But because of the people who care
It's living and doing for someone else
On what life splendor depends
And the joy of this life when you sum it all up
Is found in the making of friends

We can take every day with the challenge it brings
And meet it head on with a smile
Cause we know when it ends we've assisted our friends
And that alone makes it worthwhile
So here's to our friends far and near
And you know that our wish is sincere

AN OLD BRIDGE

The columns of the bridge were wallowed in clay
Here the ground all around parched and cracked with age
At the bridge abutments were matted weeds growing tall
Below this frame was unhinged shadows of pigeons flying away
All along a deep culvert dirt had sped there
Far below the trestles a somber river flows
There was a placard on the column built eighteen hundred
This old column was crumbling with lack of care

A ways off was bulrushes with frogs leaping about
While looking West along the river deer were drinking
Standing guard was a hart deer listening for sounds
Such a road to here was off the beaten path a lost route
When I set to rest, grass frogs began leaping around
In a nearby tree a chattering squirrel, as if he owned the place
Then some cooing doves say I live here too
Out of distant shrubs came many a cricket sound

Here was a place to empty thoughts of days gone by
Have lingered a while on this scenic tour
Was such a long ago road way off the beaten track
From the edge of a wooded area wailing winds did cry
Sounds like voices resounding of a way back then
Each incident harkened by whispering all around
While unveiling new spots came more lost in time things
The day is growing late have to return home again

FROSTY WINDOWS

To remember curtains in the kitchen window frayed
In winter was Jack Frost doing scenery on the windows
Many a snow bank up to the roofs back then
The winter months of November on to April they stayed
Wandering thoughts of old times were sentimental forever
Those night prayers followed us from long ago
Sleighs with horses crossed my mind in this snow clad place
For life long ago there was more hardships to endeavor

A life is like a flag the elements make it raged after awhile
Have seeked indoors waiting for warmer days ahead
Them frosty windows was like yesterday here
Be better to wait for warmer days to have a smile
Would be nice to stop shoveling snow once more
Even warmer days being something not to dread
Was all in natures plans half warm days half cold days
From my window seen snow ploughs resume another day

Have walked through all of earths dreadful attire
Seasonal thunderstorms to pounding snow times
My old home made from bricks on tile letting frost through
Was not much warmth no matter how high the fire
The winters work in the basement cutting potatoes forseeds
For ever were stoking fires just to keep warm
These thought scene accountable to understand my past
All weekends were spent fulfilling our deeds

OFT TIMES

A morning suns blaze on the window comes to be
All family folks must be on the early morn scene
Dad's words for action will be fulfilled
Already the sun is waiting for someone to see
We have the might of our almighty to save us from harm
Our thoughts point us the way with a day so divine
Some people cannot wait to spread yesterdays news
During oft times the devil to pay with foes to charm

Many feats will be performed for most of the day
In search for better things to do will turn my views
Then comes the grand discovery most adored to do
By times it's best to be modest having nothing to say
Have tried not to be a fool with folks of no respect
Seems some days there's no one to a-light to humour at all
Best a smug routine getting most things allowed
The behaviours in the world there's things to reject

For truth as well as humour follow it how we can
Our families live for friendship, also live for love
Life has taught us patience make it better to endure
Most timely wise accept responsibility for a life's plan
We are merely struggling to display our earnest soul
An old remembered story is some what entombed
We are only wanderers for the realm of our times
It sometimes takes a whole lifetime to reach our goal

THE NOONDAY SHADOW

There was a serene host of ghostly actions to be aware
Along the pathway a follower sanctifies to a memory
Still seemed to be a living shadow walking along with me
Under the sun shall govern all things in harmony, unending there
The sun intercedes me with the company of a silhouette here
Such loneliness to respond to in our cold old worlds sake
That sun a mediator introducing a lonely special greeting
Beyond all tellings the adoration lives in my heart, it's sincere

Now have absence in my heart missing someone today
Only enthusiasm an unconscious action in the silence now
All my faith for life has no choice, shall be lost for ever
This man has only a shadow for a companion since yesterday
In the bright sunshine summoned a sorrowful heart again
With that bond of love gone there is nothing to create gladness
Yet good thoughts remain for integrity in fulfilling our life
We are all victims of mystery all life's work what do we gain

Are those who's memory we venerate representing life truly
Our wonderful journey ended so soon with passion to death
With all my confidence will persevere further tomorrow
Will be found hastening along in that path here worthily
There comes that drab sad feeling in the husbands heart
Still that memorial moment walking together graciously
With what's remaining in new adventures will do very well
Have held firm to things concerning reality right from the start

For me, shall understand that dwelling spirit remains
A voice keeps calling my name at midnight from the stillness
Shall forever remember that lady, the nicest person I knew
My thoughts seek to believe in abiding with no shames
On through them spans of generations the young days were
hard
We were not the chosen one's of splendor, only failing
goodness
While prompting tomorrow have instilled memories old and
new
In tracing my footsteps through bad ancestor land, love was in
need

WHEN SHADOWS FALL

Every tree is in it's summer beauty now
Winds blow on the meadows with a timid breath
The whole place has changed it's look some how
Day's have changed entirely to a warm tranquil sky
As earthly shadows sped in and out for a while
From a far comes an echo of a cooing dove's reply

The warmest streams of sunshine climb the air
Loud cawing sounds were heard high on a lofty spar
Then several crows shadowed wings past over head there
This sky with kept breath, held in it's rain at noon
A wisp of warmer air from the South comes blowing through
There's great hopes a nice summer shower to come soon

Each day an event of a very vibrant scene
Such a drastic all over change was envisioned here
Many a dewy morning has turned the grass so green
Above the garden butterflies flutter upon a breeze
Once again a cloud sweeps a dark shadow past
The sun begins to sink slowly beneath far off western trees

At night the outdoors seem to have a change of tune
A day has vanished leaving the night all by itself
Then comes a shadowy light through the trees from a moon
As suddenly a harsh voice from night invades the place
In the shadows a raccoon rambles along the garden fence
Soon are bird melodies as part of the coming dawns embrace

MAPLE SUGAR BUSH

In a farmers woods a few miles away
A large maple bush he tapped the trees
To the sugar shanty a horse and sleigh carried sap
Into a big open vat the sap was stored that day
Then open troves above the fire syrup came about
Some one had to stoke the burner beneath the trough
I was a boy of fourteen collecting sap from the bush
The sleigh path through these woods was a snow drifted route

I waded through snow and brush to do my duty there
Once in a while would trip over logs strew in the bush
When friends came around syrup was poured in the snow for
candy
The sugar shanty smoke blew across the tree tops everywhere
A man by the name of Garnet Denyas owned the place
Was hired here in spring for three years of work
Working in the bush and at home was no more for me
Had found a job in Sparta at a turkey ranch was the case

A life of tramping woody ground was no more to be
Worked also in my Dad's woods for zero dollars three years
Here cut piles of cord wood from noon until night
Would drop tree's that come down being elm and maple
one's
Each winter did toil in minus thirty to forty degrees cold
Another task was loading cordwood to take to the barn
Was the only boy of all three to gather fuel of Dad's sons

AN AUTUMN MORNING

Gone is the summer of things clad in green
Many flowers had shed their blooms at my feet
Groups of songsters soar on feathery wings through the morn
Had gazed at scenery of only bare tree's to be seen
Those winter thoughts in mind not to far away
Far beyond this morning haze heard a dove coo there
There on the lattice masses of morning glory fading
Then walk under a bower of roses no flowers today

Was uninspired which summer shine turned to gray
Has been the dullest day of all since dawn
No more summer showers for robins to sing in
While walking had an amiable change of mood today
To many clouds across the sun now casting shadows there
Seen frost glittering along the garden, by ten was gone
In fall seems only bluejays and crows stay around
Here was I plodding along thinking how great life is
So much better life is from long ago having people that care

Many bridges have been crossed since my elder time came on
This life most of it unfurled, a few years left
There's no old church steeple piercing the sky
All of these stone churches they are allgone
These times not like old days burning wood for heat
With natural gas supper is easy, done in a jiff
Now a days the fire stays on all through the night
It does not take hours to make something to eat

WINTER AGAIN

The snows heavy blanket has hushed some sound
Another summer passed our warm days are gone
A sky now with solemn cloudy days of white
Many white mounds banked or blowing around
Each voice muted by the wind howling through trees
All the flowers been browned from frosty morns
Without twittering of birds no songs at dawn
Every toe and finger numbed by a North westerly breeze

There's that call of loneliness beckoning our mind
That ventures beyond deadly silence of each night
The darkness calls the moon to linger out there
Here in the cold, cracking ice in rivers you find
One lonely owl hoots from within a tall pine
Several icicles had formed along my eave trough
On the doorstep came mounds of snow over night
A neighbours dog wanting in had started to whine

By chance who might wander along this stormy path
Having watched people walk dogs on the coldest day
Seems so long ago summer had turned into fall
So much waiting for a sky to end this seething wrath
These walls of winter bounding everyone there
Every day becomes shorter as we keep going along
Each hour we share friendship with love seeing us through
Sharing gifts at Christmas time takes away despair.

OLD SOUNDS IN THOUGHT

At break of dawn a milk wagon there
Them clambering steel wheels clouting cobble stone
An old horse with blinders seen clippy clopping along
Here there were other morning sounds which to compare
All along street lights of mere candles burning
They had been lit by a lamp lighter last night
Many a narrow alleys with ghostly shadow so dingy
Buses out on open gravel roads sounds of them returning

Rustic shuttered buildings marked the street edges
Windows of tutors style reflected the sun's ray
A solemn soul a whiling time as the sun climbed
This solar ember then passed above woodly fringes
Suddenly came a ringing of a church bell from far away
Recalling a long ago Christians being part of life
An old country steepled building resounding heavenly things
The church a reminder, reflecting from yesterday

In the distance an echoing whistle, clouds of smoke
Was making it's way through the countryside a train
A rushing engine speeding towards the depot
The people on board wore fancy hats some fedora folk
By the station square back cars picking up there
Soon went putting down a dusty road out of sight
Many sounds of long ago recalled to one's mind
Our tribulations have another lifetime to compare

LIFE TOMORROW

Such earthly existence had disasters brought
Some implications for Tsunami troubles tomorrow
Once again some awful confrontations for citizens to bare
More then this for the world is still unfounded
Things not revealed we must understand what's sought
With reassurance as a whole check for ourselves
The reckoning of the matters with somewhere to begin
We know someday our old world will come to an end
For now build an underground shelter with shelves

Make happiness be in todays world affirmed
Only my thoughts hold up tomorrows means
It's a big boogieman from the devil to get you
An old earth simply falling apart it can be termed
Being like a human factor having a beginning and end
We must use the common sense thing every day
The saying to stop a train, one cannot is the call
Like our atomic neighbors never knowing what they send

The beginning baby that impalpable breath to start life
After this breath comes life to seek tomorrows fate
Using our foremost to hold to all our living days
Then comes bad omens to cause that human strife
Them future days never knowing when death comes along
Have only hope wondering what tomorrow brings
In spite of it all leave out that envious feeling forever
Stay in that house of content that's where I belong

NO ONE CAME

Was building a beautiful home in Plainfield place
Here spent time clearing two acres of land here
Began putting cement blocks in a rainy thunderstorm
All alone a man in his shirt sleeves working this space
To have measured my working time with coffees and a spoon
Was a two acre clearing beside a trout stream
At the streams edge were stones shining in the sun
The sun told me it's twelve, it would be lunch time soon

Some people watched me more the five visions there
Not even one soul came near to see what they could do
The horse named Venus looked at me from a far off pasture
She seemed to be the only soul that really did care
A great old horse, that helped me scoop out the soil
Also clearing of the land with so much tangled debris
Had two brothers along with four sisters out there
There was no one stopped by to help me with the toil

Had finished almost the better part in the autumn sun
Within my loneliness croaking critters at dusk of night
An evening moon starts to shine in the eastern sky
On seeing that it was an October night work almost done
Was our makers voice behind me that had edged me on
After all was said and done slept all night on the floor
Did not disturb the universe for all this darkened time
Having a lot of work to do inside floor, doors and all
There was some time to relax for a while once more

LIFE'S DREAMS

A dream being one stone thrown into the water
Then comes some ripples forming a circle here
The circle gets bigger and bigger for a little while
A increasing circle comes to the ponds edge now
It becomes lost forever in this span of water
Was as a spent dream faded in a moment in time
To be the same as if seen for a while gone tomorrow

We repeat the stone throw for one more time
Another birth opens up to life as it did before
Being another being some years later
A whole new matter different as it can be
These streets are not the same as they were
Them known people once being alive now are gone
To be suddenly another days wakening everyone's old like you

After our circle of life goes we lay still in that pond
Have cast your life in that big circle now an idle stone
To be lost in the deep bottom for ever more
Here standing at the waters edge wondering now
We have played our part in life's loving realm
Did work to pay a home than soon to say goodbye
The dreams of it all ends one again dead as can be

If not of strong mind and body a disadvantage takes over
Must curse them they had no ripples ever to watch
A life is over the stone rest on the bottom of the pond
Them best of times gone then the piffles come on
A waiting time for the ripples to stop a stone be still
Here is the bad omen part that's always the very same

LOVES TORN PAGES

How weary are those spent roads left far behind
One's destiny applies time bound for out there somewhere
Them days forever as the sun goes down in the West
Good moments on oft times is not so very hard to find
In love has its ups and downs similar to the weather
The parts played is as good as an actor could really be
Was some wager as to who can be really sincere
Being so great married life eighteen years being together

There's always someone to greet you when coming home
The best of all things after working hard all day
So great the family raising seeing them all growing
Had to work long hours not well fixed like some
One day had phoned home saying Dad has to work late
Was told a man was parked in my front door yard
Then came on home to see who this person was there
A wife was cheating on me was that awful found fate

Our love took a turn for the worse on that dire Saturday
All the goodness in life now had turned into hate
A home filled with sadness no reprieve which to see
How can a grieving man make this to go away
The trust was not there any longer in a family place
To wonder what the love of life must do now
Here was a good man only staying for the children's sake
Forever having so much conjured emotion in which to face

That lost love whispers at one's soul each day
The love things should matter but now they do not
One cannot seek a woman's love that only wants evil
Had hopes of her leaving us to move far away
A morrow came when this woman was on her own
Then divorce put me on my own a judgment claim
Went off to Toronto for a tradesman's College degree
The courts made me pay support a real somber tone

FULL OF GRIEF

From a time long ago real evils ran around
Makes me shudder the way things were
No way to pare down vices this part in time
Have to reopen these wounds again to resound
How could a wife try to suffocate her children back then
Living in an exualtant bad light in a weird time
A man with proudness this moment breaks me down
Here's a husband trying to cope, do what he can

All this confusion has played havoc from the start
Not even a Harold's angel could change this disgrace
When alone my face had a veil of tears running down
That good grace she had none from that promised part
Also had a mother a youngster beater in these times
Was abused my whole life through, no let up
All my young days feeling poorly, try best to be strong
Should a mother have been punished for these crimes

Out of my past comes a wife of disgrace
Her boss gave her a raise with favours to pay
A twelve year home life of living in hell
So much sadness came with hardships to face
The times while at work she was cheating with affairs
Them things she did a woman deserves a black wreath
So many witnesses having evidence proving them days
This life of mine there's nothing that compares

BREAKING THE SILENCE

Another summer the smell of grass once more
Even with common sense it may go astray in thought
Seen house wrens by the roses was no better place to be
Wanted to go somewhere in a park to explore
These birds have stopped chirping is signs of a storm
Have moved to a spot with blossom smells there
Could by chance a dove start cooing to break the silence
Here to be standing on a calm day that's so warm

Hoping this quietness will have spoken before night
Only parkland shadows came to greet me there
Spent an hour just cutting a walking stick from birch
In the afar a rabbit with her young come into sight
Forever in silence my conscience keeps attending me
Here somewhere in nature is a matter of fact
In my wandering heard a slight chirp of a bird
Came not even a pestering bluejay in which to see

Went back home leaving the park for another time
Here through the kitchen window comes the sun for a while
These daily endeavours of house work will not run away
Natures forever changing but today it was sublime
My only wish is for songs to break out for forty miles around
Hoping something in this loneliness will resound before night
Should I go find a babbling brook murmuring for a while
Maybe wait until Sunday for a churchbell sound

FORERUNNERS

Must misery strive in vain for such a long time
Have come up from an old world to meet today
That frailty of childhood we have all come to know
Those farm smells here behind barn walls coated with lime
There's a short list of words describing the scent
In prayers ask for despair to leave this place
A pledge for mercy was our beckon call
Here on the farm such a simple life a bad event

Always to see farmers driving cows on a morn landscape
Such methodic ways that one should least expect
Had pondered these moments to see what else was in shape
That sprawling ground in realism on a rolling tape
Same old concept of chores for another day
The stifling of hope wagered like a time warp
With no fond endurance shall pursue nothing
To be discontented even under a suns nice array

These melancholy days of yore reeked away
Lets be gleeful farmers one knows no better
Farmer John is the nickname in which to relate
An old saying from away back then is hit the hay
A bed time expression reposed to a time of rest
Have not used the word finally since my childhood
That word hope by passed me a long time ago
Each piece of old realism is what I detest

THE SILVER BOX

The most precious box made from silver shinning bright
So much attention to the silver one, an enchanted place
Inside the mystery box profusion along with change
Here a lady stands forecasting events of new treasure in sight
Having rings, heirlooms along with necklaces of gold
In this box many were left only wearing a chosen few
Our blessed moments of a new jeweled member there
A great lady triumphs moments here so it's been told

A while she lingers undecided which jewel to wear
In my thoughts unwilling to buy any more precious things
Maybe give her some scented fragrances with odors
Was unable to mention jewels or perfumes which to compare
How should one render their feelings about it all
On down the dim hall my feet ascended like before
Have gone to the sink to wash my hands for dinner now
My thoughts of this day did not set firm I recall

Had remembered sitting by the bed to bless a starting day
Would it be better to change events to something else
Those daily ideas never finish they come or go always
Best to be clean shaven, neat hair, with something nice to say
Should someone shine the silver box make it like new
Hoping to change her mind to think about fine arts of life
There is always a better way around things I've been told
Just try to enlighten the day when someone's feeling blue

ONDERDONK LANE

Once upon a birthday in a place not far away
The actual consequences of an imaginist coming there
With lots of moments of opinion how could one forget the way
On leaving Marg's to the four-to-one an accident on that day
Some grace by a chance of fret to find Onderdonk Lane
Where in the world lives that kin of mine no time to spare
Dark was the sky on through the night we rode
Across the bay bridge to Carrying Place with lost time to regain

Seems there was not a place like Onderdonk in sight
Having prayers makes despair vanish for a while
Take a reckoning of matters as they come or go
Went hither, thither on country roads on this night
Then came the grand discovery with modest sighs at last
When reaching here it was a real place of happiness to know
At Onderdonk Lane, here there was a strong hold for love
On seeing their grandchildren, here was so much love to be
cast

The scent of apples makes me think of yesterday
Also black and white brings back the memories of our old folks
We have all hauled down sorrows of loss luster days
Such long ago realisms haunts us in another way
Most of us now have become feeble pestered with pain
Only good news delights us mostly, we seldom smile
Most old people losing a loved one, idleness comes with time
For Bill's seventy fifth birthday we had a great time at
Onderdonk Lane

TOWN CRYING HAGLETS

Those wonder mysteries never seem to be good
Almost impossible having these haglets for neihbours
How can they flatly deny things they really said
By times they speak in different languages not understood
To have the urge to ignore these haglets forever
All these town crying words are extreme from a neighbour
These by-law people are getting tired of haglet phone calls
So many frustrating moments its our lasting endevour

In my thoughts have self inscribed philosophy overtones
The live long day has no gusto, losing patience in the end
Have to reinvent ours senses to get through the day
When a frig goes out to the street haglets phone
A by-law officer comes to investigate a discarded thing
For sure there is an audience of haglets applauding now
Lets prepare a day of reckoning have it come soon
This kind of neighbor is like a bird always to sing

Sunday haglets watch us Catholics as we drive away
During summer they pull our garage signs out on sale days
All my thoughts are transcendent on doing for the Lord
They antagonize us with by-law people selling Saturday
An all summer long brooding by the haglet one
Made a pile of earth in my garden to mix my compost
A haglet called the by-law people on my gardening work
These people without a conscience what can be done

A TINY TINKLE

A wind brushes across the chimes making a tiny tinkle
Watched as maple keys twin down to the lawns dewy grass
Came songsters calls out from nearby trees
The gazebo canvas caught by the wind making a wrinkle
That summer haze caught in hours of stillness here
So many times mist has passed across this lonely yard
Then came a blue jay squawk shocking morning silence
With a crows caw many squirrels did disappear

The chimes will tinkle on balmy breezes of a peaceful day
On such a breeze so many fragrants were brought
Each day is spaced for every kind of event
Best to transfer todays moments by any way
Out of a July sky such a nice summer came
A small wind motion tinkled its way through the trees
While looking for a sense of purpose the afternoon passed
None of my summer walks are all the same

A glowing sun now heading down to its nightly fate
Here towering pines shadowed the sinking sun
A blood red sky set a lonely moment for an evening mood
The chimes still tinkling away by the garden gate
Then came the last blue bird sounds under a blackening sky
That untiring tinkle shared its sounds night and day
For sure there's unseen lovers under a moonlit scene
Here was only me dumbfounded no one close by

A DWELLING PLACE

Many a story centered on tales of woe from yesterday
Here standing in an old land with events out of the question
There is still those old lamps sitting in the shadows
So glad to leave this place standing beside the road far away
Them days all hapless times with little care in mind
All of those dark moments left behind out there
Can remember that ragged urchin his voice unheard
A place with no loving moments only the rash stern kind

Have been able to tell the story of my life in a dark hallway
The old cornerstone had prayers to help me out
So renowned were the deeds from an old home of late
I did know life could be better on that far off day
Such a rough storm shook the cornerstone of my past
Had stood in that burdened land wishing for better times
That young heart called out for new roads to be found
One's soul cries out hoping these old days would not last

Here there was no goodness or dignity to be found
There was need for a resting place for a weary man
No fulfillment for the future leaving destinies in wait
There's no place for goodness with attitudes around
In seeking reality first one has to bear the pain
Been so long for having ones back against the wall
Have gone through hell in that place of disgrace
In a place of poverty only hardships with no gain

A MUDDY POND

All miracles have might to last only time decays
Out yonder a muddy pond seeks having cattle there
Here a farm boy walks aimlessly along each morn
A pasture land filled with moos starts many days
This was a place for cattle that barbed wire closure sight
How could a life of no grace need pity as of now
Always in need of honour for doing a good deed
To do all this farm work without pay was not right

Many crows had cawed to the sun in their daily flight
Wish a gentle summer breeze would brush cares away
Are these times when the world of wonder began
The sun on metal barn roofs reflection was really bright
Here the barnyard was a sight wallowing mush
Up the path of sucking mud with cows flaps the cattle came
On through the gate to green pastures they were bound
When the collie dog came, he made the cows rush

In this world of wonder compassion does not apply
There's might for the work without any gain
It's a muddy pond after the cattle tramp through
A farm has a rotten day even with a bright sun in the sky
The grass in this pasture was almost eaten away
For all summer came steady mooing by the pond
Was the only chore boy as years came and went
When the green grass runs out we will feed bails of hay

WEEDY WAYS

My actions are stronger then the weeds that grow
Some weeds on this green earth seem never to end
Lots of quack grass comes at dawn creeping up again
A young boy working the garden every day no weeds to show
A wish is these unwanted had weedy wings to fly away
Without any sense or purpose have weed sinews in the land
So restless they are on the ground wanting to multiply
These dandelions during summer blow their seeds all day

Has a devil made weed seeds with sponk to spread
Along the garden fence some tall weeds hobbled by the wind
The touch of this human hand puts pesty to rest
Even a small drop of dew is how earthly plants are fed
How great the flower dwelling there of pleasing embrace
A rough wind shakes the darling buds of the old pear tree
All weedy one's be gone I was unable to hold a swift hand
back
Having been gone today these dandelions tomorrow to face

There's vining ivy that staggers through the fence each day
Then comes the human hand putting them to rest there
Soon comes the thistle saying hello in a nasty crouch
These spectacles have weapons trying to keep you away
What we call pig weed is good to eat we all know
This youngster of yesterday pulling weeds is a weekend job
Sore knees and aching back was always the case
Work everyday from morn to night is how it would go

REBIRTH OF WONDER

Here is some kind wonderer with a hopeful heart
When by times hands are idle, look for good deeds
Had become a caretaker on many old lonely rooms
One never knows what around the corner to start
Forever comes dreadful thoughts left on memory street
Every day passes like dark clouds on the horizon
Around every corner there's something to do for me
No haven place to stay in order to rest one's feet

Forever in dreams keeps calling me back to long ago
My old mind sighs with finally having rest from it all
Then these times refound in nightmares as if its reality
Here was I in a fearful moment of ago times to reason
Always in every life we must bear the pain
Now have found love in a rightful place while searching
From that old life restraint came new found freedom
Goodness has twined around my heart it will remain

Most often former day twilights will come my way
Remember those old days a flimsy thread of concern
Them days were with fearful rogues of untrust
In scenes of woe now is a mission one would say
Away back that earthly idle was a spectacle indeed
A lad was unfairly treated being entombed there
Back then with my gentle ways wanted to cast wishes
Better ways with better days this person did proceed

HEARD CHURCH BELLS CHIME

An urchin boy a working stiff every single day
One day fought back, lots to say no nice guy anymore
For fighting back was taken to farmer in Trenton for work
Here I slept in the loft of the barn filled with hay
Went picking stones all day in the fields at this place
Each morn carried buckets full of water for the cows
Then climb a ladder to a loft to throw down straw
So much in the nineteen sixties a boy had to face

At night went plowing fields in the moonlight there
The existence was tough, too profound to bare
Out of this bad world come walk with me to see
Wore rags and shoes with holes, nothing new to wear
Only the moon with the stars seen me at night
Would like to know where the road of escape went
Please call me dear Lord I would like to go
Had look everywhere for happiness none was in sight

The start of each day was at five, breakfast at nine
Did fill my senses with regret not to do this anymore
Heard church bells chime while working in fields of stone
Would like to run away be a gospel singer I had in mine
Had sour delights on my menu today wanting to leave
Every month my mother and father collected my pay cheque
Worked day and night with no money in return for it
With this type of parents with a heart so naïve

A DAYS FAREWELL

A creative morning sky with clouds looming there
All types of birds flying from the shadows of the trees
Several bees came from a hive by the wooden fence
Had woken up one hour ago with no time to spare
Yesterday's work unfinished seen with sleepy eyes
Here it goes again walking across that same old floor
That sun's cheering light of morn has bounded so fast
The old hay maker has climbed high into the sky's

Was a nice view from where the story stood this day
Where silence once stood my feet came to be
A better place now then those long ago means
In the silence heard a caw from an orchard far away
From life's constant journey makes old times a far
Those lost echoes have disappeared on roads of time
That noise from the stillness resounding happily
A long time past gloom day have gone on to par

Every sweet thought a general part of the day
Lets go say hello to our best friends for a while
Here on a noon time street what better things to do
Not like old times the last gasp for something to say
Have time to say farewell to a neighbor before night
Was not to tired to say a prayer as in long ago times
Those dusty roads with bad days is now all gone
That rash time for my world is far out of sight

EVITABLE SCENES

Days of yore with fishing, the brook walked with me
In the bush trees tall and short a picture of nature
Where I sat fishing noble willows dropping over the brook
Out from the dammed up waters wild ducks to see
Around these waters bullfrogs croaking there
That crows cawing never changes always the same
Many squirrels could be seen and heard all day
Left the farming chores for one day did not care

Did fish for a while then went biking in the cornfield
At lunch time here, lots of pigeons came around
Soon after went off to an orchard place for an apple
This fishing place by the orchard and cornfield was concealed
Someone else would have to do chores on this day
Heard callings far off by my parents by the mainroad
Wanted my brothers to do chores this day for a change
The wandering reason was just to get far away

Here I was waiting for colours in the west to be born
The old sun now behind the trees heading down
That collie cow dog came to meet me, like where have you
been
Was time to go home take my favourite path through the corn
Onward around the orchard bound ways to home
An orange moon rising now between the shadowy hills
Became tired that every day was my chore time
No matter what happens I will take another day to roam

SLUMBER ROOM

To drop off to sleep with a night full of dreams
Into another world of distant wandering there
Here breaths of former people onto me
How things can change after midnight it seems
A mind able to look into the night where souls can hide
Happens in dream time just when you want to rest
Every thing stems from times of old persisting in mind
Life is a wonder of change where thoughts best reside

Each night waits for a brand new dawn to show
A dream is things lost in time still reaching out
Recalling life's misery embracing the night
So much emotion reclaimed from long ago
Here in this slumber room it's being brought all about
At night a spiritual world descends from this bed
A visionary in mind supposing days whence to unfold
It seems only after midnight these apparitions come out

In dreamland life is entailed to what it use to be
Where else to be at night but huddled in a warm bed
Out from nowhere has been scenes stalking the dark
Why in this creation does a spirit divine want to be pal to me
Seems the darkness has mysteries it want me to take part
Sleepy times and old time, nightly walk hand in hand
Night times is like other times it turns into day
How to eliminate reveries would be a start

DISTANT SHORES

At morn the rolling mist came down to hide the land
Had been walking close to Cape Bretons sea drenched shore
The bones of seagulls lying like broken sticks among the stones
Suddenly the land sheds it's dense cloak, as the sunshine
began
Stood watching the white surf curling a shore a distance away
My thoughts had been tossed into the rolling sea of mysteries
Ere many water beetles brought killdeers to feed here
Such a wonderful place to be on this beautiful day

Across this windswept land heard church bells chime
In mine ears still abides a gospel message for me
Coming on through these blue cathedral skies bold sunshine
Them rolling waves thundered ashore many a time
All of a sudden the tempest raged lightning flashing around
That soiled sorry weather ails the evening for a while
The fearful storm came with restless torment for a spell
No seagulls or killdeer nothing could be found

Such fiery of blown spume, with seagulls crying from afar
Had a quickening of the heart not tuned for new events
The storm was winding up the sea to a billowy swell
High waves crashed on shore with raging foaming mar
Again came rumbling thunder, descending on the sea out loud
Then suddenly there was a colossal moment for this visiting host
Here along such a deranged shore bird's cheeping afraid to
show
This hell bent storm encircling the sea with its nasty cloud

LATE SEPTEMBER

Where ever the flea markets are we go there
Out of the constant world comes the time to rise each morn
That vendors voice inside us says go there each time
While breaking into the best of a day, none can compare
Most mornings set up on dewy grass, a beige here tent
We will set up in early morn, sometimes to the sunsets west
The prices are not set to high for customers to reach
Here we are on the road a breaking dawn when daylights near

We are part of these episodes keeping up summers pace
Out here under the sun always tanned as we can be
Each year it's nice to mingle with all the comrades again
A weekend dark highway setting out to many a place
It's wherever our senses may guide us this day
Hoping to have a long season, be able to sell things for sure
Have gone across these days in life our fortunes not high
All of these doings fills the weekend void in every way

In morning or evening rain could come to spoil it all
Whatever the course of weather it rules our fate
Here's the drawbacks commandeering our sales here
With all the odds discounted there's no time to stall
Along with a few laughs, as well as meeting the friendly kind
Was our notions to sell then finding those who buy
This selling of used items has been part of our life
Some are articles from garage sales other things we find

FOREFATHERS

These farmers known by the red barn name
Off each gravel road its plowing time again
For ages we were the people growing everything
Summer days the sprouting new crops, cultivating the same
Still remember seeing farmer and team silhouettes there
At twilight a team of horses crossing the headlands
Those dusty fields of forefathers day of toil
That workaday of long ago nothing can compare

Out past the red barn plenty of fields to be sown
While riding a two furrow plow, got bumped around
Other days readied some hay to be taken away
It took most of the summer for hay to be grown
A hay loader followed the wagon along for loading at noon
As the load got heavier these horses slowed down
There was lots of sweating for the work being done
After emptying two loads in the barn dinner would be served

From the house porch heard the dinner bell out loud
Getting meals was a woman's chore them days
In those times farmers help one another was the call
The grain crops were thrashed with all men on board
No money changed hands it was the bartering style
Every farmer's wife pitched in during thrashing times
A table full of cooked food these women were good at
This lad helped to do that kind of work for a while

GLORY STILL WAITS

When all the world is young prancing away
What's appealing to life is having a girlfriend
With them thoughtful eye's to tell me great things
Better than having meandering moments all day
To be always roaming with a loving heart it's true
Being a person with that common sense emotion
So many kindly intentions per day to resume
Was a long ago scene from dawn to dust, many things to do

There was trumpets sounding if glory was found
Was always in turmoil until I found a way
So much pride ruled my will from yonker years
Those silent screams inside me wanted out when people came
around
On me rest hopes clutched by a doubt ruling day
Here in a well traveled place was entering wits end
Was sentimental for days sitting along gloom road
With my attitude would be a strange person anyway

My sighs where a disgrace while wanting a glory spot
All those so wanted moments at once fell apart
An old gray haired man still yearning away
Somebody had told me to be happy with what you got
Are these intentions for more to farfetched to be true
Seems like a void with intended prayers on either end
Every year from away back when with it's tried circumstances
Some glory would be a blessing after all I've been through

TWILIGHT PHANTOMS

Such was the land of dreams in a pillow world race
These old home land nightly walls never to face again
Here after the lamp went out it turned into another place
Some gracious old memories by gones nothing could compare
A time ago walked beside woo's of this old time place
Was harkened by a grandfather clock still with me
Still remember those altercations after midnight
Seems mightily perks in yonker years gave fright was the case

After midnight was spirit ditties during long days past
This home with night haunts with souls from beyond
So much dementia frequented in them times of woe
Was the happiest young person to be from here at last
To recall them futile echoes from a creaky stair
Heard a crying baby in the attic in the wee morning hour
The front window curtains fluttered about all night
To be affirmed these foes from the hiply house were there

The pulse of night abides above the ceiling space
Those awful cries full of daunting restless fear
Some nights a priest fully robed in white looked at me
He was a ghost holding his hands like he was saying grace
Every time these strange scenes haunt my sleep here
One becomes fit to be tied in that hiply house of horrors
Amid the shadows folklore phantoms came once more
Always after midnight the twilight phantoms came near

THIEF OF YOUTH

This young life has missed many a splendored things
That outreach for love was left with a solemn heart
Each morning was up before the crowing rooster
Could never attend church when the calling bell rings
A sincere voice with haunted hopes seemed forever
Most roads were uphill all the way during my teens
Ere the years between five and ten were grim spoken
In silent thoughts grin and bared every toil endeavor

When I was from five to eight years recalled the forest
The making of a leaf house was part of youthful ways
Will always remember green moss facing south on the trees
All long gravel roads golden rods being the main pest
Every morning under low bushes partridge were drumming
Had a little reprieve with no parent coming around
Had to make out I was busy raking leaves here
Heard the dog bark telling me my mother was coming

After dinner took manure to the garden spreading it
everywhere
Was always a tanned boy laboring without slack
Before summer was through went thrashing for farmer John
During these thrashings was waist deep in grain shoveling there
Recall the humming of a threshing machine all day
The weekend before shook grain sheaves in the field
That relentless work for sure was a thief of youth
Working for farmer John then hours ten dollars was the pay

WOOD PILED

This was a day of cutting the winter wood supply
The frost sparkled along the edges of the woods
Among the bare elm boughs no squirrels playing now
A cold breeze through the trees was the only reply
Out in this weather a person shivers in despair
From silence came the howl of a wolf out loud
Out of a cedar close by a chickadee came to say hello
All my moods or passions not a soul around to care

My hands numbed until after the tree notching chore
The axe strokes echoed through many tall trees
At once the chainsaw brought the tree crashing down
On through the morning trimming these felled trees as before
There was ten cords of wood I had piled each day
These depths of winter reach into my very soul
Each breeze unmerciful in this cold lonely place
Through all these winter days no offer of any pay

My heart had no pleasure unfairness is to blame
Had to shudder when looking back on woodman years
Such cold winter days with the north wind howling
Any boy in this environment would be made to feel the shame
Still more elms waited to be cut during the bitter cold
With frozen snow crunching with every step was the case
No one, here to pardon me from this mortal pain
With the winters in Belleville it's true that was told

MY PAST FOREVER

On a school day here rambling down a gravel road as before
At all times my clothes smelt like smoke of burning wood
With mingled thoughts is this the way it's suppose to be
Seems every day to be dehumanized just once more
My young ideas was an illusion to this heart not redeemed
With no peace of mind condemned the real life part
It cost four times as much to feed cows then to buy milk
Being poor was my companion forever it had seemed

The time of having chicken pox was the worse part
While having the sickness our house was stifling hot in summer
With the windows open flies came to pester you
Everyday someone came to my room to see when work would start
As you walked from room to room fly stickers bugged about
Here was people with no sentimental feeling just cruel at heart
Be best to curse them times no one was really sincere
For my adult life thoughts of farm life came with doubt

Had to wear a tam to church leaving a forehead ring after
No one else wore such a thing as this for miles around
My thoughts mirrored these old world friends, were few
In church behind our backs heard snickers and laughter
Do as I say not as I do came loud and clear from a mom
Been there done that rings true for them former times
Would have liked for you to give me your world, would give you mine
To be seen and not heard was for sometime to come

ABOUNDED WITH WOE

Them old times daunted me with so much blatant woe
My heart guides me through it all with love of prayers
From attitudes to foul not better but worse to comprehend
Was a lot of wishing on hope could make better so
The rumours were right about hearts of stone
In todays world there is common equal love shared
Let there be recommened portions for young or old
Not a soul around to help had to fight the battles alone

That in which fate hides a good faith omen can see
There's not enough might in a youngster to defend them
You where unable to meet the people from whence we know
They say according to the times is how it was meant to be
This man has been to the place of see and tell, you cannot go
there
Old times always ended on a sad note for all concerned
Here many stones were pitched into a stormy sea
The folks of them times raised urchin children no one to care

This man will always adore others no matter sayings of some
A person always has faults that's part of our life
Time is like everything else, after while has an end
What we intended to do in this life has already come
Like in a day one time rain another time the sun peeks through
Some days we limp have pain it's the oldness it's true
With an ebb for a reason like words in a song
We wish it could have been better but we only have one life to
do

SECOND TO NATURE

Here from our horizon the sun appears again
Then second to nature man's added noisy trains
Once again comes black clouds, thunder resounding there
Down winding highways, passing cars emission restraints
Along the by ways tree's swaying with dying foliage to remain
Out of fireplace chimneys comes choking smoke once more
From a gloomy sky cannot predict what's really there
Us people wallowing in the midst of a world of doubt
Our nature is sick, each day slowly dying, not like before

It's a nice day up there beyond the dense haze of it all
At the break of dawn diesel fueled vehicles make smog
Now Mr. Sun can hardly peer through until smog floats away
Wanting something done about the problem there's no one to
call
To be a short answer, the waters fixed in a truthful way
The lake smells like sewer, in summer it's even more strong
Would call it a sad day because of political hoopla jeopardy
Have poured no no's into the environmental space many a
day

In a rain storm comes a pollution mixture of rainbow stew
Forever to cross one's mind, where does respect come into
being
Out on what was green pastures nothing grows well here
Had need to turn someone's crank to ask what is really true
All they told me was to pee in the flower bed keeps raccoons
away
Then I answered back pull my finger here is natural gas free
How great thou art does not jive anymore, no sentimental
value
Tell us some good news, are all the pilfers really going to stay

Best not go on an ocean cruise it's full of garbage there
Will have to rest on tomorrows mentors waiting for change
The two faces of yesterdays world are really gone forever
To subsist until our grandchildren grow old some truth to declare
Above the clouds that suns shining full blast the earths a mess
Must endorse better ways get away from doing things wrong
Best be accredit to new standards of mind to manner
Our world is going to pots, be truthful a need to just confess

EMPIRICAL TRUTHS

Surely the visible truth counts a whole lot for some
For that stature of things hiding truths gains nothing
The proof is the pudding fashioned to suit reality
Our world has milestones we endure for the best to become
Must say plausible words with smart meanings to recite
Better to abide in one's self in only things that are just and true
Who ever respects good friends shall be honoured by them
Them partakers in lies, one wish for them to go fly a kite

Lets strive to where value counts for doing better tomorrow
There is always true affection needs guidance to resist nurds
That faithfulness personally has harmony to keep on going
Becomes a waste of time when some is creating sorrow
Should partake in devotion, for sure it should span a lifetime
For the sake of good tidings leave vengeance grumbling alone
How many good actions qualify with unreasonable people
Had endured hate from far back in my childhood prime

During my out pouring hope then, have made it this far
Wanting for an image to be up to par for making of friends
There is no need for improving my mind is already made up
Here is a father with three oppressed sons not up to par
They have been transformed by malicious lies caused by one
In rendering my kindness it was unaccepted by their views
For my deeds it's an honourable life with rewards galore
Was devoted to my wife, now I have lost her in lifes there's no
fun

Whose good will could restore all things that went wrong
Everyone's all for themselves in their greed for fame
In concerning them precious times in life how long is to late
When someone ask me for a favour it will not be left this long
Have been so greatly sincere, merited by respect for people
That sincerity of heart means nothings, which my conscience
dreads
A number of years it's been hard to understand inscrutable
family way
Someone behind closed doors disobedience prone for trouble

THEM OEDIPUS ONE'S

The people's conduct was from a strange point of view
As for passion it was abandoned in their teenage years
So far fetched is the ideas about life in general for them
They accomplish that which the mother purposed, nothing new
When more friendship is pursued, they persevere it again
These forbearers of hate have lives overshadowed by evil
Here is a father that has endured an alien family for years
There is my faith with no understanding, is everyone insane

What more should a man have done in spite of it all
Those long years was concerned with the purpose intended
My faiths devotion has no mystery it's there, it's for real
Had a spouse that was permissive then one does recall
Here is an example of a wicked person known by all my kin
In that home was a father in every respect descent and fair
Trying to find the source that's creating anguish, no one knows
To be deceitful, siblings it's inappropriate, for sure is a sin

Hard to deal with futile up bringing's, no consideration there
For a lifetime initiated my good intentions always
Have tried to use kindness along with good judgment then
Everyone knows good Samaritan fathers today are rare
What this man has accomplished did receive generous rewards
The disclosure frame of mind is who despises descent people
Our wake up episode to smell the roses has not come about
yet
How terrible it is with no harmony, only those deceitful discords

112

Lets have the families become transgressors have a fuge day
Here is my final say, the whole bunch being not worth their salt
Every foundation for prosperity is the precious part of life
As for their failing part it's nonsense in every which way
Will reserve my dignity of a good sense person forever
The inappropriate relationship has a known cause in life
All them memories that what went on makes a man cringe
What is proper to good living people for them it is never

AN EVIL THEME

Someone gave them an evil lecture sermon a while ago
The alienation episode was one of a kind at their home
Was a pretence given to life starting her miserable game
All prolonged hope is lost on streets of time we know
There on Shyster street they must go with the flow here
To get fame just invent the coarse needed to get through
Here in a planned for play had to fib every single day
The unwelcome door to enter was the same to exit there

Let them wear black coats no cheerful colours needed
When she was calling the shots a fable story suited the need
Maybe leave things just use Murphy's law for best results
Only the Lord knows where happiness really has succeeded
A mother has manipulated every idea to suit the purpose
Them footsteps of faith have faded away forever more
A mans mind changes when scenes with evil did prevail
Did not go visit them for an attitude, not what I chose

Was best not to stay long if that kind of smite rules the day
When the poisoned message came returned everything to
sender
Today flipped the scene to nicer people with no neurotic brain
Best to leave my blessings with friends with things nice to say
Those who assume things will be okay, have a surprise coming
Where on earth has the love of ours gone that's now in limbo
They come in packs of thirteen, a baker's dozen, everyone liars
Them peons of evil have marred our domain

Let's throw a stone in the water watching hope rings get bigger
A slogan with values gets me through every year so far
Such a motto is to set goals of expectations to come to be
Shall bare in thought that no one's perfect it's best to figure
To call it defeat for the land of Nod so far for those years
Will think about tomorrow's ideas for suggestions to use
Out there in La La Land will wait to see what will happen
Can think about them better people when a new generation
appears

A PENCHANT

For months spent writing a stubborn stanza
Thinking it was the old age of seventy-seven eluding me
Had to reassemble for a while finding some clue
Hoping before that failing breath get a bonanza
All my dreams being dashed as in times before
Was never a spend thrift day during my whole life
Always to be in dark halls no goodness getting through
Seems there's no change traveling the same road once more

At first a family life of an unfaithful wife
So much emotion entombed around every single day
Life was a stubborn stanza every chapter wrong
The shabbiness of a woman's morals an ungenuine life
Them lie versions are hallway shadows there
Most days of regret weighs heavy with doubt
That past penchant had wagers to deal with
Always it will knock on my heart that bad affair

Such a folly consumes my thoughts once more
All that commotion of virtues love could not live
For this part of life's compassion had penance due
She flawed them vows designated to implore
Here on that long lost path one person dressed in devils attire
The repose was half a lifetime with it's end
My first wife's children have bad father thought revenge
Today's wife with all her good morals that I admire

AN ELOQUENT DWELLING PLACE

Here an Chada Avenue where I live today
A nice bungalow a stone throw from town
Such a nice dwelling with flowers all the way around
My wife, Jeanettee and me have good things to say
Have a garden with so much stuff we can grow
An eloquent dwelling place for people that care
For twenty-five years we lived in this place
There's interlocking bricks where the van does go

Was not like times of yore the deceitful kind
A long time ago left this place of ah regret
Finally the maker of loneliness set me free
Through trials and tribulations a new life to find
Back then there was no such thing as good humour at dawn
As for bygone times only flaunting moments always
Was able to draw black curtains shut out the past
That old tenantry now forever is all been gone

Now a whole new life with someone to care
We worked as a team to pay the mortgage off
Who knew that someday one could find peace
With love in our hearts nothing else could compare
The entry into a new phase being great I recall
Them kin on my children's behalf do not bother to come
They do not want phone calls or cards none of the such
There is lots of friends visit us big and small

MISCHANCE

Would like to stand a while just to whistle a song
Making a pensive mood for something great in mind
Takes away that melancholy frown all the while
Here at my place people with an attitude do not belong
After every closing day take a long lingering look behind
Before closing the door for the night wave to a neighbor
It seems right and just in a friendly town
Not like the old days when everyone seemed confined

Best to say prayers when your paces come to rest
The birds wings have quieted from their daytime flight
Every heart at peace is splendor for us all
Everywhere embraced each friend doing my best
With come of morn had passed under the evergreen tree to
greet a neighbor
Not like old times with that rude bliss of solitude
There should always be goodness following us forever
By chance ask to water someone's lawn as a favor

Help a neighbor then it comes back ten fold
Put a comrade feeling in your old fellow bones
Having friendship galore when each day unfolds
Best be a Samaritan kind of person I've been told
It's like looking forward to a robin's cheer-up time
Some have the gift for gab hoping the wife will wave you home
Have watched a neighbor hang an old black coat on the
porch each day
Be for going inside listen for the very last chime

PATCHED BREECHES

Old day orchards beside a clover field was a common sight
My life was like a willow tree growing in acres of corn
The dawn fog made it hard to find the cows to milk
To not be a farmer this man never got the right
So many people were poverty one's in those days
As a boy had assumed patched clothes was the fad
A home remembrance of lighting lanterns at night
That old time lantern light had taunted me in many ways

My mind foresaw little hope for a patched clothed boy
The wheeling West Virginia songs were a midnight delight
Sometimes stayed up all night listening to nasal tone songs
There was not to much other radio programs to enjoy
That next school day my patch britches got the attention time
In summer wore no socks or shoes was the case
Our childhood poorness restricted us to winter shoes
Having no shoes could only hear the church
bell chime

Still we believed in God saying our prayers before rest
Being immensely lonely not going to church like others
All those old days saw lack of hope with patches of life
On through terrible times unable to have the best
Was hard but wished the hurt would go away
My thoughts was to be a traveller, never come back no more
Must life always have black clouds hanging above
Had always thought positive for things to get better someday

THE HUNTING WOODS

To recall the hunting woods where cottontails ran
Then out a ways on a ploughed field jackrabbits hiding
On the winter landscape tree's like guards frozen in time
Most days went hunting with a twenty two gun
Then into groundhog holes bunnies scurrying there
My dog spent time chasing rabbits into these holes
There was a box strapped to my back, carrying a ferret there
All morning had been trekking on snow trails everywhere

The earth our mother solitude gives us all she can
By a stream another human footprint heading Southward
My assumption another hunter out in search of food
Where the tall hickory's grew, out a black bear ran
This old black wanderer headed to a gully then disappeared
A little while later a squirrel was dangling off a bough
This day of howling winds blowing snow outside the woods
Suddenly the call of a moose because his kin had neared

Was quiet for a while until a wolf starting howling away
Many tracks of wolves and rabbits showing where they went
On my shoulder yoke hung six rabbits all in a row
The North wind blew snow most of the day
During the high wind drifting a bobcat ran
He had a rabbit clutched in his teeth with head up high
Must head home now that the darkness is nigh
The wolf, bobcat and me caught many a rabbit in a one day
span

AN ABANDONED FATHER

Until some right answers come a heavy heart remains
An old Dad waits as days go on more lengthy now
Aging is not a planned time to be reviewed again
A road that comes beside me, all my love it sustains
There's been many a times have played on taunted strings of
hope
Forever an immoral mooch puts in place the fate
There's friends and the unfriendly your coping with
Only bad people make a bad world in which to cope

The belief is we are not befitting as grandparents ever
Our wish is not granted cause a stranger takes our places
One mother who deals in devious things for the becks call
A woman doing her best, the bloodline bound to sever
Such things administered by her cronies in ill repute
We know in families that bad omens do exist
On these streets of time leave a lying dog lay
When we went to visit them they conjured up a dispute

This clarity has immersed from a mother's planning team
Not to well understood is the devious point of it all
An old saying in Rome be a man or change the vow
According to one's optimism it's a ludicrous bad scheme
Each motive not being at all similar or even the same
Here was a terrible story theme that applied false episodes
For the purpose of alienation from that person which it came

OUR COLLOP KIDS

They have no real work to do as our olden times did
There is a bus that takes them to school and back
We had no bus to get school, peddled a bike both ways
A whole lot of junk food makes an easy lunch making a fat kid
To peddle a bike on gravel roads, back then was a real task
These youngsters do not walk to see a friend, see him on the ipod
Most teenagers puff and pant while walking only one block
On the computer everything is there to know, don't have to ask

No one takes a lunchbox to school, they buy cafeteria food
The fat on these young peoples arms hangs down like goose wings
It looks so funny these days, they waddle like ducks as they walk
The computer age children do not exercise at all, which is no good
Having to do chores at five in the morning, then later to school the case
Had to ride our bikes one mile to school slowly moving on gravel all the way
Since old times the gad persuader no longer exist at home or school
When we lost control in the schools and homes, now it's hard to face

Every time you turn around the children have a special break day
Even when the child does want to go to school he says I'm staying home
Now they tell the parent when they want to go to bed at night
Some teenagers become paper delivery people to receive a pay
In classes of sex education the children have been told everything
During this day of age the parents have no choice of discipline
It's all on the computer no need to listen to the parent anymore
Do not worry about where food comes from thats for the tooth fairy to bring

Is anybody qualified to give orders around a parents home
Even at school one says I am going home they just up and leave
To live in harmony, no restraints or a child will call the cops
Without obedients we have no rules to follow, how come
Tell them to go to city hall to get married, with an atheist thought
So much to persevere these days with no choice in the matters
What has to be endured why repopulate the world any more
No merit to raising a family only humility no hope in what we got

KICKAPOO JOY JUICE

In nineteen sixty five a Monarch company made beverages
Their first was Kickapoo Joy Juice said by the bottle
A person by the name of Al Capps was inspired by the drink
He published the comic book Lil' Abner for all young ages
There was a beverage called Mountain Poo, changed to
Mountain Dew
The Kickapoo Joy Juice was only sold in United States back
then
Before the drink came to Canada it was renamed Dr. Pepper
Even Coca Cola then having cocaine a narcotic, it was brand
new

Our generation with the coke capped magic kid showed up
This Coca Cola companies narcotics made people crave for
the drink
Coming up with bottled drinks has fulfilled the children's time
Was easier for children to drink from a bottle rather then a cup
Half way in every store was a trunk cooler easy access for all
Some bootleggers used Coca Cola as an additive for the mix
In the old day village stores everyone remembers Orange
Crush
The Orange Crush bottles were a smoky orange and very tall

There was song writers like Tony Danza with new lyrics
His songs derived from any new beverage that came to be
Than along came copy cats to get on the bandwagon then
Soon came a traders world for all kinds famous comics
With the collecting of bottles money, children could buy more
books
The buying of comics made up the children's world of those
days
One strives to live by what's important for every era that's
going
Will always remember the stove pipe trouser, the fifties looks

Much later came the Sadie Hawkin's formal dances trio
Also Anne Shell Marines musical album trio in nineteen seventy
Was a classic comic strip that inspired them to do these
In the Irish show band version was like a jig about scherzo
This all came out of a company called then a skunk work place
During those times we had crafty writers for a child's world
Todays world people are to serious, with nothing for happy
moments
Here the new phase seems to be heading on into cyberspace

DID DO ME WRONG

Someone had forgotten about compassion that rules hope
Them moments of decision has that awful dimension of no
concern
Even though we are all of the world theirs is some nasty ones
We must be persons of expectations helping someone to cope
Have encountered in days of old no bond of unity what so-ever
Things were not appropriate all the days of my young life
No one showed us some guidance to follow, just do what I tell
you
The home was a wholesome compunction of shame forever

How does one respect those kin full of hate coming from
childhood
A man is worthy to accomplish all that is good, always slighted
Must be involved in the routine, do it or get the gad treatment
The way wardness was ever land hosted, do as I say or have no
food
Get prepared for another day, it's always much worse then
before
As for encouragement was based on how much one could
endure
To live justly was asking a lot, pietism came with a second
thought
Always trying for an honourable way of life, but was stopped
once more

Forever searching for a more happy home with some freedom
there
Was unable to find that fathomable goodness in a human race
To justify well being to be judged by the good things that you
do
Seems parents where not worthy of responsibilities here
On the journey for happiness hope to find it some day very
soon
Looking among the supposed mature one's, wondering about
their actions
A mother wanted a black sheep to fit in with her ruthless part
If no one weeded the garden our Mom did yell like a baboon

Have eagerly intended to explore a new source of honour for
me
Shall push forward with my thoughts to only favour number one
For my sake will rise above that obligation knowing my fate
All things of harmony can be rung in, while truth sets me free
Am not the pilgrimage group of long ago working for no pay
There for must pronounce the good news have no more
despair
Them old parables lack kindness and joy, it's the way it was
At my new dwelling place deprived of a loved one will still find
a way

NO SAMARITANS

In weighing of life's merits, fault hoods don't count
For all the remembrances of yesterday, no pardons given
Out of the doom and gloom no hope lives there today
For the realm of decency pick out, what is the full amount
The product siblings for my half assume disorders are alright
Have merits of goodness to be pledged by a faithful heart
My dedication has no goodly grace, was failed to be noticed
Only the best must be called today from a good world sight

Hope someone declares the truth willingly one of these days
Hidden in the depths of mystery what makes some people tick
Some pass through the shadows of the world but cannot hide
How one wins the game is not judged by how fair that the plays
Since the grandchildren have no confidence they are manner
less
Good gestures turn a day into wonderful moments with
meaning
Whoever respects their Dad's good heart, nothing will haunt
them
Them imbeciles of a world have created their self inflicted mess

There is a reason why one cannot honour, first become known
While the father has always been devoted, the kin are rude
It can never be undone that doubt part staying in my heart
They do not know how to act with adults it's this kind of slovenly
As for the origin source it leaves me without confidence right
now
My everlasting love as a father is hard to understand anymore
If the group had honour in their life would be a wonderful thing
Shall entreat my thoughts to wish everyone the best some how

Must recover the peace of the times with a new make over
Hard to humbly expect blindsided intentions being the father
Has to be a way to change discord to mutual, well being
respect
All those who are pleasing to me, do not wish for any other
Whatever was spoken about in former days, had good
intentions
Will someone recommend a new insight, a true image kind
We are all here for the same purpose, make a life, get along
Is a mother that alienates her family, the perpetual functions

LIFE'S FOLLY

Having theory to life is get along a part of kin kind
Most of all meet someone halfway best deeds to recall
Than manner in life is complete without pall mall
Taking everything into account a caring part in mind
Best the better half to be found a person without shame
Forever it was her means to suit circumstances then
This wickedness had created disaster such an undertaking
To distort real facts with lies being that kind of dame

A woman to raise the children as galoots without much doubt
An narcissists raised them up thoughtless like her
Having distorted the fact of reality eliminating consequences
These matter of fact lies making excuses what it's all about
Keep your face always toward the truth no lies find you
Best have happy inspiration be friends with those you meet
Our creation was meant to be on a happy note for the most
Never point fingers of devaluation at life be it an ado

A deception does not belong in a family of friendship
Those delinquent episodes distort facts of honest ability
One has to maintain goodness for all of those concerned
The family bond is mostly about a good relationship
There shall be that impact clique for them fowl deeds
To hate one means you must hate yourself also
Them bad parts rendered must justify the real cause
Every good achievement in life makes it's own needs

To get attention through lies is invisible for fame
Will tend to remember the hurt like it was yesterday
Was a rocky road but did plan life honest and proper
A two faced life will have been ruled as a chance game
Untruth a impressive façade for sure cannot last long
Their potential for a rejection world comes to hard to bare
As one's self being dedicated to peace with much inspiration
For life built with goodness loves hope keeps it strong

DISMAL RELATIVES

Have peevish people being some kindred one's
That informal group an Oshawa clan out there
Must not pray for them because love does not work
Those galoots have manifested misery are my son's
So wretched defines the times made by these nerds
In reply to their objections best confront them with shame
These folks principles where only rotten dispositions matter
Seems it's unsupported by facts in so many words

Hard to understand a reason to smite elders is the case
A contemptible household not worth trying to pity
Comes down to disregard them as a pejorative family
That home settings of lying delusions has taken place
Was a appalling scene grandparents no longer visited here
Had to be bastard born to treat old people with no respect
These were plain rotten notions out of context being uttered
The grandchildren were quiet ne'er a word sitting with fear

Perhaps their mind was full of self flattery back then
To be very dotage that appeals to their way of living
Here's a group of excuses contorted by these human beings
This old world needs goodness not one of us out of ten
For everyone's sake need a common sense reason of late
Being rotten must please them a lot on aiming for tripe
To actually need an idea to advise us as the friendly kind
That welcome sign still bobs in the wind on the front gate

Cannot understand or know who brought these bad vibes
about
Most stories tell of who was the one bringing mercy times
All days must be bad hair days with chintzy idea's for all
With all of their misery times be looking for some new route
Shall put my best foot forward find people to enjoy
My ipod or smart phone not wasted on these galoots
It's the principal of how smart I am for better days
Would name them all Sue, it comes, when born a boy

THE MIGHTY DUKE

The eternal prophet was to serve all people we know
Some people try being more righteous, that embodies them
from real life
While growing up poor was put down by such people
These flagitious one's were looked on as our foe
Have been seeking the trump to sort out mighty dukes forever
They were sullen frowning people, look with faces of awe
All ruddy thin lipped humans always putting on the air
To be part of a snooty tribe, for our family would be never

Such people smiling to your face but smite us later
With them uppity words they are imitation people
As for this ok society we never concerned ourselves
To normal friends our family did cater
The revelry seemed they belonged to the deviant one
Their suggestion of being smarter than the average man
In our born days we all come the same way
It's a wonder they did not get burnt with the nose up to the sun

Them pompous one's talk with a brogue for attention
Where unable to envy them wallowing in spiteful pride
In those day's as a boy it made me laugh the talk
With wantonness to avoid them always I will mention
The family called them buffoons in them days of yore
As a normal fancy we are committed to who we are
Such egotism is a society crutch from away back when
For the last hurrah lets call their bluff once more

THE BOOGIE MAN

All alone in such a narrow orb of darkness so scary here
When night came we were told there was a boogie man
Behind the curtain comes the boogie man told to us
This was the repose wanderer of night to appear
Told to be an ugly form emerging out of the gloom
Were thought to be members of ancient times emerging
These cadences was the content of boyhood darkness
As a boy always kept a light burning in the room

The parent of the time made up of this fathomable affair
Every night kept watch in case it did appear
As for life it's woven into dreams to forget heralds of darkness
Hard to understand our folks infatuating this thing there
From out of the state of dismal so much woe came
This was the utmost extreme that anyone told to a child
Away back in old family times these are the people to blame

Was so glad when the sweetness of morn lights up the room
That demon of darkness was no longer around
Was afraid to look in my dresser mirror someone may look back
The coming of day light hurled apart the place of gloom
Such immortality exited, rebounding no longer surrounding me
That creep of imagination parents should have never uttered
the word
This example of these times was so bleak for youngsters moral
Then comes daylight where that altercate of colossal could no
longer be

WHOLLY PERCEPTIONS

That inevitable condition of humanity is create something new
The purpose of creating is to perceive essential things
As in old times plows were made to till the land
There many chambers from old days to new we went through
Our tendencies are to make life easier as we go along
Them difficult times always striving for it to be better
With faith have come to triumph through hardships and all
As old farmers striving together that's where we belong

The story of adventures in life has taken time to compile
When coming to money truth was it was next to none
During personalizing tendencies comes instinctive desires
Even with tough times we enjoyed having a laugh once in
awhile
Having common sense goes along with whatever we got
We will delve in to well being forever shall be
Avoid antagonism it creates war in a crowd
Having friends working together forever it has brought

How wholly grateful everyone was in that place
Harold and Effie Nichole's place I left the house to go
These were people less conscious of expectants to do
They loved to frolic with children was a known case
Had to get away from at home people who create crying eyes
Did wallow in ignorance for all them childhood days
So relieved to make a break to the real world at large
Was glad when I left home at eighteen with them goodbyes

OLD FASHION WAYS

These times of copper kettles and cast iron stoves
For early morning was the bacon and eggs lingering smell
Put on your bib overalls once more to go to school
Every Saturday bread baking time of twenty loaves
Them times had no conscience of a social metaphor
All a routine to hunker down to for the whole day
Well known as an idiom circumstance for all concerned
To attend the old mission call as one had done before

A life back then of green pastures with mooing cows
Such affluent symbol for the human course of woe
Comes a will call of responsibilities intended for some
Beside the barn a sty of mud wallowing of sows
An acre of garden to be weed get the straw hat on go my son
Was an amber of mist enshrouding the apple groves at morn
Had to wait until noon to go apple picking there
With crows feasting on the corn took out a shotgun

Never forgot about that rooster at daybreak crowing away
Will always remember gravel roads putting dust across fields
Them hens clucking trying to lay an egg some days
Them fond memories plague my mind from time to time today
We were them people who had survived from the pioneers
The smell of pig manure reeked for miles around
But this was the best thing ever to make our crops grow
All our clothes came from the catalog sent by Sears

FRIVOLOUS TOMES

Many people have dropped out since a new generation
began
To know we are poor modest people with a challenge in life
Above our fast pace world are our blessing still there
A life brimmed full of fancies with no hope in plan
All these new phase times befuddled in the cell land
Todays people are becoming daft in a disorder space
Say to the persons get your heads up see what's going on
Maybe the generation from them old times can make a stand

Since the old radios and gramophones we came a long way
The wandered paths of tolerance have been changed by
some
There's unbelievers in this land but our maker's still here
With the endorsement of computers life is more dire every day
Even peoples cultures from far off places rule this land
Them democratic one's do what they want we have no voice
Our country has a door mat saying welcome to our shores
When the pioneers cleared this Canada place this was not
planned

The Canadian social lapse timidly let's aliens have their way
In our long ago times worked the land from dawn to dusk
Aliens simply will not play fair they want their old customs still
Should be like old times an honest days work for an honest days
pay
As the saying goes when in Rome do as the Roman's would do
Having good manners is not a blessing for our good will
Could forever shout to the highest hills it does nothing
We need to put our foot down soon both me and you

NAPKIN TIMES

During child years heard the parents voice only as we sat
Instead of heads up it was heads down over your dish
Was always them identical plans where the napkin deems
It's a given heretic opinion if it's our house you're at
No forgoing restrictions today forgetting mostly all
Them days a father's authentic words keep your bean over
A special for visitors put the napkin in top of your shirt
At Christmas made a big long table, thirty people would call

Us poor one's windows had shabby curtains hanging there
All them taters the sunshine was able to shine through
With grace we thanked the Lord for giving little we had
The cupboards were only restocked when we had money to
spare
Was hard times, a sceptered race working everyday
Being plagued by war times of rations was the case
If us children left some supper went to bed for a while
Every meal time all had to be proper with a napkin right way

We always had a tentative list of who sits where
Each napkin had a name written marking the spot
With hit and miss them many days we manage to strive
To ply the question about the loss of a pet that faithful friend
Even the cattle seemed to know their buddy had passed on
In edacity days everyone had to tow the line for sure
Them old time traditions still intend to haunt me now and then

LOFTS OF NIGHT

An old man here in bed thinking about a long ago place
Have gone back to yesterday unlocking old time scenes
As I stare up from my pillow remembering old snow days
To live back then we were a real tough hearty race
A horse clopping along with the cutter going somewhere
These days of winter commotion of hame bells ringing
The infatuation of these old times has really made my night
Here sleigh track after sleigh track marks here

Such an outrageous venture turning back pages of time
So much pulsating motion spent in a mind set era
From an old time page so many people now lost souls
An morning church bell many sleighs heading toward the chime
Out of my lofts of night comes an old how do you do
There was something about another episode back then
That long trek over the snow to school we had to go
There was no excuse of the buses not getting through

Went to a one room school out in the middle of nowhere
Still wide awake looking on down that old road
A honey pail in my hand with a lunch inside
Here looking out from todays world nothing can compare
Again pulled my head higher on the pillow to think on
Thought about old big pennies along with small ones now gone today
To have actually stayed awake the whole night long
Here to lay wondering where them old friends had gone

ONE SUMMERS DAY

The near by catfish creek a good fishing place
Here sitting on the shore with my pole waiting for a bite
A warm summer day the water barely rippling along
Hoping this day to get a nice brown tan on my face
There was an old iron bridge to cross to get to the fishing hole
Before fishing I would put set lines along the way
Clipped to my belt was a pouch for a can full of worms
My fishing rod consists of a reel on a bamboo pole

Here was the Denya's woodland the creek ran through
There was very high hilly land reaching the water below
A great lot of crows in these high evergreens there
On the steep roadway hill there was always a road crew
Most times the gravel washing from the hill filled the ditch
There below in the glen was clover and grass for cows to eat
The cattle did not like climbing the steep hill to the top
Every evening came milking cows driven up the hill with a
switch

If carp were caught we buried them to make flowers grow
Every flower bed around the house had fish put there
At home there was plastic stows holding hundreds of worms
With lanterns at night on the lawn found dew worms to stow
Once in a while went fishing left chores for my brothers
A man needs time to reprieve once in a very long while
I regretted at home being called Skipper the nick name given
to me
Was a deserved break, meeting people fishing have a reason
to smile

A BONA-FIDE MAN

Was authentic on recovering from barbarous long ago day
Have abided hail to the dawn a creation for my glory
Did find it best to make a self foundation so it's justified
Be like the wind scattering the clouds get right out of my way
There is no need to serve mama like it was away back then
To abide with people shall pass the trust of them all
Had no sense for reposing ways of comfort in an old life
Those passed times of benevolence a man will never see again

One's mind continually thinks while waiting quietly alone
It remains to see if a humble heart will be honoured some day
Have tried to derive at better answers, siting here by myself
My days are precious, serving them with constancy hope of
somber tone
With many talents no one can take that away from this man
How you ought not to understand when you deal with an
honest guy
There is actions speaking louder than words for one
Better to be a harsh person trying to make it through any way
you can

A long time participation enabled one to grasp things untold
Did happen to find imitators being inspired by the liars group
Do not regard people having partiality, it's not in their genes
Have conquered them long roads in time almost by ten fold
This man is in the changers chair making a farewell speech now
When the name skip passed out of sight equity came along
Now call me by my sir name I will not answer to any other
In accordance to a man's ability he has plenty of know how

Had no one on my children's side to share a Dad's distress
back then
We have world tenants with only understanding for themselves
That prolonged summons a long with fate have recovered well
Whatever is grateful is honourable ever since this world began
In these elder days have made every foot step count so far
For sincerity of heart this guy has gone the whole one hundred
yards
Having been betrayed for a life time the source is well known
It's noted in life's motives for all times who is not up to par

THE HAGGARD HOOLIGAN BOY

Being an astonishing thing someone done this to a mere boy
No one knows how it's to be alone with no love from anyone
On a farm is where my parents put me in rags upon my back
Took a teenage boy here for some farmer needs to employ
Had shoes to big blistering my toes and heels, becoming so
sore
Each sole had a hole the size of a quarter where dirt came in
Was taken here with pants two sizes to big, with a rope belt
Much anguish in thought of no remedy to get away need say
no more

Such a place of no hope, without choice, not eighteen yet
Today to proclaim such an awful deed done by my kin folk
As for a young man's sake so much hate ruled a whole day
An example of humility from a parent something not to forget
Was never any good Samaritan that ever came into this man's
life
This be something yet hidden, nor forgiven, being kindled in my
heart
The farmer was miserable cursing and swearing the whole time
For more income the farmer prostituted out his young wife

Had taken me their son working as a hired hand that day
Here my bed was the hay mow for six hours before working
again
Would work cleaning stables all day then plow half the night
When people came to buy eggs they called me the haggard
Hooligan boy
On weekends went with tractor and stone boat clearing the
land
Had hands chapped and bleeding coming back from that
field
There was not any gloves given to me while working at this
place
At nine the farmer in a loud voice go back to the mow he did
demand

The parents where not worthy of having dignity ever, I know
Those trails and tribulations had no justification at all
At the end of every month these parents show up to collect my
pay
Had work for a months wage but had no money which to show
A whole life time of kindred curse as long as can be
remembered
These thoughts in mind is that the way all families were
What were their intentions with money belonging to a son
Even as distraught as things where will get my life
reaccessioned

WHO KNOCKS

The most scary of all is when in bed a knock comes on the door
My thoughts go back to yesterday of nicky nicky nine doors
It's this time of night bad characters are prowling around
When you put your house coat on to answer the knock no
more
During the old times a Watkins man had his monthly call
He had salve for animal healing as well as the family
If you had congestion on your chest, medicated ointment for
that
That petro carb salve would heal cuts when you would fall

Who knocks but the bread man every Friday afternoon
Back in the fifties when Canada and wonder bakers came
They had vans with racks inside for bread as well as cake
At this time waiting for Sears mail order that would come soon
As children we were barefoot for the whole summer through
The order was for new shoes we got for the winter months
Every poor farmer had bought children's shoes at this time
When this knock came we were in our glory having shoes
brand new

Was on Monday the iceman knocked to hold the door open
wide
From his truck with tongs he brought a block of ice on through
An icebox kept food from going bad from Monday to Monday
The ice truck was huge with eighty blocks of ice inside
When the wonder baker came knocking he sold socks as well
Them schools back then were a three mile trek in the cold
We were mighty glad for these socks and long underwear
Being one problem the socks were mis-mates, under trousers
could not tell

OLD MEN'S DREAMS

The urban gloom confronts me to utter disgrace
Just dreaming that tomorrow be paved with good intentions
That state of man depends on where he is living
Each day wish for better not always misery to face
A young man's feelings always looks beyond them doubtful
days
In my long ago house them bad images wanted stilled forever
Forever in dreams keep shuffling back to tough times
If so in dreams could not it happen for reality ways

The dreams could have compiled a pattern for another day
Has mystified my thoughts with no hope at all
Had contemplated leaving sourpusses alone forever
Some days it does not even make any sense to pray
Being this old it's to late to look into any crystal ball
Here is a senior man plying his way along an old lost road
In the real world my body has shrunk down to five eleven
Some how in a dream my image shows me six foot tall

Such wonder claimed in dreamland still pesters you
While venturing inside the depths of time found misery
Always will woo the days long gone for the abuse there
Went off down a lost forever road the only thing to do
Became an engineer for the University of Toronto pleased me
well
This old man's dreams now came true in the big city Best to be
a realist even though a sad song was sung
On my long road from misery had a real story to tell

AT TWILIGHT

Only one mind and heart awaiting in my lawn chair at dark
Them divisions of the heavens push clouds aside was able to
see all
Always have partakers in our twilight zone all of the time
Out all day but twilight has brought me back once more to
park
The prompting of night is suppose to give a notion to fall asleep
It's the mean while time with all the street lights all coming on
How spooky now the man in the moon was looking out of the
sky
Seems this man had company in the tree was something went
peep peep

Was awesome when the sun was downing in the West once
more
So much splendor the sun had put to rest, on it's going down
Once again came to standing coping with loneliness all over
again
On the ground in the midst of it all an opossum came to
explore
That Northern star not forgotten you are seen up there as my
host
Did have the night scene to rule from our sky all the way down
In the void of that darkness just me with some parading
varmints
When this man had turned around an owl was sitting on the
clothesline

So appropriate having the lighthouse light still shining there
Every time something came along a motion sensor gave me a display
These animals lurk like a spirit in their nightly shadowed place
At night my garden is an animal sanctuary they come in a pair
Must admit our maker made them too for some unknown reason
Was their domain before we barged in sometime not long ago
Have watch them with their quiet hearts in the silence of it all
They have to survive because they are here no matter the season

To recall at twilight in the cedar trees many birds twittering sound
That world of life has it's animal night shift part, begrudged by all
Will forever pronounce the varmint scene, they are part of our life
Have neither gripes nor mastery over what animal comes around
As of now my good thoughts rest with me on my pillow once more
Best initiate concern waiting for morning to arrive out there
Was that heritage pride with ancient words love goes on forever
Our answer my friend is written in the wind as our tomorrows before

LIFE'S CRUX DAYS

To be able truly to understand partiality more than some
Have dealt with it in youth days with a bias mother
Such an oppressed life constantly from morning until night
Only me to participate in chore time whenever it did come
One son got all, the other degraded to the utmost, so unfair
No one to faithfully understand the problem back then
An older brother was honoured with kindness, no work for him
Must rely solely on hope since age five, no one really did care

For meanings to life was in fulfilling deeds the whole day
Would like to announce my birthday only the elder deserves a
cake
There never comes respect for services rendered by son skip
Forever she recited intentions telling me to get on my way
Some kindness or compassion was not for this household place
Still worried about tomorrow though tomorrow will worry on it's
own
Did never grow to understanding the conduct of most
everything
The one doing nothing gets highly graded for merit was the
case

So much disappointment had seen all of my yonker years
Every family has a buffoon a crafty smiling person there
It's whom has the right to exist made him refined in every way
What was customary just favour that son of a gun it appears
Being too shameful to mention our world of long long ago
Here was life such was this gloomy place always to remember
All things were governed by the gad method always leaving
marks
Some one greatly disturbed should never have any children we
know

In my mind and heart the brunt of such a burden was not fair
So much tendency in praising only one person up to the sky
Took a while to bypass that host of yesterday, half life's years
Was taught by example of how to attain that respect to care
As for today have found people worthy in which to praise
Here is my dwelling place of goodwill, come if you wish
Is still a fungal beast lurking down a forbidden road out there
To say what one thinks about these people it only takes one
phrase

A STREET BRICK HOUSE

A dwelling in the country near the village of Sparta
The whole of our creation was a garden with livestock
We were poor unable to possess a more abundant life
The person that worked very hard supporting us was our Pa
Seems nothing was ever finished from dawn to setting sun
Our growing up part was always filled with wonder days
Did accomplish only the necessities of life for ever
This household was divided by dissension since our life began

One day the grandparents moved in with us having no peace
Were told to have mutual respect for old people back then
These grandparents were grub stealing off of our parents
So much was bestowed on our father that did not cease
Sometimes us children went without for grandparents sake
When someone is oppressed they cannot function good
Them words used did not inspire us in the very least
As we walked our by ways life had all the grief one could take

The grandparents passed away in their sixties with mercies
With what little money we had paid for the funerals
No sooner they were gone our mother's sister moved in
Had no confidence of any source just victims of the times
On our families journey there was a lot to contend with
Her sister went to the landlord offering him more money
That intention was to have us kicked out of this house
Our landlord evict them instead, it was Mr. Mills' good faith

This foretold future was bleak, ongoing duties had no end
A writer the host of realities, delivered the consequences
For sure integrity through endurance of hope we got there
As for my unfailing goodness a message of thanks I send
Today came the gift of everlasting freedom found by me
Had no prompting only devotion got me this far today
I roamed and rambled, as with all my footsteps made it
Have needed that lesson in humility as far as it could be

CAPTUATED MOMENTS

Some how decided on a precise time to wake up
The circumstances unshaken, only splendor for a goal
Have accomplished life's importance of the working part
Nary a rife to bother me, as for coffee have one more cup
No cark moments eminent to a days planning schedule
There will be a shining example of preservation if needed
In plain sight have seen various ways to overcome monotony
Had always looked toward honourable things as a rule

That forsaken part of humdrum is now lost in the past
No one to appoint me what to do in them dawning days
Am old with all my faculties to arouse perfect harmony
Are amazed at worth while events that have come at last
Here them imponderable moments do not irk me anymore
Forever the anguish of former year oppressors is gone
Let's not be ashamed it was the moralities of the times
Better to instill honour in life then encroach as before

This man came looking for a Samaritan city for his journey
With plausible words shall abide with some good tidings
The author of life has told every by gone story at this point
Only can rejoice with it's completion with brand new today
A man is solely privileged to choose his very own plan
Whoever respects this man they must be friends of this world
Our coarse of the world has changed must get used to this
This span of life is for today, tomorrow do what you can

Comes the imagined future encouraging respect in it's wake
Must come to know who's who for the sake of believing them
Need no such going's on of testy denials from them akin folks
The reason for being here was through a devoted way did take
Will remain influent until the fabrications are all over
By a worthy conduct will pursue good effects on the kindred
Them authoritative oppressors no longer uphold any of my ways
In accordance to my age took almost a lifetime to recover

MY SPARTA HOME

At Sparta our home was made from bricks of Ross Street
The scene around me was country with dung smell in the air
My mind always purging my subconscious of days gone by
Had a whole day of trudging with rubber boots on my feet
A lassitude of miserable times wishing they were extinct
Beside the barn housing cows was a huge manure pile
Each day before dinner had to wash my high clad boots
Coming from the barn my clothes still had an awful stink

Seems my grandparents were children of pioneers
Every morning bacon and egg smell filled the air
An old coal stove chimney sent smoke skyward curling
Oft times I would be astride in thought, knowing a weekend nears
On the weekdays what was done depends on the time of day always
These old traditional ways gave no rest on the farm
Remember harvesting days working under the blazing sun
Was not forgotten the pitch fork in the hot hay days

Sometimes had notions of just wanting to leave this place
Each morning the barn door was strung with spider webs
That old wooden privy with Eatons catalogues for wipe
Every weekend a heavy smell of bleach from the clothes washing space
The squawking clothes line pulleys was all day long
A winter wash had frozen clothes on the line hard to recover
For a moment came a spunky thought with a rouged face
So glad for modern days where this kind of living does not belong

A COUNTRY CREEK

Was a forsaken creek until a weekend came by
No place was so remote having clay shores with rocks
Them old days with my fish pole heading to a fishing hole
Most of the summer days with no clouds only a blue sky
Another weekend febrile fancy takes me to this creek way
Such a leisure day to rest my weary bones once again
Would always reach that fishing spot after dawns light
So much was told that I had to do reneged the whole day

On that dewy path bound for the fishing hole was best
Here was an old time setting with cattle grazing by a cedar
fence
It seem they were trying to understand what I was doing
Beside this fishing spot was a patch of grass for to rest
While looking at the farming fields there was not content
A victim of circumstances plagued my ever living soul
Even though I had caught a trout felt like throwing it back
Should one count his blessings with so much to resent

In wonder have pitied my fate with more life to go
Again my mind held me in tether go home as before
Well knowing my mind will be made up one day
The saying abide with me is for some not for all I know
That person who said home sweet home acted like a child at
play
With frustration skipped stone after stone off the water
The sun must set behind better things than a world of haystacks
Here as a teen looking across green pastures, rued the day

THE GRIMMEST ONES

Without any say did reside in a confound place
Here was not really ancient but naive as it could be
A setting of old rambling houses with cedar roofs
Being as elder as the time you imagined that walking race
On going to the old house feels like kinfolks are here
Maybe one could shake hands with a shadow or two
Wish this was not a place where gaunt episodes occur
An old window came crashing down giving me fear

While on a walk seen grass growing up through the gravel road
An old straw stack was growing it's own crop of oats
The cement block silo had most of the top blocks falling away
Every fence post was laying flat was the next episode
Went through the barn door seen cow stanchions rusting away
A family of mice had taken over the hay filled mangers
Had a feeling rambling ghost might pass into my space
That bedding straw reeked with mold every inch of the way

Maybe there's an unseen world to inspire their fate
Would be impossible if something convened me here
These rattons have avowedly gone without a trace
Them old sodbusters left far far away they could not wait
They rode away out yonder into starry skies above
Let's try blowing Gabriel's horn it could bring them back down
The boy that looked after their farm came back once more to
see
Better to forget about them they never believed in love

VERSIONS OF THE TIMES

Many a dire events took place no one could imagine
My thoughts that perhaps a mother's sternness was woe
Was a creation of raw courage with standing the test
That life's scoffing unjust was all their fashion
For sure poor children follow that golden rule so far
All days taunted with untimely plans to follow to
Wanted chanted moments to let people hear it all
Having whiled away striving through that befuddled mar

Them feuds with attitudes were the rage of the time
Forever sorrows with miseries pledged some souls
These long lost echoes to smite finally they are gone
To abuse a child in long ago days was not a crime
Even youngsters had suitcases under their eyes
Everyone had to work from dawn to setting sun
So many ungrateful events were always taking place
If boys work like men not even one person cries

Was this son that was sincere but no one gave a damn
Them old times must have rotted into hell
Such a grimace location has claimed the sigh today
If this man could go back there today the door I would slam
All them versions of the times have many kinds of foes
We must enter this story without passion in the black book of
time
Even though there's grey above my brows I still have my pride
When the last dying embers occurred God only knows

ONCE A PEDDLER

Was a peddler with many a story part
Here was me on the road going somewhere for a sale
Have them kindly gestures on this merry morn
Me the Watkins man out across the gravel roads to start
Each day passing having the gift of gab when I came
Some drudging moments to be driving on wet afternoons
Maybe whistle a song to cheer me through the day
From old times until now all the products are the same

Watkins man me was unable to stop talking until a sale
Was simply a countryside needing vital things
From old time bounds with fame was the Watkins man
Me the peddler had everything under the sun to entail
If noon was right for clocking time it was meant to be
An old theory is ring the bell then get your foot in the door
In winter for chest rub medicated ointment was good to see

There is them malarkey stories with their funny parts
We are blessed with Watkins products of old and today
The Watkins man has excelled from horse drawn buggies
Hence from early morn that peddling he starts
These elder customers recall old tales of events
Here was a man of his word was sincere as could be
That peddler is somewhere out there waiting for a sale
Being out there today with still good products makes sense

AWAITING FOREVER

Such humility in awe walking them roads of time
So much untendered mercies in daily episodes for all
Was only good weather friends for people in need
People were all for themselves when I was in my prime
Had never forgotten those days of belt punishments indeed
A boys wishes were dashed hopes a disgust for me
Here in that house of wrath a disgrace of them days
Them prayers at night on my knees almost like words to plead

The reason for being poor having money was a sinful thing
Our church only wanted the down cast of the modest
As believers in the sermon our poverty would be forever
Being poor under this wrath an everyday sorrow it did bring
These child sensations for the era was relived in nightmares
A church creates this portentous modesty of this kind
Best to have renew the script be money eager people
As a child have no need for money as well nobody cares

Was hard to believe that church quote the priest made
He said go out in the world to multiply but money is evil
How vain is hope just pray for mercy stay poor is it
Be poor give up your money do not become afraid
Turn people into the frail ones just pray night and morn
Always fear that part of being the holy righteous
The best theory is use plagiarism then bless them all
That awaiting forever part being blessed, poor and forlorn

DILAPIDATED VANS

A nineteen fifty-eight slant six Dodge van, light green colour
In it did carry tools along with some material for the job
Had heavy duty roof racks to carry the forty foot ladder
When the extension ladder was twenty feet on the rack carrier
Just one week later while crossing railway tracks heard a
snapping sound
On over the tracks two front coil springs came through inside
the van
Then these coils springs danced back and forth with a
twanging noise
The front tires scrubbed against the fenders with tire pieces
flying around

All of a sudden the front tires blew like a cannon blasting away
Went to a farm house to call a tow truck to the railway track
sight
In an hours time the tow truck showed up to haul me to be
fixed
Soon the van was in the garage to be fixed some how some
way
A man there braised new fenders back onto the van, then
sanded them
Then he braised the spring shackles under the fenders, solid as
can be
In about two hours time now the wheel alignment had been
done
After replacing tires and tubes was six hundred dollars parts
with time

Took the contracting money paying cash right there on the spot
Later that week did an all over green paint job on the van
This old Dodge slant six ran for another four years no problems
Being a subcontractor for Maurice Rollins at that time needed a van
An old man could not drive anymore so he wanted me to have his vehicle
When I offered him one hundred dollars for Volkswagen van he took it
This bus operated very well, burning very little gas every time it ran

My children loved the van, they always rod on top of the motor seat
They would say "hey, Mr. Bus Man, hurry up a little bit, hurry up a little bit"
Most Saturdays all of us would go fishing with the van by some creek
With a small mattress they could sleep in the van it was so neat
The van fenders were rusted off so I body fitted the spaces
Went to thank the old man again for selling me such a fun machine
Easy on gas, giving me sixty-five miles to the gallon, a big saver
This van was a fun vehicle taking us to some far away places

ERISTIC EFFORTS

Some people are not in their right frame of mind
Each one cooks up an untrue story to fit the occasion
Their morals are zilch on a daily basis for them all
Where does the love of God go in a situation of this kind
Those made up stories to fit the times even though it's fake
Maybe they cannot find a spot in the world where they belong
These people look through you not at you for some unknown
reason
Have seen strange people before but this for sure takes the
cake

When wonders never cease one does not know what to say
We have ask what is wrong with them nobody really knows
Being a pooper your bound to get rings before to much longer
They are down casting on elder people, ignoring them every
day
We are not around forever we have to make the best of things
Such a contradiction coming from misfits in a society trend
If you say something nice naturally they change into something
bad
All should rely on common sense for all of the happiness it
brings

Every beginning has an end depends on how long you can
wait
The rule of thumb do unto others that they do unto you verse
What's out there on memory lane how can they just live with us
A father always wanted to share with them now it's become
late
It's not really a misunderstanding it's just a clueless episode
How does one respect these kind of abnormal people
Give me a reason and I will give you a truthful real answer
Where to go from here it's a dog eat dog situation mode

For a conclusion it's very cheeky a deliberate kind of way
Your sense of humor went out with the dishwater long ago
Best you cut some slack before you choke on your nasty words
You cannot buy happiness it will come from the heart some day
After all that said and done then comes your kind of end
Have counted my blessings but regret for you the black sheep
Will be no place in the realm saved for your meager kind
In hopes there comes someone real nasty not a good friend

A NOTABLE SIGHT

The social strut of people with their airs bugs me
They inspire only their social friends no others
Every one with distinction Lord knows how they got there
Maybe look around see where we would like to be
Every so often a gnaw wish follows you around for a while
In old times the elite had thoroughbred horses to pull the surrey
Them with paltry means used what they could to travel
These notable one's are always to serious to smile

That old saying is we do not have to prance their tune
Even with money they will never banish our ideas
Only priest have their own way we built churches for them
We are so many old haunts wandering through my mind
Forever wondering on a merry day parade who's in town
Him being rich came to see what our family could afford

These people ate the good eggs, gave us soft eggs from inside
the hen
The loveys wife seen me eat two cherries off of their tree
As for me never tasted cherries before they wanted fifty cents
each
To give fifty cents was a great deal of money way back then
This man came to our house every Saturday to look around
We were unable to grow a garden on his land it attracts birds
He always pulled weeds then put more grass seed on the
ground

164

METAL CLICKERS

These metal clickers sounded like horseshoes going there
In the old days this was the fad for farm boys
Them bib overalls a working class zoot suit of the times
The Kep buck heels with clickers, boots today do not compare
They were called our ramblin' boots we Dubined them every
day
Always had to be moving forward with more work to be done
Always heard a woman's trumpeting voice with a command
Every errand was one of a kind, doing chores with no pay

In yonker years was work or get the belt on your seat
After all the chores were done cleaned my clicker boot as
before
Was clean your boots, eat, go to bed back to chores on the
morrow
Every morning clean manure from behind the cow's stinky feet
Had to Dubin the boots every time to stop the smell on school
day
With metal clickers on the toe and heal work boots never wore
out
All the farm boys had metal clicker boots polished with Dubin
Up at five AM do chores then walk to school a mile away

During autumn the metal clickers were good on stubble ground
In the cornfield after the corn picker went through corn cobs
were left
To bag corn cobs from this place these clicker boots were
needed
We had to pick these cobs up before the crows came around
The fad lasted up until I started high school in Sparta place
Found a special box to pack the clicker boots in forever
Now the clicker boots were put to rest under the stairs
Here was a dress code everyone in school had to face

HOME HOW KIT

Being a man with skills has the lingo to do it all
From a teenage boy my father taught me mechanical skills
We had a ramp made to fix our cars and neighbours too
The home how kit we were taught to fix and install
All saws on the farm, buck saw and one man saw sharpened to
a tee
These were our consequential deeds in those years
For cutting stove wood had a circular saw three feet across
Had a chainsaw to sharpen then set to hew down a tree

Our axe handles were honed from a hickory tree
I sat on a stool carved handles for all our tools
A single tree was also made for a horse pulling logs
There was no other choice we were poor living in the country
Had a big tank full of blue cheap gas to run vehicles on
We were self dependent for all them years gone by
This dangerous highway curve was cut back some more
The highway department come, this house and barn are gone

It seems for a safe road our place stood in the way
Those memories have been wiped away forever
Only the sound of a little babbling brook passing through
So much came to an end on that fatal summer day
Such a nice white picket fence all torn down gone
That small gate to the yard being closed by the wind
No trace of where my family used to be so long ago
Only a rounding curve going into Plainfield from now on

BEHOLD THE HOUR

All my thoughts are on youthful friends of long ago
At times had that feeling my thoughts were undaunting
That era has come to lasting rest with only memories left
How great were the times of horse drawn cutters drifts of snow
The world declares more worth then away back then
Must my conscience hanker on with lost feelings ever more
So much remembrance about trains the ploughman and all
Have been viewing them old times since today began

Them old train stations have remembered that hissing sound
On these open tracks hearing that loud trumpeting whistle
Again the world declares a great love for the iron gallant one
For ever comes the tenfold moments of the eastward bound
The smoke blowing with a wind over pines far away
Waiting at the station have heard a train coming down the line
In mind that wailing whistle stirs up my senses
See a huffing train at the same place on time every day

Is such a privilege to turn back them pages from old
Almost as if a living thing had past it's time
All these moments of thought to resume the old iron lady
That Wabash hearing the mighty rush of her engine it's told
Would like for just one more time send a steam train through
Even though it's the future let's not forget about yesterday
We are members contributing to our own find fate
The makers of our lost world there was only a few

THE THREE CHARACTERS

There was three boys once called the Brindle brothers
The three characters showed off manly spunk by times
To pass the nights we must have them dates to go
We were a noble squadron sticking together fighting others
Most times together to Kibitzer in laughing a lot
As for us we were not concerned with the parents knowing
On Friday nights the amusement was going to the drive in
Still today them good time friends we never forgot

By times let out loud uproars when our school ball team wins
Way back then Coles school played other schools always
winning
Well blessed be them days we got through again unscathed
Other times we were by shores of a stream killing frogs, such sins
That lead us not into temptation path was for ever more
Where never humble lads there was not much sense to the
word
In that old home our talents were mistook as being hellions
A life come with misfortunes it's best not to explore

Never tweedle-dee sissies ever in that day
The answers were sometimes nay would never do such a thing
Once in a blue moon comes that serious face of relenting truth
Have had quiet moments as raptures rise nothing to say
If we left well enough alone a better future await out there
Maybe politely ask us grow up act your age
The question of the day was how is the model A Ford running
Every dollar earn kept the car running along with a lot of care

RAPTURED HOURS

Was already up as early morning broadens pushing the sun
The old collie dog had fetched the cows waiting for his meal
His morning treat was fresh milk on some kibbles
The cows were milked and fed only by this boy one
Down the gravel road off to school again until four
That manure smell made me feel out of place there
Even though I washed the smell still came through
Another day with them raptured hours here once more

Sometimes being so frustrated wanted to run away
Wanted to grasp onto some nice place working in a city
As for my thoughts they were passed through corridors of time
At the end of each episode tiredness comes only time to pray
Only the darkness of night changes things here
If our maker had not conjured up darkness I'd still be working
How many times does one's heart beat before the night's over
Had to do the daily work or have the consequences to fear

Above the house in winter hear that North land beating down
At five AM with snow boots on went to the barn for chores
No ones budged except my father to stoke the fires
Others stayed snuggled in bed only one up was the clown
Made a snow plow from planks to clear the walk way
There was no bus in those times on through snow drifts to school
On down the road with howling winds and drifting snow
The school hours where from nine to four on the week day

CROSSES FOR PETS

In yonker years thought of pets as family always
All the children were so sad when this death came
Had to have a special rock marked with red paint the name
Everyone of us would put flowers on the grave for days
The white cross stood up three foot tall with a ribbon tied
Our school friends would ask us about the pet brought tears for them
Even the other pet that came here looked awfully sad
Someone would tell a sad story about the pet everyone cried

One day a fox killed our pet white goose a real crime
My first thought was to catch the fox kill him
Bob Garrod lent me a couple of muskrat traps for this
Day after day wait with a wild rabbit for some time
The wild rabbit hung with a rope from a tree limb over the trap
Went to bed then the next morning this fox chew off his leg
All that was there was the fox's leg in the traps jaws
So had to give up on the fox idea was left with a bum rap

We had a pet ferret who escaped the box place
Our dog Mickey had eight puppies two days old
The ferret went ate some puppies then killed the rest
No one knew really what to do about this case
After we went through burying four pups this day
This ferret was sold to Mac Fish for a sum of ten dollars
The head land of the garden was full of crosses for pets
We were so glad Mickey had eight more pups right a way

IN MY SHADOWS

When a shadow has passed it shows no more
I shall console my heart with lost memories
My soul left with silence waiting in despair
When joy keeps the loneliness alive as times before
In the forgotten realms of days gone by
All our life moments are so precious day by day
Friends are in my shadows with every prayer
There comes sometimes a reason to sigh

Wish all my relatives where in my shadows forever
To be part of my days sunshine with a smile
Old years be left in empty rooms wanting someone there
A man not wanting to be front and centre or be clever
For each day wishing for each new blessing to start
Want to portion our love for equality in this life
Form good times both for you and me in our hearts
The compassion over all falls always for our part

In my shadow the pathway has good intentions
Wanting joy to keep loneliness alive each day
Everyone's life has a little sorrow to deal with
Hate we must rid, by finding some good preventions
Times have turned the tide from bad omen days
Now to interpret a different tune for our feud years
Mr. Nice Guy was for a long time, now my piece will be said
We no longer deal with people that are strange in their ways

TOPPLED PRIVIES

In the country privies marked our landscape everywhere
Halloween was privy time for trick or treat or else
There was no angels for ought to or not to boy will be boys
Once in a while a privy was moved ahead with mash there
The horror for Halloween tom foolery for that night
The restoration of old times would be a bad thing to do
One night being extremely bad, three hundred sixty four good
Many corn stocks where pushed over, making a messy sight

From the beginning of Halloween orange with black it be
That was the year of pumpkins, spooky mask pranks
Was a night to become terrible pranksters was the case
The incentive for doing tricksters was a yearly spree
All these folkways came from our Grampa days
The yonker years were indeed a Halloween to remember
A farmer blasted a shotgun over our heads one time
To be done from a long time back Halloween these ways

Today maybe children soap a window or two
So many kids with gum spittin' on the sidewalk everywhere
Those long ago hellions are guys and gals being bad
These times parent groups go out there that's what they do
Them days a farmer would elevate his voice "get out"
No one knew us with our masks and costumes on
The farmers cursed that day it for sure was wrong
Maybe turn back the pages to see what Halloween was about

A TYPICAL DAY

Along our ways we play down the past to define lost life
Maybe old spirits should come to gestate unsolved problems
All that slippery wax that paves hells roads pulls people down
To have the final say is a tradition of the ages for a wife
Had managed through old life, am more then ready for the
new
Have always believed that a syco is listening to my ideas
The false hopes repeats themselves on up from the past
There was so many trails with tribulations we had gone through

Sooner or later seems every kind of omen passes my door
In history most scenes are fostered by legends on going
Some word instances are not everyone's taste it seems
For the most part drab moments love comes through once
more
As for the real world of creation pettiest is all the go
Having for saw obstinate people thinking their right till the end
Did see occasions them kind of humans are full of themselves
Once in a while restore the past where discontent did show

Oft time images provoke my thoughts from yesterday
In life one is a traitor the other a saint seen everywhere
For todays realm of oddballs, being uncanny forever to be
Our egotistic one's still have on tic unreal ultimate day
The maker of life made some people wrong it goes to show
Have planned a future of not paying attention to self conceit
As for good friends they will have welcome times forever
Will always have the best of days when colossal one's depart
No matter where you live there's awful people on every street

A WORTH WHILE TROW

Every warden in life is here to help us along
For always giving of themselves with wanting ability to do so
Have been always ready to shake a true friends hand
Knowingly them bad perks need not really to belong
Beware of bearers of evil fancy it will corrupt your mind
Forever keep in mind those avenues of good grace
Many of the demented wanderers from reality is out there
Where cults dwell there is also them real evil kind

From a place of confession there's lot of room for more
The general feeling for the cad one's just let them be
Perhaps what's best in mind be ruthful only for some
Every church keeps on calling with a bell, as well an open door
One day long ago was made remembrance day for good
men
That vision for well being is so perplexed for most of us
A wonder of triumph shall rest on us for all times
Out there a church with abilities to confess every sin

At will can open avenues of grace on our part
Up from old times hark comes that voice of peace
The old farm life was helter-skelter, all literate one's
All the smarter boys knew they would leave the farm from the
start
So many left old time plowing pitching hay routine we know
Passed out of grade thirteen before being able to go on
Made honours in order to grade with a great profession then
Being an engineer at age forty-five so much greatness to
bestow

EMBERS OF OLD

An old one room school with a class of eight
Being the Union Jack our sovereignty then
Also there was a picture of King George on the wall
We saluted him for a commonwealth place which to relate
After this came the Lord's prayer bowing our head
Some time later foreigners changed that tradition for all
One gets so tired of being Canadians with others having their
way
Has left a bad feeling, you are not allowed is what they said

Made us feel we've been had putting us to shame
Cannot possess our freedom saying it's discrimination
Would like to blurt out fowl to decline this fate
Our dress codes are tarnished nothing is the same
All that's left in Canada is just our broken pride
A void of disgrace the land we fought to save
We are the Simon do this fools of a lost mission
Have lost our sense of dignity in this land we reside

Must have lost our almighty senses to let it be
Telling us how to pray in schools as of now
We are the idiocy of these times no vigor in our will
Why does the national anthem say we are glorious and free
Our countries anthem does not relate to their prayer
All of us hypocrites letting them blemish our great land
We are made laughing stocks with resented blessings
Is it them or us that have given rights to declare

THE LIVE LONG DAY

Was here in Vancouver as morn breaks over the mountain
peak
At a distance seen water roaring down from rocks above
For a time went trudging along a well used deer trail
Our son had plenty of mountains to show us this week
Had plenty to see on the winding path through a park
Here seen high flying eagles diving for fish beside the river
Their shadows followed behind me across the broad flat
On the path a rabbit carcass lay telling me an animal made it's
mark

A pair of raccoons passed under the dwarf cedar tree
Their masked eyes kept looking around at me
The snapping twigs on the path put fright in the pair
When all of a sudden these mates you no longer could see
Beyond the path a warning sign not to hunt here anymore
Farther was a swing bridge where people went going to and
fro
Here the trees were about one hundred feet high
Up a long the mountainside was wild berries galore

We were driven to a place there was rock climbers about
Some people even climbing upside down barely holding on
As we looked across these mountains their most highest peak
had snow
Just a little ways down the road there were pools full of trout
It was getting dark now went to a high outlook seen city lights
below
The outlook was over a thousand feet above sea level we were
told
Here was like a fairytale place with giant people of woe
There were street lights along the mountain road all a glow

COPPER PENNIES

Our post office man carried big pennies every day
We always waited until finally he would show up
A handful of big pennies here and there he threw down
He strew many of them while sondering the roadway
This man had a slight limp a war veteran from the past
Still remember this man with horn rimmed glass on a big nose
Where he got all the big copper pennies from was beyond me
His sack was empty of more then fifty coins all threw at last

As the old man walked children gathered all around
Sometimes he would whistle a merry old tune
Was thought to be an Irishman had broguey things to say
Seems the pennies were taken as soon as they hit the ground
An old saying, pennies from heaven is where they came from
Would have to go a long ways for a sense of humour like him
For instance the village store keeper would short change you
He was a very nice chap not a real hypocrite like some

Be for the old post man past on pennies had filled a cookie jar
My thoughts were these coppers some day be worth a lot
On the coins was English kings that reigned at the time
This old man was kinder than my grandparents by far
It came from the heart that was big as the outdoors
A life is begrudged by a chosen few galoots with woe
Today could not find my cookie jar of pennies lost forever
Can still see youngsters scrambling for pennies on all fours

INTEMPERATE EARTH

In the blind wait of time no telling what's there
We all have a purpose in life to do our best
Should we have a room to gesture in thinking of what to do
Onward we paddle through rivers of time with care
In the quake of it all has tumbled my soul in time
There's that high door of hope we want to walk through
To have already traveled about only found poor mans gold
Makes a person think of long ago when a church bell will chime

The intemperate earth houses us all for time to come
For the years weather needs to have the farmers almanac from
now on
What Jesus said I'm a shepherd for the sheep these sheep were
like me
When there is earthquakes or other it's not good for some
For sure be nice to everyone so in hopes there nice to me
Some have been called gracious but only a chosen few
Do not do the attitude part try to keep right on smiling
Other words have expressed whatever will be will be

During the time of Noah must have heard cries when floods
came
So much devastation came to many living souls
The clock is ticking from long ago but who knows
Our world can lash out or just stay real tame
Without understanding, a Tsunami struck that day
Any earth's sleeping giants can awake once more
When nature gets out of hand victims are the case
Having no assumed moment no one will have time to pray

HEINOUS ONES

To imagine there is heinous ones in everyday lives
In our midst they ruthlessly will come around
A happy heart presents itself with love for all
Them heinous ones create trouble they never give
Our known mutual friends forever have been the very best
There are those who alienate children against others
Envy as well as shame makes up Anubus persons of our world
Most people are good them evil dorks makes up the rest

The fame with honour needs the most attention by far
Them somebodies who are liable in creating deceit for victims
All my life to be shrugged as a misfit in that society
Then comes along the famous boy chosen as their star
Are quirks in life made for a black sheep boy put down there
In regards with faith have enough courage to spite the wrath
Always use the word adieu now that to have risen above it
Like saying the last will and testimony it's a hoot to care

A heart adds a lullaby suitable to the occasion sight
Here have been going many years away from dusty roads
How one loves the city so much since becoming an engineer
To have struggled from youth to win the greatness of life's fight
Now can carry my everlasting worth in my heart
So much did the heinous one's make the grief last in time
A man needs to be put in front and center when he's smart

HERESY LIMBO

For reality sake wondering who is right or to confide with
Beyond all telling it's a mysterious world of disorder now
For complete adoration can be accountable for goodness
expected
The manifestation of different religions, who with most faith
That dedication of striving have we really accomplished a goal
When you are forsaken, no worry, someone takes care of you
Making everything wholly pleasing is what it all amounts too
To proclaim we are believers, for what things that's all toll

The bond of communication reflects different kinds of limbo
Most children are victims of circumstance, do it or die
Such as the aid for mortal beings need to correct the remedy
Must be that humanity is at it's fallen state of mumbo-jumbo
We all have different proper functions to get us up there
But who in what religion retains the merits of true standing
Who is bound for glory among these most gracious believers
That true of heart announcement has become to be aware

As for the eternal inheritance who claims the most right
Some say that religion is only to bring harmony to the world
Even being a devoted one have to admit there is mystery
Our life is not for whatever we choose, have to earn it
Seems there is host for sublime glory, what is the willed fact
Who really are the chosen one's for what belief is real
Be holy in order not to provoke the Lord, he could lose heart
Let our true to heart theory be the best given peace pact

Could have been mortality itself that's caused our downfall
What ever church some do not attend, giving heresy limbo
Such life has amazed me having human kinds many categories
Unable to establish a firm family is not my protocol
Our humanity over the whole world has an awe of wonder
Given words as well as deeds has brought every life mile
From being a footstool in life did challenge this disappointment
What my life has gotten to be let no man ever put asunder

PERSNICKETY PESSIMISM

Have not lost concentration even though loneliness nagged
me
The arrogance of people provokes me as all get out
Eventually will establish perseverance to get me there
No one seems to be aware of the malice of hypocrites to be
There is an alienator among our kin, heeding to make problems
Have girded myself with strength to withstand everything
Here is one that is sincere as well as concerned about the truth
Forever participation rules my day, then be consumed by lies

By my surname you know me as the mistreated father
Had not justified the purpose or understood the cause
She best not live with selfish ambition it will eat her up
Whatever is contrary waits with eager longing of a succeeder
A discerning mind for pessimism creates concern for us all
Let's separate people get rid of the nerds if we really can
The manner of our life has mystery, my thoughts, then your
thoughts
We need guidance through all despair, can I give you a call

In any circumstances my dutiful service, you can depend on
That unceasing anguish in my heart is a father's sorrow
There is a divine word that challenges me is absolute
Nothing concerns the times or the seasons, now it must be
done
Always had someone putting sighs into my life, on going
This love in my heart cannot be numbered because it's so vast
Amid the uncertainties of our world nothing now can be fixed
Whose will can restore all of these commitments needing doing

Being like a remnant cut off from the family by whom
Cannot a soul be faithfully united through goodness of heart
Once again have summed up those years not understood
Such unhappiness creates all of that gloom and doom
Through observance seen their mother's trait of being retarded
All of them kin are like strangers in which a father regrets
Here this man is directed by peace as well as devotion always
She had done all types suicidal things before we had parted

WINDOWS OF YOUTH

In my memories time stands still in legends of it all
Our house heated by wood stoves everything smelt like smoke
A aluminum coffee percolator always was in plain sight
At age five seemed like such a small world I recall
Still remember hearing my parents voice "it's your bath night"
The square galvanized tubs were brought to the kitchen
Then came the bucket brigade making many trips from the well
All afternoon spent hauling water to the store tank sight

The girls numbering four always had the first bath them days
Us three boys would bath in the same soapy water
This method was carried out because of water shortage
At seven o-clock at night was bath time them old fashioned
ways
Then into our pajamas then off to bed each of us would go
Again up for morning breakfast of bacon and eggs with
porridge
The same ritual for me eat, chores, then off to school
As to only me that had to do chores I do not really know

During summer holiday months went priming in the quid rows
Was long grueling work out in the scorching sun all day
After work with soap went for a bath in White's pond
Back home our model A Ford in the cinder lane it goes
Had many scrapes from a cinder lane going to the barn
The bike slued in that cinder lane then down you went
My ears can still hear it's your turn to wash dishes tonight
While washing dishes one would crash to the floor, I never
swore said darn

THE RUNAWAY BROOK

The winter's passed, spring arrives for a tiny brook
All them summer months water gently murmuring along
Tranquil days a woodpecker pecking away on an old birch
Here was bulrushes made specially for a dragonfly nook
In the calm stream seen four bullfrogs all in a row
Then a couple of spiders walked on water near water lilies
Came that summer shadow maker a cloud over the sun
Here a brook babbling the summer away so slowly it would go

One spring not a brook no more had a roaring water sound
Seems the brook waters had rose into natures provoked
tempest
Had made a raft to respond with natures onslaught
Heard the pounding of water had debris here all around
The raft built by me was launched with me sailing along
Here comes a tree branch, quickly ducked my head in time
There was a smell of frog scum smelling up a breeze
At this moment in time realized that here I did not belong

In a place such as this could very well rip my bones
My raft went speeding along dragging debris in it's wake
The golden cross around my neck was my good luck symbol
Stay afloat was among things in mind with under tones
A shaky religious voice praying to make it through the day
The conclusion if I make it through this episode never again
Having wet clothes made me shiver right clean through
With my long pole maneuvered the shore to stay

AN OLD WORLD

The growing up part was invisible to reality was a fact
Had brothers and sisters thinking we would never part
Our fellowship part sometimes had calamities to deal with
On our journey of life had no harmony or passion type of pact
Never any happiness to spur us on or to respect any one
As for an image it had no honour to pass on to the world
That poor people endurance indeed was hard to bear
sometimes
No one ever raised up new hope, that part was never done

Only an awe filled mystery, we dared in hopes to come true
Did assume some word that morality took part in then
With our eager intent never amounting to nothing like nonsense
Came the sorrowful part there was no money for me or you
Nothing new in those times always had to fix the old
Was the fixing of old cars taught by our good father
Must be better remedies for young people of the times
An example of vice to rule the family just do what your told

The parent never instituted a pattern fair to everybody
As for a downfall no loving affection ever it had seemed
Them parental foundations never changed with the times
Not like today disobedience was not tolerated by somebody
Then came perseverance to get jobs done with a gad
Some work not to pleased to except, but we had no choice
Life has it's blemishes once in a while a well known fact
Had the more conscious part be satisfied with what we had

There was all kinds of elders who had no inheritance to offer
Not always a good memory of grandparents that we visited
For them it was here today gone tomorrow remembrance
Seen it all on my journey where every family seem to differ
Our human intent ever hasting along steadfast as it can be
The remembered part of different types of faces, some
bearded
Was nothing truly worthy in existence for honour at any time
That thing being professed to be the best had it's troubles to
see

A SUBMISSIVE WOMAN

The potential act of a submissive woman has no logic
She had no compassion or respect in her heart for anybody
Being a victim of circumstances, what to tell the children
That radiance of good people will remain forever is my verdict
How a woman's conscience works while passing the truth of it
all
While some abound with noble understanding, she alienates
her kin
Have distanced myself from this lowly person as a mortal being
When one presumes to botch up something, repercussions is
the call

An atheist does not repent, so there is nothing to declare
So many sighs of wonder in ranks of life that's unjustified
Did abash to make somebody more concerned about untruth
My sincere heart is in wonder awe who she has bewildered
there
She would call a man while I was at work, away he would go
Is there someone that confirms rights to lay anyone you wish
There was an eager part many years ago who she took to bed
Going beyond all tellings how can a human being sink this low

Here have an announcement of a bad deed that cannot be
washed
To commit adultery she though it was make love to your
neighbor
Then do not worry about tomorrow, tomorrow has worries of it's
own
A villainy person should be condemned is my real true wish
She thought better to tempt the devil then be vain with the
Lord
They will not except penance in the Netherworld it's useless
Even being a victim have enlightened my views for tomorrow
In order to keep up a good image, to people pledged my
word

Any good person would actually be disappointed with her
Such shameful acts during them hours a man was at work
These partakings were not assumed they were at my house
This sort of life reeks, what did she get married for
Our pledge for marriage made no difference to a filthy mind
Will not be inspired by forgiving words or good faith actions
again
Must be aware when man is betrayed trust goes out the
window
For all her ills of a villain spirit, for sure a submissive kind

MOMENTOUS DRABBLE EVENTS

Those uncertainties determine where reality belongs
The mediocrities of life, is say something to good to be true
Must judge beyond a joke, beyond belief and beyond doubt
Maybe some how we can canonize rights from wrongs
From a purely hypothetical perspectives there is opinion
Using persuasion it can be both morally right or the best thing
There is a sign of character quality, is make others feel better
Good types of everyday trajectories sets a right direction

Put the best parts of what you want to do into a panorama
Be a realist it's a right direction for you of importance
Some who know nothing take false judgment into their hands
There is a place called irksome with a hasta la vista mama
In this case get lost into a world where no one needs you
anymore
While being deep in thought found a way to fix uncertainty
Stay away from these hubbub Goths, they will spoil your day
Best be inspired by rambunctious, it's away lot better then
before

A day in fine form is some what fan fic some way
When you are feeling good, it's a best time to do something
Cannot claim that dignity is essential for one's greatness
Did find precarious diversion, with nothing really to say
As a matter of fact with no decisions it's a toss up it seems
The charisma always is how are you on this very fine day
In accordance to finagles law we can do anything we want
In hopes something will come true like wonderful dreams

We are not apt to focus on circumstances to be better
Best to do other stuff where faith might get you through
All in the purpose of influence you get where you are going
There is a perspective of everyday dealings as a go getter
Some days you want to wear black clothes, walk in the shade
Have got tired of aligning everyday life priorities again
Now to focus on the end of my own journey now forever
Here is an essential life thing ultimately call a spade a spade

A PICKWICKIAN

Help find your life's purpose, put time an a perspective
As a Pickwickian person to be only understood by choice
Show no difference to no one, regard all with partiality
What my conscience dreads is the uncertainties of love
Must ignore hoodwinkers, it's a matter of good choice
We ought to surpass unconscionable conceited people now
When people become wretches, go find new friends somewhere
The manifestation of lies, you grow less fonder to residence

Have become immune to being hated, will turn the other cheek
All my honour is dedicated to conduct, which is good things
For one's own accord strengthen our faith when we can
Being a builder of good habits, some people a pain in the neck
Will not believe in hiding something, everything above board
Some acquainted kin will find substitutes for them some day
Their wayward home is out of bounds apart from me
To go far go slow, with determination comes your award

Always be conformed with a good image, it makes the person
Some bad mannered people belong in a hooligan tribe
Am a believer in good thoughts, the more we have the better
Having sincerity of heart it's better then a featured lesson
When annoyed just sit quietly until the wrath goes away
Was that portion in my life had forgotten what happiness is
Those ones that say trust me they are infatuates of sorts
Sometimes was encircled with doubt, then it's better next day

If hope comes finally, rejoice, otherwise it's a circumstance
Must conk the monkey on my back off, it's long overdue time
As for one person our single purpose is recovery from the past
For a splendid day come hither to my nice dwelling place
The netherworld mentioned fulfills it's initiation of doff vows
Those who walk during the day don't stumble they see a world's light
Our world has only a few good Samaritans with stood the test
Are some of us really going to a better place, who actually knows

A POOR MAN DREAMS

That wonderful world with magic will never be there
All of them morn until night were idol worthless dreams
The country place has for some time been a demise
Old days had the most doubt as well as despair
Such a well worn path of dimension in my past
On that special day of surrender gave it all up
Have liberated my senses on to the better world
Had them put downs for most of my teenage years
Was able to perform my best with no one to interrupt

My life was like a window pane the light always goes away
Some members thinking they were the chosen few to be
The usual current sent got me through old times
One must follow their dreams to make it someday
Have life play you a much more better song
The foresaid destiny of belonging all come on through
Them peers of yesterdays actions had nasty plans
What happened in my younger years was very wrong

Alas what one man has achieved no one can put asunder
In the realm of conduct persisted my way through
The old farm reeks from awful smells of resentment
When coming to pleasant awards mine was the unfound
number
On every farm lived poor people regretting each day
Woke up long ago to roosters that crow, had cows that moo
Was away back when dirt roads had these dusty scenes
There was two cloppity clops that brought in the wagon of hay

THAT INKWELL DESK

The memorabilia of ink wells back in my day
To remember the first day of school everyone used dip pens
Every desk in the classroom had a hole in the right hand corner
All my pens were lined up in a groove a very nice display
Used these pens made by Esterbrook until grade five
The girls wore pig tails back then this guy would dip them in the well
Seem to be my chance to get attention from a shy type girl
These dip pens when fountain pens came they did not survive

Than Sheaffer brought out the fountain pen the next year
Soon Esterbrook followed the trend of a Cartridge fountain pen
For a gift could buy a mechanical pencil and fountain pen set
These Esterbrook sets made great gifts when Christmas was near
There was boys here doing mischief put chalk dust in the well
Every well was a solid mess at the start of this class
The teacher laid the strap on her desk who did this was her call
They would let air out of some bike tires if anyone did tell

Mrs. McClennan was the teacher in charge eight grade school
Them flunkeys finally got the strap some told the tale
There was no modesty ever in this class, stern was she
She was a stern lady never was anybody's old fool
Did parley in studies with this teacher right through grade eight
My thoughts here to identify reality with my thanks to recall
Her invisible spirits up until today have touched my inner soul
Wanted to send a birthday card on graduation she died was to late

SPIRITUALLY REFINED

All modesty of good grace is pent up inside me
Parts of my rare talents can be dispersed for critics
As for an onset for bad youth there's no place for it anymore
In regards to bad characters it will never come to be
Every element of violence has been tamed a long while
No more bad tempered elders detesting moral pride
As the graces of me being old was not like youth times
The composure my associates was to greet with a smile

For the most part have been graciously become old
Them days away back then were not this great
Have revolved my manly spirit to a proper phase of life
No such oddities in stories, so long they have been told
Was no consideration or well being in them long lost days
Had vowed to resurrect a much better kind of life
With new found friends pursued a better sense of humour
Such scrooges in them old times ranting in forlorn ways

Had a good sense of humor to while away a dull day
For brazen people have lost my pity for a long time
There will be no clamant voice giving orders to me ever again
Always had the mighty duke in every high school concert play
Having confided in myself there was no put downs whatsoever
During that coeval my brother was awarded quite well
Through the years became spiritually refined I had an honours
degree
The teacher of them times with sixty percent said he was clever

AN OLD CLOCK

A stay at the grandfathers house one summer time
In the hall was a tall grandfathers clock with a brass pendulum
Being a small boy this time piece seemed so huge
When I was sound asleep it woke me with a loud chime
May thoughts were about shadowy spirits by the clock there
In books had read, fount members coming out at midnight
Was an old house where fud people did pass away long ago
These by gone ranks come out from the elements to scare

So much pathetic demise to arouse me here at night
Those lines read of the mystery says ghost parley about
Parents delighted in telling children many ghost stories
Was a child's thinking of envious things out of sight
In that hall of shadows the big clock bonged an immortal
sound
Always was told that guardian angels kept rivals at bay
My dreamable night, with nothing bonging near to morn
Could never fall asleep until after midnight with this clock
around

Them terrified arouses was that month all summer long
Will rearm my thoughts when I have reached back home
To that old grandpa place next time never again will go
Shall quell my stubborn brawn make the word no be strong
From portals of shadows a mere child imagines something there
Other tales of woe was the boogieman is going to get you
Would of much rather it be ecstasy then a prophetic moment
Some parent long ago though up the shadowy peeper just for
a scare

WHERE EAGLES FLY

Was in Vancouver place for a to weeks stay
Saw huge wing shadows across some mountains were eagle fly
Here they were diving their utmost to streams far below
On down scooping a fish, then pounding wings aft to the sky
Upon these mighty wings they were carrying a feastly load
Their plumes straining there high above a deep valley
Such a beautiful bird to present this wonderful day
I was caught up in a spectacular scene on this mountain road

Here was me caught up in such a picturous place
The mountain scenery and trees high into the sky
A gorgeous holiday get away made just for two
Had toured most of the day between river and mountain
space
This was a deer trail that followed the mountain so far
At the mountain base soft moss strived in bunches
After touring for a while found the main road again
From where I left till now had found where we left the car

In this land of mountains is where my stepson dwells
He drove us to all nice spots in the land where eagles fly
High as we could go was an outlook seeing city lights below
From the outlook so high up winds brought salt sea smells
Far down on a North side heard pounding waves against the
shore
Here we go on an adventure again across a swing bridge
Could not stop looking up, tree's seemed to be a hundred feet
high
Now the darkness was closing in on us was home time once
more

WEST TO YESTERDAY

Here was our home constructed from bricks of Ross Street
Was a blue jeaned boy that carried on his duties there
Wanted to playback the mooing from the old days
Along the merge of old times here's me with boot clad feet
Before each meal came the voluntary sound of grace
The image of the farm was cow tails swatting flies and pigs with worms
Out on the veranda each morn was rotting slop for pigs
There was no human courage working in such a hectic place

One reason for having flowers called mums, mom weeded these
In my mind have knotted a strange pattern like a galoot
Nothing makes any sense for them times it's a no brainer
The buzzing of houseflies on a screen door one forever sees
An average Joe farm boy by living here is all you're going to be
You knew who left the house at morn with a screen door squeak
Before they left could see bobbing shadows in the dim lit hallway
My paces of life was someone commanding it for me

Out at the barn was always manure a hectic smelly place
So many carrion flies swarming in stables within
Every morning the doorway strung with cobwebs galore
Was hard to put up with the humph of everyday disgrace
That parity old world so full of many depressing days
As a matter of fact no one had much pity or shame
Do not say no to a parent you will be sorry for it if you do
Use a belt or slap the behind hurts with old fashion ways

DAYLIGHT VEX

The dawn springs from behind the trees once more
Our front window rattles when a train passes through
On the road a milk truck's brakes squeal on every stop
A gust of wind all of a sudden blew open the barn door
Was a mysterious morn brought a skunk to my sight
That retriever of light brought crows cawing again
Many a flock of geese flew over the house at noon
A lot of nature had passed by this yard since daylight

Here at my Plainfield house not till Monday work would resume
A jet plane passes over resounding against grids of silence
At the same moment some sparrows flew over my house
singing away
On Saturday morning this shepherd dog it was time to groom
All these happening around me in such a short time span
You do not feel like doing much on Saturday from morn till night
The neighbor Bill Rollins gave me enough gravel for a laneway
To build a house here took some time with this plan

Did build a cedar fence fifty feet for roses climbing away
Pass the fence was a trout stream babbling along
On the east side a trellis was the roses going to the garden
The garden had many chimes ringing through the live long day
Here was wanting to raise a loving family it never came to be
The daylight vex lost it's greatness in such a short while
She stole, she cheated and lied the whole nine yards was bad
A two timing woman playing the field on a husband me

A NARROW WORLD

From our coffers politicians puke and wallow each day
To become tired of pompous voices ruling us forever
Always perky vises pondering over us with push and shove
Since youth seems we were humble servants of low pay
Even after our culture is scorned sovereignty will prevail
Being suffocated through the ages with morality put to shame
That of traditional nature monopoly now has taken over
With a lack of understanding seems we are nomads on a lost
trail

We should be boasting heroes remembered from wars of late
From the countless beginning of time is our Canada place
Today we wander in lost shadows of our former pride
Our merits of requital from old have been rendered to our fate
A nation of less words more deeds than anyone on earth
For sure our maker looks at them good works down below
As we withstand humility keeping our pride never to awe
Introducing our old time lore for all that it was worth

The lewdness of aliens has made our country a dive
Them long ago pioneers cleared and cultivated our homeland
Had those days of weary, but these task we had to do
We had to work by the sweat of our brow to stay alive
Here people strived long hours from dawn till setting sun
Have been averted to another phase unlike them former days
Since these aliens came have made this a narrow world
We came here with our flag and prayers since Ontario begun

THOSE SUBURBS

Must be a final perseverance enticing a man on back
Here a long country road winding through the suburbs again
To remember back here times of joy and sorrow, now lost in
time
The family happiness back in those days we seem to lack
Very inclined into wanting that country road to take me home
Need sharers in what tomorrow brings, should be so great
Them good things the eye cannot see, for sure remains in the
heart
Was in nineteen seventy seven away from here a man did
roam

There was no other thing that a man needed to do next year
Shall look favorably on getting established in the new home
Todays manner of life has become generous better than a
wage
So indeed the outcome of wonder and awe is now coming so
near
It's not a selfish ambition it's getting back what was taken from
me
Being a weary elder my merits have all been sustained now
Best be contrary dedicated to one's liking in a victorious way
Will accomplish that which a fellow purposes you will see

Can be steadfastly devoted to establish some plans all new
My adopted urges was to complete the journey of hope some day
Not like the old days of a shattered world, improper as can be
Has remained in my heart a choice for happiness for all of you
Hope to share together my thoughts that brought me here once more
Here for now then go on back to a place where a man belongs
Let there be no doubt in mind, traditions as a boy are now gone
The precious concerns are for lasting happiness not like times before

Once more in hearts of believers had been a sonship incoordination
Everyone had failed to understand that un-favored life back then
Did have courage when our task were different in wayward days
To complete my journey of hope have adopted an explanation
There someone needs to rejoice in good faith for what lies ahead of me
Those days of past had no purpose in rhyme or reason
Shall only do what is pleasing to me these days, is a desire
This way hope does not disappoint life as things use to be

OUR FURTIVE KIN

Them clandestine people are irksome to the better half
Are we to remain with credulity, implying we are the problem
Those having a mother sedition does not help matters much
Someone who deviates from what is considered normal are
daft
Am not a person with supposed power to foretell the future
As for the understanding part, one remains pessimistic now
These surreptitious parents have almighty deprived us elders
The outcome with debauchery intentions is not very mature

A mother's stead does not come close to a real fathers stature
For years have been higgledy-piggledy about things in
common
In a figure of speech quarreling is resisting our reality
Some stratagem of exclamation really for sure has to occur
Where there is rational conduct we find real people here
Someone's bequest would make an aversion for years to come
Have to suggest a befitting splendent for a needed change
over
As for my place can render every good feeling needed there

Might have to rendezvous as part of an elite to over do it
Them foofaraw situations they irk the general public
The foreshadowed generations does not understand the
outcome
Have not established where a father stands in a group I admit
These personal cinches should be put into the works some day
Sometimes regret these people not standing amongst friends
Always have been an amicable Dad taking part in others lives
A pervious man is waiting for an answer in a protocol way

For some unknown reason relatives manner stealthy always
Unable to find out what's wrong by asking with no answers
So be it, in need of a communication insight from intellectuals
Must be a rife of a chain gang bumpkins for each of these days
Maybe malicious pleasure made some days full of only gripe
Has our kid gongoozeler made an ass of himself forever
Until one has been privileged nothing ever will come to be
Everything is not a matter of choice, some must choose the
type

WHAT EPISODES

There was a game of strip poker at the Tordoff home
When our mom went over there a lady was naked then
Our mother accused the dad of having an affair with her
The mom stormed out of the neighbors house told us to come
In the afternoon she took the train to St Thomas her mothers
place
A neighborly poker game turned into some real fiasco
At the village of Denfield is where our family lived then
Now the father had to work along with care of the family to
face

About a month later a phone call came, come pick me up
We had an old Plymouth car not fit for travelling to there
All the way had motor problems, but we finally made it
At the grandmothers she invited us to chicken and dumplings
sup
Was brother Tom who went away with his mom on that day
These parents kissed and made up, being happy once again
Had such a mother being sensitive as well as be defiant
Every day came ad hoc rules with gad in hand, us with nothing
to say

Her life had contemplation along with much rigorous discipline
There was trouble justifying some of her harsh actions every day
Seems her family had a bad twist of what passions all about
The story about her father's molested her, being a pervert bad
kin
One day she almost killed the Tardoff boy on a barbwire fence
Very soon came dad to stop this woman from tearing the boys
flesh
When she scrubbed the floor us boys looked on in such discuss
Her thing of not wearing any panties ever did not make sense

One night had a house full of company staying until morning
No one cared about me gave all the blankets to the company
Go sleep on the leather Morris chair told by my mother
The stove fires were allowed to go out, the cold came no
warning
This cold caused me to pee on this Morris chair, shivering there
In the morning our mother found out about the accident
With a piece of cordwood almost beat me to death
Had to go to the hospital for twelve stitches and medical care

THOSE FLIM-FLAMERS

There is so much deception in life as a whole now
Forwardly came to understanding when a bad message is sent
Whoever honours flim-flamers they are a divided generation
Before the eyes of all nations humanity has changed en-how
Unity through an honourable way of life, will always be best
Must dismiss disgrace wherever it may be found today
Be a sustainer let no one pull the wool, better to justify
everything
These patriarchs of false images they are different then all the
rest

So diligently have established various ways of avoiding them
Once in a while one is worthy of finding bad authors in life
Therefore truly ignore two faced messengers, just shy away
Being like eternal charity, with their hands out will come
Whoever respects all mortality see what they are all about
Must reveal everything not up to par, know the real truth
Do not assume things we are not sure of best confirm it first
Some earn your anger with an advantage part where there's
doubt

But out there is always flim-flamers attending to their trade
The grace of your kindness someone takes advantage of it
With hope in friends let none of them put you to shame ever
When you buy a new suit never tell them how much you paid
There is perseverance to make people understand not to bug
me
How nice is what you see but be aware of what's behind your
back
Where by have been there done that, recognize scams in our
world
But here on my journey do all good work always you will see

Let's all gladden our days through participation of a good deed

It's a dedication day of pardon, must stay happy no matter what

Here there will be good motives worthwhile for all concerned

Much rather you recognized the shame of your past greed

Using some confidence will defend my part of faith always

Here is my claim to fame is love when all else has failed

Thinking something is wrong when someone has turned away from you

The humbly commended part in spite of it all, it's their miserable way

CRYING OUT LOUD

To be followed on my olden footsteps these days
Those seeking me out for things being left behind
Have we them one's that truthfully are sincere as can be
Did they really love my better half as the letter says
Then comes a phone message how could a man be so rotten
Is there money not known about by me stashed somewhere
Knowing there's very little cash in my possession for them
She said this man is greedy, there's no bucks to be gotten

Out of the goodness of my heart bought her a bed with my
pay
One person has her hand out without even to really care
Here being an old man struggling to beat all of the odds
To come what has to be there's no money here anyway
In the streets of time people turn old with a final day told
On that long road one travels love seems is not always there
When nothing has really changed some are being content
The times it comes down to money people turn very cold

The truth is in what lays ahead which everyone can see
Best the greedy one's not over step their stride wanting all
Have a heart would be better for your own sake
For there's only a misfortune that comes later to be
As is crying out loud nothing in our world will be free
These cast of thoughts waiting for a myth to come around
In the goodwill package their dream not to come true
What one suggest as protocol will never ever come from me

Them shell outs have no grab bags at this household place
It's hard to play your song it has the wrong kind of beat
Just have a nice day it's what life's really all about
There's no gold at the rainbow's end in this kind of case
She wants what coming to her, that you've already got
Who in the world needs this part of a family's tree
It's the best that can be done for those without care
Just keep on digging you will find your needed spot

HOPE PREVAILS

Did rise above the circumstances of a childhood day
Must showcase a positive theory to make wishes on
Here behind a change in life need no one to make it happen
The old poverty times did not make constant hopes sway
One's commitment gets to where possible goes too
Must do what really counts, this for sure will get us there
Had no reason for a mentor did it all combating it alone
Such a myth about some silver winged angel helping us
through

Had nurtured every decision to qualify things to the utmost
Should never use a human bridge to span all your needs
The passion in one's soul truly sets them apart from others
Them poverty days was never any good times which to boast
To forecast those old times was taking away leaving the soul
A life so remote with mostly classes of illiterates back then
Them tasks traditionally only promoted hard work forever
These parents had a set of ad hoc rules the belt persuasion role

Was the black and white days no cheerful colours there
Having no good sense these old time count down formats
There was no guardian angels where them farmers came from
The suggested daunting task was to abandon those who swear
Such large families was like an army in which to feed
These waughzoo's and doflickies had made there debunks
That heritage landmark of long ago still smells of dung
Come that new trend of better education is all we need

All that old cockamamie finally now up and went
Not a single person uses their brain the ipods to blame
Unable to calculate one thing without a telephone there
Leaves many lame brains the new gadgets they invent
When life is built on knowing our hope remains strong
The pretentions future will push us past the brink
To follow those footsteps like sheep to a pasture
Soon comes the grand awakening it shant be to long

A GENTLE HUMORED PA

All the time practice good virtues only for every a kin
Never a divine generation, some always makes trouble
We have an author who makes up untrue stories forever
Always pleased to will in compassion, let the joy now begin
Need to obtain joy and gladness then sorrow will flee away
Whoever respects a kind father for sure gets the same back
Do not forsake those with loving kindness, it shall haunt you
Someone thinks they are appointed heir over all for every day

Best we live honourably to establish much better insight
The host with ill deeds the little red pants will not last forever
In my thoughts for all times was a sonships hate created
Will abide my thoughts while staying decent should be right
These akin are urchins of perseverance having a divided heart
Much encouragement is my steadfast point to turn heads
Can remain with perpetual consideration with firmness of faith
Have always abounded with good thoughts right from the very
start

Did send a message that manipulation was in their homestead
How can one resolve bitterness with alienated members there
Cannot reaffirm those kind of people of la la land ever
In mind and heart my spirit has love forever that can be read
For their sake troubled episodes forever they will be there
A man has earned his anger being worthy of this fact of life
For a gentle humored pa he remains in normal fashion always
By looking at these perspectives when can life become fair

No one to unlock the path way bound by a source of deviance
Even the former generation was not a choice of parents then
Where does true affection start, when smite'd by your kin
Being alienated children back then, they did not have a
chance
In our midst we have a liar everything she did, would deny
As for myself this man is a partaker in peace for all times
The aims giving is for all elders hoping for a better
understanding
Above all noted problems my mind fails to understand why

THEM GOOD BUDDIES

On a Friday evening we would have a guitar jam
We are a group of four guys playing classic and country
Our group was Josh, Robert, Ed and me as we chorded along
Having good will, surpasses good unity at this place and time
Most of the songs sang were by Johnny Cash or Gordon
Lightfoot
It's nice to have some family come along with good buddy
friends
Someday us buddies want to do a recording, send it to
Nashville
In need of everlasting joy as fulfillment for the time we got

During these days a little joy with a lot of sorrow has come
My wife passed away with Cancer and Ed had a heart attack
Did ask in a prayer for Ed to get better to return soon
Have written a few songs in favour of my wife, while lonesome
A few months ago Robert went for a tumor operation, was
benign
Wanted now a get together to sing recent written songs
Have been practicing new songs with only lonely reactions
A person that wants peace for sure is like a theory of mine

The remembrance of old generation days having Uncle's
singing
On such a journey with a good sense of humour there is friends
Would like to rejoice celebrating someone's birthday again
A thought to have better siblings along with friends they were
bringing
Into the hands of those who hate me, wish them some enemies
Wish all understanding family a splendid day you really deserve
it
Better to like people who are not stuck up or even conceited
The word trustworthy is a solid foundation having remedies

If we seek a person shall find everything we are looking for
Let's bring courage to the good hearted leave despair behind
A stranger is a friend you have never met in a lifetime
These songs help to make everybody happy as they did before
In need of joys fulfillment even when tomorrow's been here
Would like my household building to shake with glad tidings
All you have to bring is ardent love of mind and heart, that's all
Our prosperity leans on hope with an elder custom, be sincere

FLIPPANCY INCITES

Having the future find me in some tentative place
Walking along a back road looking for a willow branch
Tomorrow a neighbor wants me to witch for water
The farmer was in need of water for the cattle was the case
Soon at dawns dim light here I am with a branch pointing down
There was a knack to doing witching to find a water vane
An old man owner watched the performance all the way
Found water twenty feet past a rock that was brown

At age twelve my father showed me tricks to do
Make water come out of a penny an earlobe trick
Put water on balled up tissue put it behind one ear
As you rub either arm make out water comes through
On rubbing one arm pick the wet tissue good
Was like the water came from the penny it would appear

Another trick was cut your fingers off with a string
A special way around the fingers it slipped out
These old time tricks I show grandchildren today
Was looking for the happiness these things bring
There were many fistfuls of card tricks them days
The cards were always handy to bring tricks about
No ipods just games with losers and winners that's all
Every night there was several card games everyone plays

SUMMER DUST

Dawn springs from behind the pines once more
Overnight coming upon a new moon more house flies to see
Always had an eight day clock beating like a heart
Here in the windows spider webs catching flies as the mom before
Had open the lower pane to let cool dawn air in this place
The night setting moths now had flown into my room
There was hanging fly stickers had caught some of these pests
This a place a young boy called home with frayed curtain lace

Put my bib overalls on went to breakfast downstairs
Must be windy outside the chimes are clanging like hell
From the kitchen window seen the plowed field dust blow
Out the door seen mating squirrels running in pairs
By the eaves of the home a house finch whistles a tune
Came a robin hopping along chirruping then flew to the fence
Not much to do at this Hipply place but view nature
In open dusty field Jackrabbits came here around noon

Seen a doctor doing house calls along the dusty gravel road
There were clouds of dust travelling with him all the way
Our place was a frame house out in the middle of nowhere
A laneway with grass in the middle beside it wheat sowed
By the east side twenty walnut trees in a line there
The roadside had elderberry bushes for the whole mile
Here there was so much road dust it coated everything
From elderberries jelly was made, the juice strained through underwear

BLIZZARDS RAW GUST

On a long ago winters morn the rage of nature flares
As the week unfolds has a blizzards raw gust setting in
The cold duties of the wind are always made seasonal
Every morning snow shoveling is essential everyone shares
Here bounding snow deluge came in for public view
Many a howling snow orbits whirling astride our old world
Far as our eyes can see the land whitened with snow banks
A North wind pounding like the devil drifting all a strew

Out in a back in time place Denfield snow up high
Here looking at banks of snow to the top of hydro poles
Was no plow in those days to clear the roadways
Every so often would see a horse and cutter pass by
Some people with big families the bobsleigh was the way to go
Had felt there was reason to grumble isolated each day
One should nod then yawn seeing the sight of these winters
From November until April everyday trudging through snow

In the old world people stored and preserved food always
Those days in winter hibernated through it all
Had to weigh nature's fury for sometimes six months
Outside elements was a real down trend in those days
The misfortune in them days there was no snowplow
As for walking people had to follow the sleigh tracks
These dwellers had to stoke wood fires to the utmost
Never heard a voice of humanity complain but they do it now

IMPARTIAL SEATS

Being social is to convene with good friends forever
Even though there is comfort in our circle beware of the rest
The spawn of low brow people are the intolerable kind
Have those raptured moments enjoying such good faith
We are the noble squadrons to help friends with whatever
Those people like us from the old school stay in touch
Each day try to be happy soon better things come at will
With the awe world have to seek one's with understanding
Ones who conspire towards others are not worth very much

Being born in poverty of old times have seen a rueful face
So many scenes in life where there's no love at all
Once in a while wanted to loose the smut of them times
When people act obnoxious it's really such a disgrace
Only want to enact for happy days raise my spirits high
One's conscience say do not bother with inconsiderate clan
How blessed are days of smiling better results in the end
An old man with only love in his heart best say goodbye

Keep what's left of patience be a Grampa stay proud
Such eagerness has been quenched slammed a two face door
Old times had taken impartial seats in life but not now
Take your zealous opinions as hypocrites I'll yell out loud
Those kin of ill repute are not worth my time of day
Having both hands on my hips makes a stern real meant report
From way back then spunk has brought me this far
After initiating my good will a Grandfather has a lot to say

THE LAND FOR OLD

A diversion out of the hither here's an echo day
Time has moved around an eternal sphere out there
The spirits of good will rest on our shoulders now
Them precepts came while we were getting old per say
This good natures face is not fair pray for the best
It's a possibility most old folks have seen a display of woe
No pity our pasts relenting days only heroes are not there
There in a field filled with crosses is where they rest

On Remembrance Day chant songs for lost lives
A melancholy wreath placed on a special day
That saying of our country was the most glorious part
The only difference in battles or now it's later death arrives
In the land of old every day walk along that thin line
To be always told to us once upon a time in relations too
An expression of great joy the birth of a grandchild
Them days being called Grampa seem so very fine

The old realm of things here today then gone for good
Life moves around that get old sphere once again
There is brief factors resting upon time that ends
Even with a grateful plea change things if we could
Only memories rue the day for others still around
Those daily duties Grampa showed me before he went
In his books them childhood days of what went on
Was so many treasured awards in his things we found

FACED THE MUSIC

When you have given it all, you have no more
Would never slight anybody with them hasty words
Today's living in idleness makes most people a beast
Those days of wishing gives you ample time to explore
On behalf of life seems you have barely started that dream
With a hope event that tomorrow will be better
Our agenda plate seems it's always full day by day
In a household from young to old should work like a team

Get ready for hardships by chance pop up once in a while
Those dilemma matters is when plaint comprehends times
The martyr system is what matters to understand good deeds
Having a buddy system creates goodwill with a smile
Common pithy sayings is ideal for a hasty word comment
A saying best for handling insults popping up without notice
Went to a family councilor informed us to go to my sons place
Can still remember those nasty words and the day it was sent

For a Grandfather's friendly modesty only came remorse
That day was like a bolt from the blue for us
All the discursive reasoning recommended by a culprit
To understand it obviously was a face slap of course
The sequel is a negative ponder similar to them old days
There's one instigator that controls their whim of circumstances
Somewhere prelibation of former kin went through the same
Here one mind of that deviant presenting these false plays

WHAT A CONCEPT

During weariness there's quietude to dabble with here
With unfurled times through harried themes ending
Should a mentor give up his hours if there comes the urge
Some blot out the soul of man if he is not really sincere
Let new planned idea's rest on the future just by one's word
In a common place for creation puts awards in place
Comes hope for sustaining triumph for years to come
As a noble bearer of these deeds you shall be heard

One should reside with the self esteem goodness will prevail
With precious thoughts can revive whatever it takes
Be careful not to do the old farm trick with the hay wagon
The arrogant should remain on the random speculation trail
A false box was built under the load of hay to deceive
Was a long ago story of beware of good weather friends
In life sponsor good concepts using faith as your guide
Always be leery there some neither to trust or believe

Those who pray together will stay together it's true
The youngsters now bolster moments waiting at ex call
A whole new world of electronics doing thinking for them
With all these gizmos the mind is dumbfounded what to do
Yesterday's thinking cap has gone with the wind somewhere
Our computers punctuate and spell-check these days
Having a creation of lame brains it will all come to be
We had to figure out everything down pat this student was
there

DOWN AT THE VILLAGE

Many things going on down at the village square
A taxidermist fixed Muskie lunge plaques for the wall
These fish were caught in the Moira river on a steel line
Mr. Collins had a shop by the riverbank, made boats there
There was two stores one hardware one grocery store
Ina Palmer ran the grocery store, Charley Beatty the hardware
The lady Ina sold chickens, beef along with lunch meat
The man Charley Beatty had pipes for stoves plus much more

Another small shop in the back of Palmers store sold fishing
gear
A good place to fish Muskie lunge as well as cat fish in the river
here
Here at this spot the river was over fifty feet in depth
Also sold firecrackers and Halloween stuff when the time was
near
This village of Plainfield had stores like a movie set
At this church was where my family was baptized back then
Also a church reverend Cursey had a Sunday few to come
Even roofing materials at Charley Beatty's you could get

Just last year when we passed through the village place
The stores were gone the church was torn down
Seems everyone had deserted this quaint country side
Them people that greeted you were gone without a trace
Was it that the people died or simply just moved away
There was no one at this place to ask a mystery of sorts
Even the house that I built went knocking no one answered
It made me feel sad when we came here on that day

A HOUSEHOLD WORD

William Morgan DeBeck the best cartoonist of the times
All his characters had giant feet and bulbous big noses
For the best comic ever Billy DeBack got a Reuben award
These were the years that the nickles were size of dimes
Then Bunky, Snuffy, Smith and Sparkplug a racehorse scene
An audience called Sparkplug Snoopy of the period
Soon he belonged to the National Cartoonist Society in 1980
The man was the first creator of comics that had ever been

A newspaper man Arthur Brisbane said DeBeck's work was bad
After traveling all this distance to see Brisbane then turned
down
Every so often he introduced catch phrases like "heebie-
jeebies"
When DeBeck came back up with the cartoon Barney Google
he was glad
Then to add to it his buddy said Barney Google with goo goo
googly eyes
This made the cartoon a Tin Pan Alley pop hit admired by all
DeBeck's very best friends John T McCutcheon and Briggs were
comics
He then came up with Bughouse Fables for great enterprises

When DeBeck introduced Sweet Mama the strip was dropped
It was meant for sure by this man for humour and suspense
Next was introduced the comic strip called Finn An' Haddie
His comic world ranged from 1920 to 1948 and it never stopped
He was known as the best creator of comics for those days
For neologisms he made up sayings such as horse-feathers
DeBeck kept readers on the edges of their seats in suspense
Was employed by many companies receiving several monthly
pays

Other cartoonist like Walt Disney got on the bandwagon
The characters Mickey and Minnie Mouse copied big foot styles
His best employer was the Chicago Examiner when it merged
One of DeBeck's newspapers Show World, forever carried on
Before he died did Bughouse Fables with parlor, bedroom and sink
As a character he starred Bunky for the Bughouse fable role
Forever DeBeck refused to join the Hearst empire media
They only wanted to pay him thirty-five dollars until he put up a stink

WISE DEEMED PASSAGES

There is a good conduct that shapes life's framework
Each journey summons us to become not perfect but better
Amid the uncertainties of the world your best image counts
Be aware when your conscience dreads somebody, danger
lurks
To challenge common sense all the way with confident hope
Maybe look beyond the present moment past the loneliness
Need no prompting only general knowledge gets me there
No matter if people become impatient all you can do is cope

Some times it's music to your ears, other times is melancholy
Only great thoughts remain in my heart it's the best choice
Our life is precious, a little hope gets us through alright
Will remain truly sorry if someone is offered in any way
Absence makes the heart grow fonder in a manner of speaking
We are predestined people no one for knows our destiny ever
Want every footstep guided to wonderful moments of splendor
Them talents make me the man for what he is, as well as
seeking

We ought to get something out of our efforts with good abilities
A steadfast portion is putting one to the test following rules
In as much must attain good merits of a life style each day
The earnest endeavor is a daily conduct filled with stabilities
Seems forever a person passes through traits of conversion
There is kindness with generosity needed for every civilized
person
Have to strive wholeheartedly for an indescribable future
Only great thoughts remain in my heart a choice of intuition

Learn to respect those who help you they are your real friends
Must take action no matter how large or how small the task
Best be inspired by ordinary things to have unending joy
Shall rejoice with happiness an esteem, wishing there's no ends
The doing part teaches us to learn a lesson by our mistakes
Let's dismiss loneliness think of tomorrow with better thoughts
Takes consideration when a man is eager to accomplish good
fortune
Will confirm every stated part is true for goodness sakes

GIDDY UP GO

A chestnut coloured horse that was always ready to go
Summer was Picadilly's resting time to romp in green pastures
During the summer came up to the fence for an apple or two
In winter she had the job of pulling the sleigh in snow
Her head was held up high bells ringing every step of the way
Seems Picadilly was proud to take the family anywhere
On school days went to the place all by herself to get us
She knew her route of where to go for every Sunday

To Mardith Stables where my father worked she liked to go
On through the windy trail of the bush for about two miles
When Picadilly got there she nuzzled my Dad's arm
She whinnied at the stable horses she would know
The horse at morn whinnied from the barn everyone get up
Seem the horse and rooster made noise at the same time
We fed her first being the most important of all
Get me harnessed lets get on the road you lazy pup

A long ways down the road Picadilly became old
Some days her legs could hardly carry her around
One morn she could not get up laying moaning on the floor
Our father called the bone man to put her down we were told
We all cried so much when she was taken away
This was our friend for them growing up years
Being not like an animal she was family and friend
When I think about Picadilly there's still tears today

YESTERDAY'S WINDOWS

A life near a country village a mere child then
Have counted many confounded days with regret
Was beyond dire feelings scrupulous as it could be
Them dismal suburbs having gravel roads which to contend
Living in a country place is hallowed from any charm
Had listened to foul cursing voices all of my child days
So much bad attitude to contend with the best of times
Have worked hard upon this green patch called a farm

Must be better people beyond my guardian walls
The jest of these times seems to me it would never end
Here in my heart felt moment a sadness cries out
Forever in yonder place of regret is where the blame falls
Them rooms with open closets infested with moths I recall
At night in summer June bugs flew in through open windows
A host of flies came in all day long buzzing and bugging
Was so glad when the windows could be closed in the fall

There was hard covered books under windows each day
Never ever any niceness each morn waking flies all around
Such circumstances were a degrading style Mom tonight
Both parents were smoking every time you turned around
In every table in the house being full of butts was an ash tray
Had no gentleness on awaking get up I will not call again
Be the silent one, do what you are told or be punished
Them sleepy time walls had no peaceful dreams within
It's been obedience with consequences since my life began

WONDERING DAYS

For a fathers world you wish for the best of times
Another birthday has come and gone as years before
There is a bottom line we are not young as we used to be
Mrs. Schmooze is at it again a blabbermouth of ill wills
Again sense loneliness that plays on your mind daily
If I had my druthers would have gone to Florida again
Wondering what's up back on the country road this very day
A wish to have those imaginary thoughts brought to reality

If you tell a white lie in the winter time nobody will notice
Always liked the song send me the pillow you dream on
Lets cut it out then put it on the fridge it's face painting
Best call their bluff sooner or later it's mama pop quiz twice
Have kept my chin up this long wondering what a Klutz will do
Some one went and pooped on my parade some time ago
In the antsy world it's full of yes madams state of the arts
For ages she has bad mouthed me now it's my turn to do so

The dawn of a new day gives you allotted times for doing
Some friends call to see how the man is existing today
We know our kin were not royalty, was a far fetched story
In future days there will be some demise were you are going
As for siblings at their place made them beds now lie in it
You've got to be kidding are my son's really in cyberspace
How come mama has the lying part down pat, was it for
shame
Who cares when winters over the birds songs help a little bit

The what's up is sooner or later is Wiarton Willie shadow
All things come to he who waits with bated breath now
Been there done that, must beg a question where to go
A camera cannot lie, go buy one to learn from it tomorrow
Do not go there as a friend your as different as chalk and cheese
Someone could teach miserable people how to suck an egg
On going to Hell there's no worry for a deviant clan just be bad
Imitation is the sincerest form of flattery wish it would cease

HOOK OR BY CROOK

Seems ancestors had unity for uncertainties in this world
Todays kindred are like between me and you and the bed post
It's hard to understand the growing apart of families
The image we set is what we believe because we are old
There is no great steadfast concern as long ago pride
A sorry sight not to acquaint ourselves by shaking hands
Who judges justly for good or bad examples for a corrupt
generation
Nothing thrives without a true to heart member's guide

Shall bet dollars to donuts that dignity is a birth right
Best say gadzooks for enticements, nothing is in good fast
For whom the bell tolls some never ever go to church
There is a green eyed monster still infringing a family sight
Ne'er cast a clout till May is out because birds know better
Some people have to be told to take their clodhoppers off
An ill wind intercedes on our behalf for these aging old hearts
Have no eager longings for any intents or a purpose matter

So many obese collywobblers walking down my street
Had many a periods of remembrance of darling buds in May
What was suppose to be done today was lost in a dream
In accordance to Hoyle there is no indication of being sweet
Always have unending axes to be ground just waiting for my
turn
We wait eagerly for someone to put a feather in our cap
Therefore being essential is not worth a tinker damn today
A legend is one's whole lifetime that should bring some
concern

He who can does, he who cannot teaches what he knows
Such as being a foregone conclusion who do you trust
Wait for something to happen by confiding in hope for now
Having abandoned folk etymology my impediment now shows
When Murphy said to be will be it's a finagler's type law
One can be noticed with fifteen minutes of fame, better then nothing
Was a grim reaper in the fields of time then become a bard
Living in an urban town was an ophidian person that's what I saw

DOWN THE HIGHWAY

The dawning sky will take me on back home
There in a country place where a brother belongs
Seems though he had left forever such a long time ago
Will be heading back never more in this life roam
Hoping for a welcome home sign put up by my kin
Now with no love one by a man's side to help me out
Knowing life needs a partner to see him on through
With a new home a lone one does not know where to begin

So much love in my heart with so many a sad day
Them slowing times reminds one he is an old man now
When life's gone there's no need for shelter from the cold
In hopes there's truth of heaven in the sky far away
Making gifts with love wrapped inside not not be
To wonder for our sake in every new coming of a day
Shall have counted the steps taken in the streets of time
Soon only flowers at a graveside there for to see

A wish to be able to walk back to yesterday one more time
Was many things left unsaid returning to some morn
Would be a whole world of glad people alive under the sun
Each Sunday gives them bad vibes, when the church bell did
chime
Comes those days of clouds for gloom then blue sky's brings
the sun
Our life has it's bad days then comes some of them good days
Whatever will be will be it's how life stands for now
These old days with so many aches and pains is no fun

On down that highway in April to start again brand new
As for this country road it shall take me again back home
In a place where a brother for sure really does belong
Here with all my family around things are not so blue
The moving time brings back old days to this mans mind
Them day our parents paid fifteen dollars a month for rent
Us children home owners a lot of difference in what is paid
Nothing comes cheap in todays world all of us did find

MARK MY WORD

Hard to be nice with those people who cause problems
To have them come to their sense is to much to ask
Trying to outwit seniors, trust us we been here to long
Every two faced is a misfit that's where trouble stems
We need family ties it will come out better in the end
Them goody two shoes people are a misdemeanor group
Must have goodness of heart makes living worth while
Need truthful people they are someone in which to depend

To follow the road of happiness it's the only true way
There's no found hope on them troubled paths of life
It's better not to carry a grudge it just wastes time
Be that welcomed friend it helps to get through the day
Our families had many a grateful moments for long ago
The enjoyment was having one another to come around
It only takes one bad omen who brings about bad vibes
Cannot look on my family's side that put on this bad show

Here as elders stand on the threshold of best thoughts
Those with turned backs live with so much disgrace
These commotions defeats what life is really all about
There is sometimes those bad ass groups to call the shots
It appalls all of the righteous meaning for our families
The passing of the buck blame is caused by bad ogres
Comes a blessing for elders well knit homes, not for others
Everything for my offspring's gives me nothing but the willies

238

Only a sense of blasphemy that speech uttered by them
Bear with us my good people we declare our true blue part
From the hell ago home came bad scriptures told hence
There came an obnoxious phone call out of her podium
Did send the best of bad wishes right from this gentleman's
heart
What in their world possessed them into doing just that
Keep paddling your own canoe till it sinks some day
From your house to our house bad vibes keeps us apart

KOAN DILEMMA'S

Have contributed already to a whole life of strife
There has been no comparable times by any source
So ironic the mottos that are not normal circumstances ever
How the courts found a woman worthy with her traits in life
It's rather a horrific choice for a dilemma of deviations
Have formed my manners that suit the purpose is discussed
That descriptive approach has it's interpretations to go by
Somewhere must be a general theory of strong traditions

Them formalities of reality for all this time were niched
For sure a father's evaluation calculations was all wrong
My dictums are not distorted they represent the truth
May the ambition of a father become to being enriched
While emphasizing aspects of it all no one confides in me
From latter times people wondered about her moral stature
When someone creates a dilemma there's formalities not true
As for all sense or purposes have voice my opinions you see

Must the challenges out weigh my concerns in this case
Had seen in plain sight the ignorance of an environment
That mode of this oppressor is somewhat strange always
There is a figurative meaning referring to a two face
What's usual for offspring's is not being included here
A number of initiatives, try seeking a dominate approach
Will find alienation that suits her purpose every time
With no comments of consideration seems no one's there

No one could ever imitate a kin never having respect
Comes that harsh example being subjected to all lies
For this concept in life could there be a possible ending
With no conscience for behavior ever what do you expect
Will delight in the best things, want a good reputation forever
Shall take my best stance in life admitting I'm not perfect
Your benevolence is a nerd creator in that wretch's house
Must grant these one's a miserable day also likewise whatever

IN FOLKLORE TIMES

The Lone Ranger series premiered on radio 1933 year
His side kick was Tonto an Indian character played
This man on the white horse wore a black hat and a mask
The man on the paint horse wore a head band and feather
When the Lone Ranger spoke to his horse it was "High ho Silver"
When Tonto spoke to his horse it was "Gide m up Scout"
As the story goes there was a Lone Ranger then an Indian
friend
The Lone Ranger had a nickel plated 5.5 single action revolver

Tonto's breed of horse was a paint like real Indians rode
A word Tonto used a lot was Kemosabe meaning my friend
For a weapon Tonto had a bow with arrows back then
As for Tonto's horse it remained in the movie being unshod
His arrows were carried in a leather mounted boot holster
These two characters never had a home they slept on the
ground
They represented the law and order of the old wild West
The Lone Ranger it seemed was never shot down ever

Still recall in the movies bullets ricocheting off of rocks
If the bullet ricocheted twice there was a whining sound
The made up word Kemosabe meant good scout or good
friend
These men were rough riding cowboys taking hard knocks
Seems Tonto got grazed one time having to be patched up
As the saying goes Kemosabe related to Indians is the good
scout
This actor looked like a real Indian riding along there
When the Lone Ranger was talking Tonto would not interrupt

The Lone Ranger and Tonto were pop culture symbols
At first the Lone Ranger was played by Luke Hartman
Then the first Tonto was played by Johnny Depp in 1933
The guns shot blanks with sound effects were done by gizmos
This army 45 long colt revolver was a Bruce Beemer model
When the series came on radio at first Kemosabe was used
That word was meant to associated Tonto as a real Indian
There is a remembrance of Lone Ranger revolvers on a forum
lapel

A STOUR ROAD TRAVELLER

A long road winding through the countryside
The Canada bread man whirling dust clouds as he came
Every Friday he came our way for a weeks supply
From bread to pastries was the goodies he supplied
Always had a package of cupcakes gave to us for free
Seemed like a big event of Friday to have such a treat
He also brought us cheap winter sox for a little bit of money
In this far outreach there was many peddlers to see

Out in the middle of nowhere came the fish man next day
He had fish already scaled and cleaned ready to eat
Our mother bought enough fish to last one whole week
Heard his truck coming he had a mouth organ he did play
Could still hear the mouth organ playing far down the road
Do recall that man with the beard on a Saturday did call
He really looked like an old salt from the sea man
Was just an ordinary man, civil as could be not really proud

Next in line was the Watkin's man on a Monday he came
On his truck he had something for colds and back aches too
For sure best of all was the root beer powder mix
The things that he brought along were always the same
Was also baking produces be brought along every time
Them cans of pepper were pure no fillers added ever
He brought not vanilla extract but the best there was
Then was the lemon meringue pie filler that was supreme

FIENDISH FOLKS

Was no one that said any prayers or said goodnight
Such doleful wayward times for one summer time
My grandmother sat darning sox never a nice word to say
Then telling me to weed the garden was not right
Went to my grandfather's acre garden worked dawn till noon
After lunch pitched manure into a spreader he took away
Cleaned the cow gutters until this man came for another load
This person cursed and grumbled the whole afternoon

By no means can forlorn people have happy days
The time that this grandson went there was in nineteen forty
nine
On Sundays was given a bath in a galvanized tub of cold water
Seems these people liked torturing someone in many ways
Here all they knew was manual toil from morn until night
After lunch the grandfather worked he chewed then spit
tobacco
Everytime the grandparents met they would argue and fight

My grandfather was a butcher, had dead animals hanging
around
Was a frightful nasty place for a boys summer vacation
His plough horses were almost worked right to death
They had children at their age each one miserable I found
Mostly bad moods comes from wretches of this kind
Had to give up with modest defeat be like them forlorn
That place of circumstances beyond the norm will always be
A boy was never so glad to go home leave this wrath behind

THE THREE DUKHOBORS

Come lets rally around some real Dukhobors there
These be the meager of such an uncommon home
On Jeanett's side of the family doctors and lawyers to admit
Have much more in common with educated one's which to
compare
The best guess is they were not smart enough to stay in school
Just nobodies is what their lives have really come to be
In trying to better themselves really there's lots of doubt
When you are uneducated it's pick and shovel jobs as a rule

To bad you should have applied yourselves in younger years
There's no turning back you must shovel away your time
These doctors and lawyers are now having their hay day
Best you Dukhobors work on with blood sweat and tears
You cannot turn the tides for loveners money best to say
The degraded part suits Dukhobors right to a tee
No need for some dumb people in an Irish family role
Just getting paid by the hour makes it very little pay

Here's what that awkward family stood let life pass them by
In the house with Dukhobors a degraded place to be
For that minds eye of it all we seen that family result
Was a place without reputation this we cannot deny
Our educated people sought to understand all of it
Not an ordinary place for cohabitating lacking morals
Them three Dukhobors could tell a story to us about it all
Such a bad parenthood scene for a household I would admit

Should put it all down to a case of messy circumstances
Had watched the Dukhobors eat from mother finches place
Partly eaten dishes of food with hard sandwiches everywhere
Knowing it was not like a real kitchen eatery at first glance
Hash it to this family sure glad when I got out of there
Give a hoot to it all this sad state of awkward affairs
The old man with her say they are parents to all of this
It's an odd world according to my place in which to compare

PAR TO THE COURSE

The persistence of a work day is par to course
Best to apply yourself it will get each job done
Must arrive at a job early to prepare for the day
We are bound for our own destiny as one life source
Having the best intent will see a man right on through
For always doing gets everything caught up for the time
Became pleased with each time using might and main
Tomorrow could be somewhat different with taboo

Those people that rest on their laurels nothing gets done
Each night review the tomorrows as to what you can do
Earn an honest man's pay leaves a good feeling inside
But all work with no play really one needs time for fun
Some prayers wanting things to be better is only a mind set
One's life needs nice song feelings that comes from the heart
Them chosen few our maker has set them apart forever
This world has hard working people that strive for what they get

What you do not plant will never ever start to grow
Tend to our good habits helps us every single better day
Best to mention about it but is only a matter of fact
It comes without saying on your mark then ready set go
One can only send good thoughts have yourself a nice day
Must not tell other people yourself does not want to hear
There is that special road that has a nice sunny route
Let's have a friendship home place near or far away

So many hard knocks during those days of my prime
Just was no bouquet of goodness for a sorrowful heart
Seemed the blinds were always closed dark on the inside
There comes luck that makes it's way in streets of time
Having pressed all whistles and buttons but things came late
Had my pillow to dream on where wishes never came true
So much schism should you believe in it or not left some doubt
With lost values in life as a whole was redeemed to one's fate

GEORGE IS DAD

While cohabitating with another man still George is Dad
These logical terms remain forever in a lifetime
For all times blood is thicker than water it is said
She has been trying to mold a new Dad, that's real sad
A cogency does not work in this real world of ours
Here's where the animism is above all other ideas in life
Takes some audacity for plans in acting against a real Pa
Must be a person creating one little world called hers

Shall make it clearly known yours is not a real world
These days of grace were dead set on botching it all
That quality of being decent does not suit her stature
In the awe of it all for her is limitations for human dignity
A woman who's callused, canny, conniving as well as cold
One's life as a father protected by deva gets me through
Foremost the last name is important for persons known
Mine is the best characteristics for mind and body
The importance in living is to have values that are true

You did set up a game with no rules from very start
Was a handful of lies being played against it all
Some day will rue all things when an ace falls into place
The best of life will suddenly just can fall apart
There is a difference of how we interpret this life
All things about people knowing if it's truth or all lies
Her faithfulness reeks in those days now have gone by
Not being true to one husband, what about as another man's
wife

To make life worth my while have done all that I could
Did bare all my crosses while suffering with the rest
Will do what she has to just to get her own way
Everyone knows where a woman stands it's not with the good
Had to treat her like a child so things were done right
A lady that stole things every time while being downtown
T'was a never ending battle talking to managers in stores
Would steal cigarettes or gum when out of my sight

OUR JOURNEY

There is so many miles we tread in a lifetime
Each year the outcome is not the very same
Part of our journey was with so much happiness
Then another part of our journey being very sad
Here left to wondering as each night we did decline

Those friends out there we shall always think about
Also people we will always remember away back them
We could dwell on these times forever in our minds
Soon after night we peer out on some brand new day
Then comes more days of growing old there's no doubt

Also songs that can put happiness in an old heart
While most other days memories unfold once more
Seems we let the clock tell us what has to be done
With a new day coming must find another place to start

Here comes the sun over the horizon to welcome this day
Again thoughts of lost events getting to me once more
Was like standing at crossroads wondering where to go
On this welcome day a breeze whispers like a lost soul
The significance of thought seems still so far away

Those former steadfast days had encouragement with hope
Along the old path of harmony comes father grumpy again
The circumstances of communication most times are
somewhat rude
Hold fast to what endures by partaking with constant friends
As for manners they remain blemished hardly unable to cope

There is people who say it's your own fault be a man take the blame

Recalling the back life immortality ran rapid with adoration

Seems obedience left with the changing of the times up to this day

At meal time youngsters to be seen but not heard a custom of old times

Unable to utter a word or even joke around when company came

IN A HEARTBEAT

Behind me is left the failing flaws of past living
By chance the moods of peers are out of sight
Not like the past troding along destined to survive
All my life people having been taking while I was giving
Them days long past with a frater feeling finally gone
Lets raise up the bonnie one the hell with the rest
Would the real virile man tell about the coddling times
In todays world of what's what the reality did dawn

For the next youngest left with a toil beat body of old
The terrific scene to meet the moral part of it all
Such was the muckler for fame he reaped everything
Has left a brother profoundly egotistic as well as bold
As for me hours of woe were stretched to the limit part
Would like to cast over again a wish for Murphy's law
That facetious or satirical proposition for something going
wrong it will
Hold everything with honesty right from the first most start

Still hear peers frequently saying it's hard to believe
He has put on a jolly good show all of these past years
In a heartbeat could play down this folly episode
It's always best to be truthful in what you achieve
Have always been sincere with all due respect given me
Was never a front and centre person to infatuate a crowd
Has been done quite a plot for charm in past years
A boy graded sixty in school having parents suit his fancy

LIFE'S BACK ROADS

To ascend on a place far off the beaten path
A frame house sitting on a landscape of clover fields
Walnut trees lined the eastern boundary line fence
The winters here of high snow banks so much wrath
Had no front yard in the summer it was full of fruit trees
If us boys climbed in the trees our landlord yelled at us
Had walnuts to sell in the fall, at the road a sign walnuts for sale
Our father wanted some of the trees cut down no one agrees

During winter months mice would come into the house
The closets of this place always smelt moldy everyday
Had to put mothballs in the closets to keep down the smell
We finally had a cat to catch every eager chewing mouse
One day in summer a hay mower cut off our cat's legs
Our landlord killed and buried the cat in a field
As a stripling did not think much of a place out in nowhere
We had butter and milk kept cold in the well in wooden kegs

Up mikes and down jikes my attitude for it all
Maybe become a clouet with all this nature around me
The dog was always busy chasing rabbits everyday
Not such a hunky dory landlord waving with a call
Get out of there was the man sitting in the truck would say
Every summer the well went dry had water hauled in
Still recall the grass in the middle of our lane two feet high
These suburbanites of hell ago land hounded us every day

ANCESTRAL EMBERS

The church during old times was built from limestone
It held a congregation of twenty people in all
Not all people had patriotic pride, mostly women came
Seemed most people went up front to pray alone
Every prayer was a secret expectation from the heart
A minister read the sacred page at the top of his voice
There was always a prattling enfant crying our loud
We touched the cross then prayed right from the start

After church would have home made soup for lunch
Had tea biscuits made from sour milk also for this meal
Them egg salad sandwiches really top it off well
Our family said grace with head down the back in a hunch
The act of being strict was the language of the soul
That one small church created so much goodness each time
A dad went to the holy place once in a blue moon
Women came to church also played the home time role

When the newspapers came a dad read it first of all
Dad cut the meat then served everyone from his end
He was the first one to this table also first to leave
Every child had to come to the table on the first call
No one reach across someone it was always past to you
One must eat all his meal or go up to bedroom
The table scrapes were gathered to feed our household pets
Any dog or cat was left outside until the meal was through

FLAGS ALOFT

Many names passed in remembrance of the flag
My Irish relatives fought under the Union Jack
A sovereign salute in kept memories of long ago
All us Irish fought battles to be free a reason to brag
We have cast iron pride in our living soul ever to be
Those vet tombs where hero's lay with crosses row on row
Our kin faced the enemy they were not cowards to renege
People that ridicule our country are deranged it is plain to see

As a child during the war we sang "stand on guard for thee"
From afar immoral grief whispered in our Canadian ears
Had to beckon strength to put us through depression times
Even through we want peace terror will not ever let us be
For the most part our rights a true citizens is in doubt
Seems in my retirement years sovereignty no longer exist
To remember the forties we were rationed to the utmost
The good fortune to bring us fame is simply left out

Being open gates left with no constraint for a few years
Them current reports of constraint on flags being flown
Having their petty means wanting dress codes changed
Seems we are affright to talk up because of terror fears
Our ancestors for passed war deeds were proud of the dress
My remembered thoughts of us saving the world for what
While our kinfolks lips are pressed thin the insult climbs
Such a mockup of disgrace our homeland is a real mess

THE BRINDLE BROTHERS

Our mother was not best of friends one does recall
Here was our country place, the smell of dung filled the air
In July clumps of elderberries in our hands each morn
The Brindle brothers lived here three guys that's all
One brother always wanted to leave home, with bags off he
went
Then some time later he would be back, saying you're here to
stay
We called him the atom bomb because he was always upset
This brother always wrote to Kellogg's for miniatures to be sent

All chores at morning and night was a routine farm thing
Early evening the collecting of eggs at the poultry ground
Had continuous oinking of pigs wanting to be freed again
Then the cows next had to be walked to the hillside spring
After all was said and done garden weeds pulled at evening
Every few hours went for drinking water fifty feet away
Last of all the fish caught on Saturday to buried in flower beds
The Watkins root beer for the summer days we were enjoying

Our Sparta home was built from street bricks of dull red
These St. Thomas Ross street bricks were heavy duty kind
Our father was hardly home, working, supporting seven kids
At the supper table get the chores done our mother said
Those summer weekends consists of gathering hay for cows
In winter bucksaw wood cutting keep our house warm
The house no insulation in the walls fuel burnt very fast
A summer collected hay for the barns over head big mows

During June picked strawberries at a farm near by
Soon tobacco harvest was in full swing for some work
A mud pond place to swim in summer to get cooled off
Three bikes lay against the side door wall every single day
It never failed the cinder laneway gave us all cut knees
Always remember our mother wore no pants, seen a bare ass
Us two brothers try to keep peace for others in the family
Our younger brother likes to pick a fight with anyone he sees

SYNERGIES IN LIFE

Have a stature recommended a devoted part of unity
Shall reckon with tomorrow whatever makes up the day
Better to grant a reward, condemn some being nerds
Take a recount of those deserving every payment of gratuity
There was those dark shadows causing bad weather for all
On through our journeys while hope rests on our shoulders
Lets work on love to fulfill the happiness part in our life
Make a good gesture time, remember to give a man a call

Will take gloom away from noon time see who comes after
dusk
Total the recount on all them wonders, while you go the mile
The common things indeed, do accordingly to what's of value
When someone is throwing their weight around best to duck
Seems some found their own town to pick friendship in
As for remedies best concentrate on what to do next
Will have to depend on fonts to redeem the best for all
Must justify the rights as well as wrongs, but where to begin

Best sustain good habits, leaves unfailing goodness
How to choose the better way for moral descent
On pursuing one's conduct, things are not always up to par
The whole hearty living is by prompting some real happiness
There is a generous gift in life obtained by your friendship
Be it like host times treat them like members forever
Our best part of sharing let it be as dignity of the heart
Always tried to be faithful to create a someday relationship

Life's cooperative passion brings out the best in people
To represent a meaning gives us well beings something good
Let's all work together to make everything be possible
With those who cast malice each day all they do is grumble
For the sake of all friends revere rules this entire day
As for sonship they cannot fill the happiness part
What rules the hearts of pagan one's of a harsh domain
That's why the honour of a father is not their way

A HEARTS JOURNEY

Hopeful eye's scan down corridors deep in thought
Seen so much grief being a martyr of old times
In olden days had to whistle to bring my spirit up
There was no common place with goodness only doubt
Every wall has restraints while waiting for hope to arrive
Again will unfurl old times with all it's harried fate
My days were like a wandering train not going anywhere
With all those beatings of abuse be thankful I am still alive

The haze remains when thoughts of inside those doors
That place was so obvious encased with doubt forever
Here was an eager boy plagued by moments of ah
An old saying sometimes it rains sometimes it pours
If one got away went fishing okay at home was bad
Every element of theory like the sun always there
Each day tried to be happy until a better day came along
Once a year someone sang to me happy birthday I was glad

Would have liked to build a chanticleer then chant away
Do away with any milieu bring my spirit to a higher level
Should be a beginning for some new trend of patience
A wish not to wait until fud times to make my play
Somewhere in a hearts journey make it to there
On through the trail of lost dreams seeking the anew
So be it pondering with roads of times free at last
It's been a real battle but this man still has wits to declare

WINGS OVERHEAD

Such a warm summer afternoon being infatuated by it all
Had built a new home in Plainfield with lots to do
Seen geese with fleeting wings up from the river nearby
Was twenty miles in the country with many a crows cawing call
Behind my house Indian fences of cedar winding their way
Was so much tranquil peace all their freedoms granted
Looking for a place to build an arbor on a hopeful corner
today

Along the back of this property was spacious for winged flight
Heard many a hawks echoing cries out over the land
Here hawks bestride searching for game far down below
On this nice cloudless day hawks had climbed high out of sight
So much to see with nesting birds taking up lodging near my
home
Twelve cedar trees along the East side many songsters there
Once in a while heard a quake coming up from the trout
stream
Every evening with my gun to the woods I would roam

Was a place for wolves, foxes and bobcats around here
Like the animals had my freedom days in which to relate
Not a farm boy going fishing on a weekend could go when I
want
Here was my place could live every day without any fear
Some days would pull up an easy chair rest the whole day
Am as free as them wings overhead one has that choice
Saved my money while working for Harvey Nicolson bought this
home
These foible people since the sixties I left, found my way

IN A DAYS SPACE

Was like a scene in an old play want the curtains shut
That element while being young hoping for a change
Could not reenact bravely a mother's fist knocked me down
Have finally got out yesterdays plenty deep rut
A day back then like leaves pressed in some book
The bad humour folks some would call nerds stood there
Them dreadful scenes are like out of the movie Godfather
Be best to shame all the abuse that a youngster then took

No by chance to parley with friends was not the thing to do
Here's where strangers walk as friends, friends as strangers
Those bad humour folks always utter shameful words
In this part of the sticks straw hatted farmers with out a clue
Everywhere brazen makers with grudges which to seek
Comes another days duration regretting the mooing and
oinking sound
Shall tomorrow find it's way to enact better on my behave
You can tell they are farmers because their clothes reek

On down a gravel road to see what is out there
The sheep in the meadow cows mooing so forlorn
A farmer could not wait to show off his smelly crew
Was a day when all the bulls went to the county fair
One should have other means in life much better to be sought
These people treated humans like the animals they fed
For your days space must be a better way which to go
No need to stay with miserable people be thankful what you
got

AN AFTERNOON'S CAPER

Was only yesterday sat on a book of pictures of lost ones
Then soon after stared out a window of a forgotten world
These hands with wrinkled fingers turned pages of time
This day could come alive again seeing videos of reruns
That empty room has no elder people around only memories
there
Each life is like a shadow passing through then gone
A noon day represents itself puts a shadow in the hall
In a corner in the dinning room Grampa's one time rocking
chair

How blessed them times when people came then had to go
Here's me in an afternoon caper snooping around
Seen pictures of elder years seems they were looking back at
me
The curtains where old fashion dragging the floor very low
Everyone in this house were very poor everything always the
same
An old Grandfather clock had stopped at ten in the past
Wood was still in the box beside this old cast iron cook stove
The front door was hard to open these hinges cried as in I came

One days wanderings going forth not one soul around
Old boots having cracked leather still on the stairwell
Was some kitchen chairs tried to sit it cracked away
A few moth eaten suits in the closets no others to be found
So long ago this a bustling place now rack and ruin
Here was me on the front step in the depths of an afternoon
Being a country home away out there no one came or cared
Old memories of someone being, will crumble away soon

LOVE FINDS A HOME

Those moments of memories lost in the past
Each sad thought poised like a pondering shadow
Was in a time to reason as to what life's all about
As to reality coming about not the greatest to be cast
Came much emptiness with unjoyious beliefs there
Them embedded emotions always around to fill our days
Our unloved youthful times for this life so long ago
The need for love in a family role with elders to care

To view more over what the goodness of love will bring
No advantage of good fortune succeeded the past
Every gracious might failed during hardship years
With only hope of good fortune show kindness a good thing
Seemed always the endurance of heartless gestures so cold
Forever hanging on to frayed hope away back then
Good thoughts with hope change would come just by waiting
While pondering life will alter dark days it has been told

In the realm of years did triumph as one will recall
Then came a special virtue to entreat one's new life
Was a woman to believe in with loving thoughts so true
So precious our lives came to be with no hate at all
With all loves courage heart true thoughts made life complete
Had created a new bound level such great love in mind
All of life had altered leaving a wonderful fixed mark
Our love did find a home a place called forever street

UNITY FOREVER

So humbly coy did exist in descendants far back in time
By having worthy conduct you can pursue much better means
So much devotion is known to me that commands my thoughts
All along our paths journey it has been endowed with memories
sublime
The author of peace rules this heart for some of us as of now
In former times oppression had showed it's ugly head forever
Be worthy of those who come always sustaining those bad
vibes
Them intentions to despise a father forever it has reaped sorrow

Go ahead make your day by disappointing all of us friends
Them hidden lies told will effect all of us folks it's known
These kindred prudes make awful remedies to contend with
Behind the shadows in life there was much evil it always sends
The memorial of bad people rest in my mind award forever
more
Must attain happiness in a home truly it's our place of honour
With kindness wondrous union comes to be here for all of us
Be those who stray humanity by that meanness they have in
store

Let's be gladdened having only honoured ways on our mind
Whatever makes the end peace always prospers in our life
The merits being devoted to dedication is requirements
needed
Shall bind our inheritance only in the world devoted as good
kind
On friendships journey let there be kindness poured out there
Here such damnation being set apart from the rest of people
Give them no mutual respect of generous moments for our
sake
Best not liberate those afflicted personality, best be aware

Once again unity lifts up good hearts with dignity as a son
Better not bother to pity wretches that are not worthy of trust
Be always worthy of those who come sustaining such bad vibes
On in life became customary to receive awards of best things done
There's eager faith as a citizen to always keep me going on
Was worthy at this stage that my conduct pursued better means
From out of old nasty closets a truthful man has arrived
The peaceful part of life now announced the meanness now gone

OUR BALDERDASH ONES

Better to bound for awhile keep right of their way
Had come to air good news when bad news had just begun
Hark lets rejoice in trying to increase joy in the world
Use a gesture to make non sense go away forever today
There is a hinder moment to yell at pagans, the honour's mine
The dawn will come again to lay annoyance on our doorstep
How much humbly will it take to make everything normal
Here is the burden we bear tires us enough to decline

Our pouring out of love now has moved to daft state of mind
In all sense of the word nerds now are their only host
Hope it's alright to loose heart with it, no charge it's free
All the days of a lifetime no one came wanting to be kind
The miseries rendered must have a place in which to land
A person who is honoured needs rewards when it all ends
My fullness of faith is like a painted scene it stays the same
At home space is a mans splendor it's not hard to understand

That messenger with love from days of old, failed on his part
So weary are they that make happy sounds to be heard
Them circles of expectations are perplex for every day
All that electronic nonsense is our oppressor from the start
Did you ever encounter someone texting in your travel time
Have held my breath while they cross the road head down
It's customary to see the stopped one's in our part of town
During teen days would go to a phone booth that cost a dime

The dawn from anew will come upon us to share together
Out of an old virtuous life the technical world abounds
Within the human state of affairs will be no sweet accord
To every sensible thing in part no need to think it all over
Here on our paths of exercise have become vacant and
untrod
What's been created good sense is not required anymore
Where has the precious things in life got to just surpassed now
Have chosen no vows for a guide now, nor believe in God

OUT OF THE CLOUDS

While waiting for a days sunshine came her expression
My Sun come out with your two eyes out, as she waited
No one any more to say get out of the fart sack to me
Heard the get up call, it's Sunday it's an off to church session
For heaven's sake she would say our house has to be squeaky
clean
All the duties for me had been listed from a days start
Our kitchen was hers to cook she did not want me there
A person doing anything to make a dollar that's how it's been

Would be a Valentine card right on time first thing at morn
Was not allowed to do everything, we shared the load
If a neighbor did something wrong she told him right off
She was up at six, long before a new day came to be born
Had a love for gathering strawberries from our garden place
Break a leg was the gals favourite saying for the to does
Then came that voice water the garden it's getting late
When it came to picking vegetables, don't touch it's my space

In the evening our front porch was her favourite spot
Sometimes she talked about her life at home it was not good
The ladies eye's welled up when she told me the story of home
While playing with her favourite doll at Christmas she got
A father grabs the doll from her arms putting it into the stove
Told me she cried all day and half the night, sobbing so much
Later on her aunt Lill brought this girl to have a doll there
Then after the weekend, back to her home place was drove

Here was my partner now lost and gone forever more
I could have done this life all over again if let to be
For many a day shed a lot of tears, was such a long span
Wished we could still go to flea markets as times before
My dreams seek her forever she was the very very best
There was evening then comes morning so lonely here
Such a solace place with only the clock ticking the hours
Could not sleep at night, but finally had to go to rest

HIDE NOR HAIR

With a century past have hallowed a special day
Maybe narrate better words to rate friendship again
Our faith makes happy hands with a sharing heart
The world is full of wretches wanting to lead you astray
Knowing that to find grace you have to be one kind of man
Never curse or swear you will not be wanted on that call up
time
All this befuddled talk is discusting forever they say
From the forties up to the two thousands is quite a span

So much debunking folklore was the case so long ago
Neither hide nor hair so be it for this time of being
As for old times do not even think of frolicking it's debunk
Every morning was a goaded hapence in the kitchen below
A father cursing because the stoves went out over night
The house was not insulated fuel burnt like crazy in wintertime
My dad would shake the ashes out then start the stoves again
All of that grumbling with swearing for our sake was not right

In today's world was hide nor hair of wood only gas
Every day tripe episodes confronted me from early morn
To think about changing things is beneath ones dignity was
thought
Was delimits for going modern more or less just stay an ass
After walking the streets of times found a better place to dwell
Have stated the unpleasant facts each slightly a different
episode
Be damned the forgotten it's much better in every way
Be better to find another place on earth then this living hell

SLICKUM QUICK

Our father cut us three boys hair for many a year
For a summer cut had a brush cut it was more cool
The clippers were hand power for a very long time
We only had a trim when winter months grew near
After the hair cut something was needed to hold hair down
My dad took Vaseline from a jar in the palm of he hand
He rubbed his hands together then slapped in on our hair
This was called slickum quick the best hair gel in town

Every Friday afternoon the village boys came to our place
Was hair cut time, each played cards waiting in line
It cost a dollar trimming each head as the line up would go
Sometimes six people a night he would have to face
From the dollars earned my dad bought electric clippers one
day
These were away lot better then the pull out hair type
If some one had a new baby we were the very first to know
Our place seemed to be old new news things to say

These long ago times still stay in my thoughts this day
The Plainfield house had a welcome mat at the front door
Many a friend came around to see us all week long
During quit times remembering them seems only yesterday
Now the house and barn can no longer seen there anymore
Also Mudcat Lane is a highway now, new houses built
All the store owners have passed on at Plainfield village
Was the department of highways took it in nineteen ninety four

LEEWARD WHYLES

Have taken a short trip to pastures crossing streams there
That notch of revolving time beneath a noon day sun
All prospects twice forty times never a dull moment
There's always a bull in the field someplace it's best to beware
Down the daily path this farm boy went in morn then at night
Me with my dog drove the cows to the barn for milking
Under azure skies this day was a blessing in disguise
Was told to do the farm work because my oldest was much to bright

You are the one that should never have been born so she said
Here was suffered so much abuse made it hard at school
There was ebbing faunts treating me as not being normal
Where I slept was in the commode room with a bed
Those awards of grace where enshrined for my elder brother
Such a daunting world for that matter of fact quest
With the enrapture for him there was no love for others
So much emphasis for the perfect boy endowed by the mother

Seems abandonment of loyalty for the other children of kin
Was this the existence on irrational grounds here
Had promised myself earnestly never to give up
For the last ditch, was looking for a place to begin
As part of my inner nature just waiting for my turn
Here comes my seventeenth year with action for freedom
No one pushes my buttons any more have escaped from it all
Getting as far away from despicable people was my concern

MODES OF PSYCHE

Have become a benign messenger with unfinished scenes
Was unable to enjoy the lonesome part need some reprieve
Recalling old folks fairy tales Santa and the Tooth Fairy
You better go to sleep or Santa will not come down the
chimney
The parents telling us about Santa Claus but spanked us for
lying
Always thinking about foretold events that were nonsense
Them entity moments come as visible notions to rid old folklore
That figurative sense of portent irks me even as of now
Some kind of visionary takes us back to those untrue events

In this providence place of origin still understands logic
You cannot combine life with fairy tales expect it to work
Even going to the sixth sense extreme wishes do not come
Only leprechauns know how to create the real magic
Let's go pray for a sunny day sooner or later comes on it's own
Often comes the whim of nod to please your oppressor
All of us dread loathsome things that spill out on life
Most times wrestle with poverty in this we are not alone

Have recited episodes telling of unusual galoots
How can an Easter Bunny lay coloured eggs for a child
Maybe a hen follows the bunny around as a mascot
Them days here was the stupid one wearing rubber boots
Our daily minds relate to poetry to say what you want to
When a child flies the coop he will then sense the real world
Those fairy tales have played on hearts of our time
Things applying back to youth days on a large scale untrue

IN MEMORY TIMES

Along a rough lengthy road good days appear once in awhile
My liberties out of the heavens of old still have pride
A life's script where misery was always an open book
Always have the intent trying to be happy with a smile
While in open fields came raptured moments of being free
Have pursued thoughtful judgment to change a mood
Such lessons not guidelines crisscrossing wayward roads
The word wretches suits suburban bumpkins to a tee

Old granddaddies were dull folks with no logic in mind
All them hellish days racked up in them memory times
Seen other children being hugged by their peers often
Here boundless places of silence sincerely the dull kind
Self plied events bring on rewards every so often cases
Out of ranks of it all comes best parts of all holy prayers
Them days as a stripling was unable to see the logic
Would be nice for people to be nice bring on happy faces

Was a countryman a rival of rural grace syndrome
If this man was to grow up to be a grouch would hide my face
Someone to make me feel good enough to dance with delight
For every day growing up thinking of a beautiful rival place to
come
Come showeth me good fortune for possibilities to come about
A field of wheat another one of corn a terrible place to be born
Still remember that day by the barn with manure on my boots
If one was granted one wish never live on a rural route

WAYWARD HOPE

Have knocked on doors of time with wandering thoughts again
Wanted to find an answer to the whims that abound me
There were always grumbling words with hyper answers then
As for the refugium matters there became hope to refrain
Spent some days trying to get buster to do some chores
Such a smart boy had no times for mediocre type jobs
Here being left in the lurch telling me to do what was told
Had ended up doing the work only got the why's and
wherefores

Was told to grasp the workload or suffer the belt
Such a crude landscape with resuming hardships all day
All that dirty work load was spurring me from morn till night
Wanted to say shove it was exactly the way one felt
Every day armed consequences to guide my feet there
Hope was a stubborn space that never showed it's head
Tell it to the marines was a common expression long ago
They were all time subordinates no one in my young life was fair

Them frigging people accounts for a group of lubbers
To forecast the nitty's you would related to the burgs
Do not leave the house without them you will be sorry
Everywhere you went was cow flaps you must wear your
rubbers
This is where a teenage lad was, as of today more happy
An old man of seventy seven no one can never put a sunder
We love what we are doing while loving those who love us
Here is me in a big city very happy as a great grand pappy

QUAINT REMEMBRANCE

Out from that country place was not much real charm
There is nothing so humble from the lookout of an urban porch
Each morning the sun ascends to greet the time for chores
Today horseless ploughs rusting away on some old farm
Comes an occasional sigh thinking of the laboring days
During them old time laboring hours no one ever said well done
Was a case of subduing the gentler to do the errands there
Must relinquish it all, no joy, no hope, nothing that pays

A beautiful rose blooming was the only love giver by the
wayside
Was a grasshopper sang his shrillness at Mom for a while
Had no comfort in my own circle the live long afternoon
The forsooth part had gumption showing one had tried
Was a mystic day encamping thoughts of days gone by
Seems the plough shears of life unfurrows thoughts forever
It could always be heard from across field of time still echoing
The same old afternoon shadows greet me like a windward sigh

Quaint remembrance follows me around all day
There came my morning footsteps on the same old path
A mind full of doubt with hither diversions of remorse
Have passed the depths despot got up then got away
Placed a lot of heretic opinion for what a life endorsed for me
Where the dorks hung out wearing straw hats for ever
Here was me living in this land of woe bearing my cross
These fellows even wore straw hats in the house for tea

CROSSING MY MIND

When some days are scheduled, leaving crossed my mind
In the old days behold what was in store from time to come
Mark each day with a cross wanting heaven to forbid the comings
Every day is emotional because you never know what's to find
Hush what's to behold in your space in the course of a day
Never suppose your days of rest it will wreck someone's plans
For mystery is a starry silence of wonder reaching far out
That fate to be happening tomorrow seems so far away

So many residences cross my mind from day one
That list Denfield, Yarmouth Centre, New Sarum, Sparta
All country bumpkin places with gravel roads everywhere
Wished my family would settle down not be on the run
Our school days were a mixed up affair moving everywhere
Still remember plop piles of horse buns on the road
We all carried honey pails with sandwiches inside these days
The three mile walk to school we had to just grin and bear

Had a school teacher Miss Barnum who used the strap then
Ten smacks on the hands it hurt like the dickens
Was so strict in those times you best behave or else
At recess played anti I over beginning at hour of ten
In those times only a few people had a car to get around
The roads were narrow persons walked the ditches mostly
There was crank phones with party lines in some homes
Having no place to play ball like a nice sized playground

FOEMAN TO FACE

One who has pondered in time nothing ordinary at all
For many reasons good judgment is first to foremost
Such a pledge always forsaken, blind as he who will see
A child must obey their elders from fright it's the protocol
Our world with it's inhabitants none of which are the same
Some pass the buck it suits their fancy it seems
So much controversy with awkward sentences to answer
Each foeman are like gladiators they lie no one takes the
blame

Be discreet in the old world put on the modest act
It makes up common merit but not truly above board
A made to believe story come from the mind of the beholder
Everyone's wretched in elder days for sure it's a matter of fact
That diamond in the dark maybe a regular stone who knows
For good luck we must seek then we are bound to find
To master faith makes better days ahead for everyone
Someone who lies once it's not much until later it's grows

Things on the back burner for later comes to be forever
Do not put off for today what you can do tomorrow
In ponderous grace we never come to terms with life
When people get away with things they think it's clever
In long ago times claim for fame was never thought about
The building remained drab covered with residue stuff
Them old clock towers bonging the hour morn until night
Had to pass another day the only signs to life was doubt

IDLE DREAMS

The experience of the heart with capacity preserved
That strove of it all having old time shadows fall
Back to the days remembering all that blemish in life
Hiding somewhere trying to get these notions of parleys
unnerved
Knowing right well things resurface like a mirrored image
It's not hard to identify prudeness when it hits you in the face
How sacred is things that crave flunky partners
You can make children believe in anything until they come to
be of age

When people of the oddity group are never obliging forget
them
In my idle dreams see my patients wearing very thin
The foreseen future rest on everlasting friends not misfit ones
It so unfortunate one odd Brennan lets just call him Clem
Have run into a few fops in my day a may hap dilemma thing
Read my lips from an idle dream let them be pissheads
Shall have no reason to subterfuge in any shape or form
Never in a life time has it came to this kind of partaking

What a rotter this relegate of sorts stay away from my home
Again to sit with idle dreams taking a human view point
My wishes are to believe in real people with love
Want to create a wonderful theme meant for a tome
But had nothing to go by because of malice intent
Have already crossed these bridges then burnt them
Will always count our blessings for the real people we are
There was no alternatives but send back the pictures they sent

THEM DOHECKTABIVIAS

Here is a hegemony ruling with radical tactics forever
Must understand kinfolks to who is pulling the wool
Had an old time buckaroo spouse who rode them men then
Glabella will do you there was no morals for her ever
Soon came the busk part, those little red pants was found out
Have set forth the facts presented by her awful fame
To finagle historic wellbeing takes a lot of tripe gull
Once in a while people segregate kinship leaving a lot of
doubt

Such a chancy one life's iffy woe be gone as can be
Here is a messed up creation setting it apart from others
Would have to lobby forever for a sad case of immortality
A sycophancy woman made her own fate, wait to see
Did trade off a father so this lady could finish her game
On back to square one for her allegories with no principles at
all
Was able to make up those barefaced lies to cover each day
Seems this father's lad that block to socialize had came

All of them family blokes have surprises dawning some day
Without ordinary people how should one handle the insane
So blatant a story with no normal radical host from yonker times
Not knowing why screwballs create this hassle meany way
Went to a restaurant in a togetherness friendly nice display
Had a thought to mingle to show gratitude that a father cares
Here were the wonders of the times with only greed in store
When those thingamabobs meal was finished not a "thank
you" to say

Best just mickle while smiling with them as a host
All had been badgered as being better, not a chip of the block
Such dominance is freaky all two faced as they can be
Are they the wonders of the world thinking they count the most
Here is my limericks to judge people as to who they really are
Was not one to pass the buck nor pretend whom that he is not
The man does not appear on their list as being a kind soul
Have a high range of good thoughts that is much better by far

WAS NOTEWORTHY

Come sit at my table of peace it's best a man can do
In presenting good thought have done all of these things
Here is a place of good stature call me when ever you can
Did walk the streets of time once in a while just like you
Lets follow some destiny with all of our good will aims
Here is my front door with it's forever welcome signs there
So much happiness in mind maybe could send a little your way
Trying some how to bear the brunt of many loneliness times

Had placed some dreams in the wind, fly them to a sacred
place
Before a night of a ticking clock, drowned out by a midnight
train
There is no boundary for good hope it comes out of nowhere
More than meets the eye out on those streets of time to face
The sobbing part means some sad tale for life right here
On leaving the house in the middle of an afternoon smile away
Today have good thoughts, tomorrow glory will not be far
behind
Came an old folks saying "go slow go far" they were real
sincere

Somewhere there is a road place where weary travelers stay
While out on my journey seen elder folks had gone a last mile
Was able to notice then off beats resting in a cruel world there
Their luggage was light only had pen and paper writing away
That mirror image tells the sad story we are looking old
Where many a blue Mondays with no happy faces to be found
To remember a fathers fathers land cultivating it every day
So many times over and over again this sad story has been told

Today a North wind knocks at my front door saying it's cold outside
Never seen the sun come out today with it's two eyes out
Out from the wrath of winter need joy in the heart, started to sing
Keeping everything neat and tidy this man had really tried
Many neighbors old like me came by to say their hello
Those friends at Home Depot are glad to see me each day
They said we will really miss you moving away out there
Must do it while one is able this man really has to go

IMAGES AWAFT

On announcing my presences everyone knows the foot step
Let's take a small glimpse into yesterdays old world
A boy trudging along heading for a sultry place called home
Was me walking with flowers not knowing which ones to keep
Had picked some trilliums as well as wild roses that day
The old Moira River had it's soft summer sound so nice
Every time the scent of pines blows takes me back many years
It's a very sad story that goes back such a long long way

So much remembered in times of old patched quilts there
During Saturday people took turns having quilting bees
Was so many hemp bags of rags brought by everyone
Those days you could not go out to buy goods anywhere
Once upon a time will recoup the solitude of that place
We wore gum boots in winter went barefoot in summer
Had winter Mackinaw coats shipped from Mackinac Island
A pegboard rack for Mackinaw coats in the porch space

During the winter used a ferret to catch rabbits for meat
There was always a pot of rabbit stew on the cook stove
Our basement shelves were full of canned preserves
Some apples plus potatoes made our stow complete
Other days walked to the store for sugar and oatmeal
We had two jersey cows that kept us in milk all winter long
Then there was Piccadilly, where the cutter went we had to go
The hard times with little to eat, this was then for real

AN UNDULY HOUSE

One's life is all a variety of characters on the loose
Have kept my courage, but not so cheerful among the
grumpies
Is there a just due reward to inspire human dignity
What could one expect having only confounded things to
choose
Here's that old path seeking to oblige with little to say
That grace proud face being sincere by having faith
Was only a country boy plowing one field go to the next
Such a relenting life getting through another hellish day

There's a reason for a bawsent face during those days
Comes a constant reminder of a poor man's brink
A merry time at Christmas then to be quenched again
Seems every year a prattling infant with dirty high chair trays
Raising a big family first and foremost makes poor years
Best just to say Amen there will never be civil best times
Every year comes a new creation in an already unduly house
When times get tough sadness is meant to shed a few tears

A blissful feeling in Dullsville is pleading for better in vain
Mostly wish that all troubles were turned under by an antique
plough
Want hurried words of love be part of an old time story
For misery flaws of literacy it's notable there's nothing to gain
The windows are waiting for twilight gloom for a whole day
In hopes that all time depression will stay in it's shadowy corner
Even erranding things are none the wiser for us bumpkins
To make things get better were told to always pray

IRONIC EVENTS

So ironic is the outlook for them long ago thoughts
Most of us have been taught one theory in general
If there's no love in the world just renew what you can
That old look in a crowd gives you away having age spots
Have tested todays limits about respect, it's bad taste
As far as people now are concerned old theories is not their
choice
All in all hearts have been set on an electronic type of world
When exercising to walk a little they consider just a waste

The especially part having no constraints for behavior times
We are all caught up with bad ass contradictions from them
Our world around me, cacophony forgets old lessons behind us
That catch twenty two, a law paradox suggests the victims
Need something's in this to rely on as sure things
Have plotted some old times on my todays landing place
Again that old reality enables us to see common good facts
With some hope gives us waiting time on what it brings

Our indescribable future challenges us for evermore
Somewhere beyond the present moment will seek wonder
Have pondered words of wisdom that need to be told
From my past spare the rod spoils the child is needed as before
Now must dismiss those thoughts of mis-de-mean, Amen
Forever my foreshadow reminds me of belt for benevolence
Have my quotes about irony days a style long departed
The method worked to make a child tow the line away back
then

During my walking caper seen an ipod person all alone
Each person seen with these are always looking down
With no safety first will get her killed one of these days
On across the street still conversing on her yellow telephone
Seen in a restaurant a couple no utterance of speech there
Let's imagine the future a whole world of people looking down
Whether rain or shine it won't matter just let the day be
What justifies the reason justifies the cause to really care

HARKENED ON MONEY MOMMA

Takes nerve for someone to ask how much is your soul worth
These are unwarranted thoughts come to this fellows mind
That protocol time what merits these moment to be told
For mercy sake marks the spot, for these claims had to unearth
If it came down to it charm was in that eager voice for payday
What you called to my mind for sure there is not any hope
Not to be inspired by an interpreter with spiteful emotions
For your such benevolence not to be pleased in your dreadful
way

All of these circumstances where really depressing at the time
Seems malice talk is uttered by hypocrites seeking money
Better not to enter her in a gathering it's for enjoyable friends
Had enough of these sort of people when this lad was in his
prime
From that time found life is a manner of being worthy, some
were not
The unceasing anguish in my heart comes from away back
then
Best to embed your intentions with the parable left as an elder
Just abide my time, partaking in novel writing that's all I've got

As a householder have no doubt in my mind having good merits
Having a clear conscience leaves just heartfelt devotion forever
So mighty is that word love, hardly had been used through the ages
Wanted family life to be adored with the best proper moments
Them days of yore for me wrote hopping instead of hoping a fault
Being the laughing stock passing the mistake as being stupid
Was like a creaking door a reminder to get something done about it
To be always told will grow up to be a nobody not worth my salt

Best for this lady to look elsewhere like buried treasure in a field
What is done by other people everyday is impartial to others deeds
Try sincere respect for a family will get you right on through
Having love for everyone never try to keep it always completely concealed
It's a portion for good intent let if fall where it may, to all know
Life's good pattern came of late some splendor came to light
A family life adored in what's proper to each and every person
Here my place of peace in which all the love can really grow

SOME WERE OLD

Had trotted down through ranks of men to become old
By all means defiance lures us to a dawning future
During that youthful phase was a sure scene of ill repute
Whatever the awkward future brings keep chin up, been told
In the old house times one enfant after another was the case
Was an untimely future whiling the dawning of tomorrow
Still remember that bewailing voice the slimy yelling
You would know she was coming after peeking out curtain
lace

Then comes the one lad request go kill a chicken for lunch
Took the axe on a stump cutting off the hens head there
Who else would be given this chore but the one nicknamed
Skip
Someone had to do it for all the rest of the family bunch
Was not a thing of honour just do it or else get a smack
A mere child had to surrender to these ethnic rules given
During youthful days no time to rest the live long day
The goodness of heart or morality every elder did lack

Have come to old man days now limping along new paths
The sun did rise once more to bless another great day
Today seems to be a feeble time for surrender to it all
New adventures in a fud world with no more wraths
An old gentleman benediction finds it's spot to define moods
Came down through the ranks of men to lie in peace now
But as for me have become a devoted Christian forever
So many people everyday belong to a society of no goods

A TANGLED WEB

To be continually blessed with opinions of good will
Had to rejoice when together we paid the mortgage
With our mightiness there's a future when you care
A strong affection among two helps success each will fill
Had counted our blessings working hard to get some place
That nightmare stack of bills together paid them off
Always used nice moods even on disagreements of such
Here we were in our love nest that was full of grace

Not knowing was left to become beyond tomorrow
We always posed in a good light of things figuring it out
No issue was to remote just analyze it as times before
Then olden golden days suddenly changed into sorrow
The dwelling place we had finished all projects there
Very suddenly with cancer she passed away
Our destiny was sincere but this put a kybosh on it all
Now with her gone have no one left in life which to share

To confide in a helpmate that was my right hand
We were real soul mates in a world full of goodness
Here along in yonder doorway rendering my thoughts
My fond heart pausing on life's threshold here I stand
The ticking of clocks puts me to sleep at night
An evening of watching many shadows find their way
Our life is not forever always having loving embrace
That aversion of thought reaches beyond human sight

FELLED TREES

Here hard work to be presented from early morn sunrise
The lad a tree cutter, a chainsaw was my machine
Hard frozen ground crunched under these boots of mine
Out in the bitter cold during dead of winter was no prize
That ruler of the realm wanted my cords piled here
Such a woodland of wolf echoes back at that time
Did urge myself to notch some trees then fell them down
My grimace dire moments that bush every winter to fear

So many lingering heartaches in the place of long ago
All that dreading encircling a young boys country life
Seemed forever an unkindly veil shadowing me
Each winter trampling while cutting wood in deep snow
The wind blew out from the North cutting like a knife
Here standing in a bush of elm as well as maple trees
Wanting to subdue this questionable hellish trite fate
Work a day even on Sunday bound with lots of strife

The enlightened history of goodness was taken advantage of
Did think about changing my attitude to being harsh
Often wondering is there's better beyond a tree world
Seems there was no place beyond that comes with love
Should one reside where nothing makes any sense at all
Where in the dickens can you find a real friend not a foe
Every page being fixed in my mind which way is to out
No need to stay here with a hundred more trees to fall

SAME HUZZAS

Are certain measures to symbolize approval of
Wondering where the passionate portion of humanity is
Mottos are needed to muse most characters out there
To be frank would be better to do it with a kid glove
Nothing unusual to presume in the wake of a day
Sometimes events have the saying oh my God no
Whatever invades our conscience sometimes slips out
Comes the day of feeling out of sorts not having much to say

All the same old huzzas good day bad day go away
When people invade your space wanting your thoughts
Their bad reckoning is naught take your coat here's your hat
Seems they have ensured your good will on an off day
Looking back on old sense of always on the defensive side
Should never have a sense of belonging no one owns you
Let's try absent minded it's possible it will set you free
Always going out on a limb, obviously have really tried

Wanting happiness to be like ever blooming roses at dawn
Have been told that venturous days were huzza capers
Them ambers of will should come when you are young
The whole of lifes gladness there's need for cheering on
Those bad things belong in memories not relieved today
We are members of our destiny proposed to events
An old saying and the farmer drew another load out
Almost a whole life time has been gone from that land of hay

AUTUMN GOLD

Having a brimful of willingness to get me started
It rained for a while at dawn with a rumble
Here comes a days demure formatted with coolness
All the songsters had sang their last songs then parted
Seems everyday there's something new to explore
Not only autumn gold but the real McCoy red ones
Us old people watch leaves fall then rake them up
Our Canadian flags leaves were falling down once more

During my growing up years seems every yard had a leaf hut
Had brimfuls of willingness in leafy corners of old
Was always the same bib overalls with rubber boots
This guy could not have fun to long to the barn he did strut
Here one goes again go do your chores there's no time to play
Always can do grief here without any defense at all
That resounding voice you're still fifteen so go back to work
Without any privileges in a long ago highly miserable day

Every morning falls on deaf ears except for mine
Just a single boy heading to the barn to milk the cows
Everything would have died if this guy did not feed them
When people are lazy nothing ever is really fine
Had to part that day so long ago, go forward with a yawn
Where there's patience goodness shall always find me
There's a beautiful light shining on my new Canadian home
That hellish haven like place since nineteen sixty is long gone

A HAVEN

Comes a memoir so old fashion turned brown with age
Here's an old car park on a gravel road with a crank
These elements of time so draped in black and white
Being a small boy things look so big and scary at this stage
Such a haven with flies and spiders always around
Was able to gather the eggs once a day from the hen house
So much fun to see a cackling hen lay an egg in the nest
Each Saturday to go fishing on Sunday dug worms from the
ground

After we dug the worms the chickens followed behind
They were like children finding something to fight over
If one chicken found a worm they would pull it apart
To remember visions of it all with the urban mooing kind
The rooster was the morning guy crowing before sun up
My dog Ted would follow close behind me for protection
A young child with bare feet had stepping in cow flat in mind

The days a boy hates the most was dressing for church times
Had to wear your very best suit in those long ago days
A tam that left a ring on your forehead after church
Us guys had to be in church before the bell chimes
It was a haven house using lamps for lighting there
Where walkways of flagstones to each house doorway
On out to the privy was a well worn path of dirt
As youngsters were counting our blessings with some to spare

NOTHING TO WORSHIP

Them heart stories in a golden diary are worth while
Each unblushing moments of moderate emotional glories
Amid a panel of peers your conscience rules the day
Where will we be if the future changes the clothing style
Be better to develop a sense of humour then the mode we wear
To walk along the paths of tolerance of low set jeans
Every day we listen to some forbearance of derated fashion
The sensible dress seen in my day there's nothing to compare

Let's say farewell to the shops out there that make skimpy clothes
For cultured groups they will linger with their drab attire
Only a daft system makes world disorders such a bad trend
We must hie the thither, disregard these perks I suppose
Do others pout to get there own way without repents
Look at yourself as a quest of honour in a golden chair
All wit has substance with feelings, some in bad taste
Where there is good ethics, old worshipping ways make sense

Still to remember yesterday, many times what we went through
With a computer spent today just resting gazing at a screen
About regarding religion standards seem to have an end
While searching into tomorrow for sure no one has a clue
There was many amorous times with errands to work out
Most daylight vetoes brought forward a strange demise now
Only the rich bewail the day because their money rules
There is nothing to worship because everything is in doubt

POVERTY'S PAIN

Have accounted for the trails with tribulations that remain
Once in a month comes a sad face with a choice to miss
Lets open the pages that declare them long ago realms
Spent every year looking to be better off staying sane
Could do an hurrah to cause some effect on our life
To know if hope had feathers to take flight sometimes
But merrily ticks the clock seeing no worries to regret
Maybe look at grace under a rosy bower to rid this strife

Everlasting haunts from the past still trying to shun away
Those little words such as give with nothing makes no sense
Have remember those empty rooms where poverty echo's
there
To wander back to yesterday poverty was the message that
day
These old wrinkled brows know all about poverty's pain
A strange place is a place you have never been I have been
there
In the depths of social lapse there's nothing to damask things
Would like laughing on a dingy day in pouring down rain

Life is like a book once it's opened it begins and ends
On through trails and tribulations shunning the nerds
In the wink of an eye the buddy system is best of all
That phase will go on forever among those good friends
Our common sense is like a black board erase bad things
Cheer has washed the drabness from an old mans heart
Been so many sad days in a mans life now for sure changed
During idle moments whistle a tune just for the joy it brings

THE POKA BLOTCHED FLOOR

In a house with a family of nine walking around
The kitchen floor was cover with linoleum for easy washing
One day the coating had all worn off leaving it brown
Our mother decided to resurface it with whatever she found
First she painted the whole floor with a gray acrylic paint
Next she blotched the floor with a paint brush different colours
This woman had only finished half of the kitchen floor
From the fumes of acrylic paint she was ready to faint

When my father came home he opened every door
After this he opened every window in the whole house
It said on the can's do not paint in an enclosed area
He finished painting the kitchen she was sick could do no more
The painting was finally all done the floor shone like new
We had another problem the floor was very slippery
My father's decision was buy the friction floor wax
Our problem was solved this was the best thing to do

Can still remember doing this floor in nineteen fifty two
Such a great floor it last for over ten years of wear
By this time we moved to Sparta in a brick house
The house was made from Ross street bricks no insulation all
through
Was a cold place in winter not like the poka blotched floor
place
Ice showed through the walls during a very cold night
Had your boots beside the bed to slip into every waking morn
Our new house took tons of coal and wood was the sorry case

SUGAR BAG TIC

These sugar bags were free in those days of yore
Also the straw to stuff a sugar bag tic cost nothing
The mystery of it all was once you were in was hard to get out
You had to roll over five times then point your feet to the floor
In Yarmouth centre was the house this took place
This home had a hip roof inside was loft of bedroom area
Was well insulated making it warm all winter long
Here the bedrooms were huge with oodles of spare space

One day the landlord arrived to tour the household
Made my parents get rid of the sugar bag tics
The reason he said was fire could flare up quick
From a least little wet then mold then fire we were told
Mr. Lovely helped to carry the tics out to the yard
My parents had to follow the rules it was not their home
They went to a place called Sam's bought mattresses there
We could keep the sugar bags but straw we must discard

In mid summer the Preston family showed up here
When we ask them to leave after staying two weeks
Was a difficult task telling them to get on the road
Had tried many many times to make them go somewhere
My parents decided that we would move out right away
We paid a mover to move us to the Hipply place
The Prestons ate all the food left in the Lovely house
Then Mr. Lovely had the police take the Prestons out the next
day

A REMOTE DELL

Freedom tells us each prospect has no public tones
Sweet twittering from surrounding trees sitting here to write
Wanted to write about off the beaten track a long time ago
A lot of quietude in this dell sitting on some big stones
Thinking about our John Deere tractor back home
Pulling logs from the woods black smoke in the air
Seems this machine had power to pull what it pleases
Just wondering how far a mind could really roam

In a more longer time ago was the ten twenty one
A no muffler noisy machine sounded like a snorting bull
The fire flew up from it's stack a fire puffing dragon
Sometimes this tractor would backfire like a shotgun
Those steel lug wheels it would not spin just grab ahold
Could not use this tractor in the woods it would set it on fire
It's front wheels came off the ground still it was going along
This old time tractor would crank and start in the bitter cold

A team of work horses could pull a great load
Remember the team taking a load of hay up the ramp to a loft
There was no hesitation they went up all of the way
First they would get a head way starting down on the road
These horse could pull ten tons on the hitch for sure
One horse was Dobin the other horse Sam a number one team
If you gave them a carrot they would nudge you for more
If you left this team untied they would never even stir

THE NETHER WORLD

Our peers make a difference in destiny's for life's sake
To spend a whole duration towards bettering yourself
This land is full of strangers until you get to know them
Them common denominators of people that just take
A lifetime that plagues me of two-faced hypocrites
Each person should be guided by some kind of meaning
Have tried with good intentions but failed in all respect
To have a good sense of being rolls some do not fit

Lets be ordinary people not trying to be who we are not
When deceit is the quality of being leave me out
In useful system of people there is better means of hope
The nether world people have untruth it's what they've got
A must create a good sense of being for all concerned
These old eye's of reality have rued the day for respect
From new life to old life been there have done all that
It's a pitiful shame these aliened people to have turned

For all thoughts in question reflected on podge things
Maybe in regards to scorn want to hurt people
In the face of honour has regards for everyone
As for that neither world there's only sorrow it brings
Looking at solemn rude hearts there is more lose than gain
Here is a man in the meanders of time patiently waiting
Seems grandparents have penalty time for doing nothing
wrong
In my mind, kin like this must have gotten on the wrong train

GLORIOUS HONOUR

Comes a certificate that's my memorial holding great honour there
Turning to future glory to have earnestly liberated ones life
With this understanding gave me rights so well to be deserved
The honour of that day was due in a man's life, nothing can compare
None other days are sufficient for praise more than this time
Before hand strived so hard to make such an effort to work
Many months did nourish great thoughts to get what's really needed
Takes great devotion to make the grade leaving a certificate to claim

Now the calibration for life has derived a method entirely to go by
With faith's hope managed every step of a well deserved best day
Was my chosen participation for such a goal needing to meet
Here a remedy had showed a man the mighty things in which to try
Having put all my thoughts into being to intercede whatever a man can
Come where in this future glory will find a special place which to be
To accomplish joy to a sorrowful heart today at long last
Wanting to arrive at a better destination was a lifetimes plan

With all due respect had been a victim of circumstances then
The honour of today had been introduced by only myself
Became a change in discourse for mutual respect in a life
Here everlasting peace with freedom was unlocked as a man
Had found happiness out from yesterdays gloomy part
In seeking did find, giving no thanks to help from all others
Now having reclaimed life as the better of the bunch it seems
A world away now humbly commended for all good work to
start

Some from the relative side think their entitled to what I got
On the journey through hell thought now was being set free
Being bad things in lateness, having good things have I made it
With hope how dare to think there was something beyond
sought
The grant of loving kindness has always a two-faced awful side
Has before again so much bestowed on me as a middle victim
Must leave make all these times be forgotten in a new nasty
world
When everything is all said and done a man still has his pride

AT CRUDES DOMAIN

The crudes arise at each dawn it's all of us once again
Has no one been aware in a family what has happened to a
Pa
Best to highlight the unjust part for everyone there to see
Did participate in having my son at your place must I complain
Must a mortal father stay pleased with such an episode done
Being not dead yet shall be honoured to welcome one and all
Having rendered these thoughts in hopes frankness surely will
do
Here is that heathen father being belittled by favoring my son

Where these is no honour virtue cannot survive here or there
Here has been the ungrateful was let pass through your doors
Will have to forgive me cannot put up with belittlement
anymore
Brings blemish to my house with many bad omens to compare
Stay away from my house bitterment rules the rest of my days
Let the kindness of a father be forgotten have a crudes
togetherness
Have lost my compassion, keep family ranks what ever they are
For the rest of time left let the crude ones have their own ways

This man must remain alone left with a true loving heart
Have been a long time forgotten in some clans real episode
Did awaken with honour while still waiting for reality once more
These farces of bad vibes has been venturing from the start
This persons eyes are wide open cannot fool me as before
A mother's confound lies will catch up it all takes time
Best break my ice make the story come out more sincere
After what's all said and done get out the truth to even the
score

Go say awe to all my son's it's a shame your father's not glad
The wholly unrighteous part to be left behind closed doors
All the way from the past comes the same wretched known tale
Better not to fret the untruth long has been said leave him be sad
Whom has restricted this goodness of heart for what purpose in mind
Will never worry about tomorrow it will bring worries of it's own
Only respect has value the rest will be left to loath shame
Must resist the wicked ones be the trusting ever loving kind

NO PRIZE EPISODES

The birth of babies was the fact of changing diapers then
Such a nasty smell every time the whole room reeked
Every time you changed a diaper it had to be rinsed out
In those times would take a galvanized pail fill it if you can
We would divide the water into two pails one to raise one to wash
When this process was done the diaper was put on a line
Seemed to be a half hour episode all through that day
You had just finished doing this, had looked saying gosh

One day had my suit on to go to church the baby pissed
My suit was soaked coat and all along with a bad smell
Had to change everything lay my suit on the veranda rail
Put rubber panties on the baby from now on I insist
On to church the family goes hoping for no more prize episodes
Could here the church bell clanging over and over again
The Hipply house was out in the middle of nowhere
That church was three mile down them dusty gravel roads

With a baby around my prize comic books ripped apart
Every card on the floor everyday for fifty two pick up
He would be eating ashes from the ashtrays around the room
Each day was a real mess did not know where to start
Would be no ashtrays today for this kind of mess
Also they have throw away diapers these days is good
Sore bottoms with diaper rash is a thing of the past
Stops a lot of cry babies, having no reason to cry is my guess

OLD BLANKETS

An asleep person under a patch quilted handy work
These home made blankets were one of a kind back then
Here comes a foot with knitted slippers to the floor
Everything else was hand made or done with the needlework
Also for the giddy up go the blanket for winter was hand made
Also the cutter blanket was hand knitted to keep people warm
The horse plus the people that rode were snuggly in blankets
As the horse walked along draped bells sounded like a musical
parade

Cannot forget the old rocking chair a patch quilt throw on it
Here's were Dad sat reading his morning paper in the forties
We were living on a poor mans dollar managing to get by
The rugs were braided rag where our dog Ted did sit
When you went to the bedroom patched quilts on the bed
These quilts of many colours looked nice and proper
Everyone had the same there was no choice in them days
All the couches had knitted afghans to cover them instead

These patch quilts as well as afghans brightened shadowy
corners
If someone said lets go back like yesterday I would refuse to
attend
Did times sitting up in bed going crossed eyed from colour
blend
When us children went to school with patches, was well to do
scorners
Each time the couch was thin would slap an afghan there
On Saturday morning each month had a quilting bee attend
The women of our village helped one another make blankets
Go to each others homes making blankets nothing could
compare

LIFES MILESTONES

The heart truly imagines what to expect some days
Having Joy can force a moment to it utmost realm
People who create woes are hard to understand why
Their bitterness befalls the true meaning in many ways
In the old days sense of mottos had bad images made
When people get out of sorts it causes a crisis to start
From long ago times longevity was people staying together
The family farm was always the next of kin had stayed

Then comes censored adventure when nothing works out
Where children in the family become educated and leave
It's a whole new ball game with no one to run the farm
As for our family everyone went their separate ways of cast
doubt
In the run of years no prospects of farming going on
So much silence out on those fields of time only echoes refrain
Comes a new picture on the horizon of skyscrapers there
That down to earth farmer has sold out, being long gone

In life's milestones there a touch of concern for judgment
Rich folks have a desire of dimension projects a money maker
They do dadoes to make events that commandeer land
On thinking back to long ago times family life was our fulfillment
All was lost time pondering while someone made their way
Comes an eye opener of a whole new episode of creation
Some day the dadoes will hold the purse strings of who's who
Was a twist of circumstances from that long ago hay day

A WORLD APART

Would like to enchant a reason for our liberties here
Come join me for a spot of tea in this Canada place
The United Empire Loyalist fought to save our land
Being Irish of the commonwealth they fought to care
As an army booter that long ago soldier would like to tell it all
We stopped the Americans from taking over our great land
There will always be that ethnic revival won so long ago
If we were one of them we could still hear the battle call

Them times of willing hearts are hallowed in our minds forever
Lets seek memorial images where there was no defeat
Back then raised the Union Jack is glory did our part
While being the British Commonwealth was war to endeavor
Here on Canadian soil are cross upon cross of the home land
race
The Irish arose from that old world to come to save us here
For the realism of long ago days should stay in our hearts
Was so much death for Canadian and American armies to
face

We waged war for nothing because we are friends now not foe
Together we have a strong bond for peace as never before
The British are with this group to join as one for all
As friends in part called united nations together to war we go
Even being a world apart everybody belongs to the buddy
system
Here we are in a loftier strain of a modern day world
Down the roads of time we have come very far in performance
If some alien starts something it will be too bad for them

ONE PEACEFUL PASTORAL

Heaven builds a retreat for peaceful pastoral days
That which cannot be divided without leaving a reminder
Tried not to hovel or groan just keep up the good work
Awaiting for the scenery to be filled with sunshine that stays
Did claw at miserable days looking in the vital day of
happenings
Have mauled the landscape around my house a little too
much
Will always have a pact of truth from my very heart
Another day with it's daily task along with the reviling's

Comes another wide open day like a flower to greet me there
To have awakened for another morning sustaining goals as
before
Heard clocks ticking away with every beat of my heart
Some days enter the wrong door where greatness is rare
Within the creation of time tired eyes lead to dreams
Here nightly boundaries waiting for hidden moments to occur
Every glimmer in the land of nod sooner or later will stir
Then comes hopes or illusions help to push me on it seems

At night comes an armchair for a tired man with peace
restrained
My heart flows in lasting waters of love going on forever
This world is too vast to be alone, there's friends waiting
There's a happy station amidst some with good humour
retained
A day to be born in the love of it all until life's final day
During the wait in time, hours fly by then be lost forever
In the depths of love is a retriever of the warmest heart
Will always have a pact of truth with lots of parts to play

MANKINDS AVERSION

There's always the absent minded professor in most of us
Some will find a sovereign remedy through faith methods
An old saying is to give someone a run for their money
Once in a while get wacked with a version to discuss
That belted out cry from the rude men does not sit to well
Has been no way to soothe the gestation of life's agonies
Always that stance for challenge defies immortal bondage
Better not to stir up trouble misery lands on you for a spell

During the unknowable, there's speculation in horoscope words
Mankind's natural repugnance awaits the futures obsession
Some way there must be a social remedy to reprisals
Upon this earth is restless men wanting to make trouble like
nerds
The old people are not just wearing antique masks they have
been there
Everywhere there is transients a form of man not worth a penny
Have the insight to terse corruption for the good of all mankind
A fluent symbol of a human course of down to earth roles to
compare

Every day comes spasms of a fracas moments headache time
One more time comes a speech with a whim questing aim
From a forecasting host of arrogants, we all try to avoid
That wanton vestige stands out, this Irish colour that's sublime
An involuntary approach from a new perspective for perfection
A striding moment to divulge one's plan for father's day
A household for a hearty dinner came about on June twelfth
There will always be traditions from our four fathers recognition

ONE EGOTISTICAL FAMILY

A group of our kinfolk being self centered uncommon people
Being conceited as all get out, unmerited from real life
Their well being blemished only to be justified for damnation
They shall have no honour to fulfill such an awful vibe example
That unapproachable group abiding in untruth times always
Only deviant ways to accomplish such a ruthful sought plan
To their sorrowful hearts can offer regret for signs of hope
Must follow kindness it claims only friendly best of days

Having love helps us through them better journeys of ours
Here torn among those family members one reaps grief
In along the paths of time Joy once was for real there
Such hatred through no mutual respect they come in fours
Seems my faith is alone unknown as tomorrows good thought
Some always to disdain that memorial grief forever to act upon
Shall we use confidence to renew life's corrupted nature
Becomes a great day whenever one wants it really to be got

Must judge the good part as how things aught to be judged
Need entire people to seek harmony out of a cold world
Are indeed raised to be truthful it's the best thing a person can
do
We have all been a close knit family with no one begrudges
Be pledged is the best stature presented to brothers all
Hoe shameful to want revenge, live with common sense honour
Make your moments the best there might come another day
Each morning restore with joy cause tomorrow no one did call

Again we ponder when life leaves it's shadow each day
The love of your life is gone only sorrow now marks the spot
That night her last moment came to this family I love you all
Will console those with unloving bad taste left with smile to say
Have prepared my heart for a reign of devotion toward love
Let the turmoil of it all come to find it's own end of vain things
Comes humility example to follow be for some never for me
Let that morning upon morning awaken me thanking him alone

BLAME THE HOODWINK

There is to many bad omens swarming that mother keeper
Was just another day it seems they turned heads away
She has nipped no love in the bud deserves nothing right well
Having sold her soul to the devil it's not good but it's much
cheaper
Hark who goes there from that nerds land of an ozalite place
Would like to be there to razilenate some lies to resounding
words
This atheist adobe reeks of damnation forever and a day
How blessed are those who seek love in our old world of good
grace

Best to crawl out of your black place of sin see our loving one's
Some how we will find a way to cross those bridges to a new
day
Lets begin the while leaving out pure lies from delegates ears
From under the rock place look what's come here it's my son
Had piled up a bad reputation stemming from some days of
yore
Come press my buttons I can tell you what my trait words are
Each moment of their intentions come right out of the land of
nod
Let's here your cast of demented ways so we know what's in
store

As for you showing up spell out the word pals referring to some
Must me Mrs. Hoodwink that takes her prudes off to the side
There must be a reason to call them back to a repute house
now
Read my lips she replied no one knows I am a fibbing mom
When you listen to common sense never mind what she did say
Wants people to know she rules, I call you don't you ever call
me
Comes to praise when they have filled every single prude
intention

In a hoodwinks world of odd balls all are for dupe it's every day
Come what must, here is me and there is she with all the say
With passion comes self confidence without palpable anger
In a sense her kind of fortune cookies have no real rewards
As in persuade urges people to do wrong things it's her loath
way
While a father was being put down he has grown in merit more
By integrity have attained prosperity far beyond anyone will
know
For my heart there is honour comforted by best things for life
Ask the hoodwink who triumphs in misery same things as before

FROM A NIGHT'S ROOM

The sun on my window pane again wakes me
With some ambition a whole day to get things done
Have no one here to guide me through another day
Them sorrowful moments have no pardons to see
Did hear despair only when a cardinal whistled away
Hard to be jovial on a deliberate moment to be sad
That esteem hard to ope anymore with a fallen spirit
Here a world full of peril, yearning for a better day

So much for the shadows that keep coming on this day
My noonday now is hidden behind a cloud adding dullness
Walking again have passed her image hanging on the wall
These haunted confines of a house have nothing to say
Have to surmise her soul will return to my abode
Knowing the sun that shines through my window is real
While thinking of love faith it's already run it's course
Have been bound to decisions along that fundamental road

Must each life with errands fulfilled just go
That very day of awing facts turned my life cold
Here remembrance overflows into nightly dreams
One will precede life's specter paths for others to bestow
Comes again a family to multiply then prosper in our place
Keep sighing for sadness or sing to become happy
We are all mortal people astride on earth's doom
Have done our duty it's time to go we are the human race

WAS A PITY

There was a doormat that said welcome to anyone
Must count each individual blessing hoping for the best
The times were askew in a world a child knew so long ago
Some moods forbade where my real feelings, that were next to none
Heard them pessimist with attitudes depressing a poor boy
Having been an optimist thinking there is better things to do
Somehow to believe Sunday would be less fatigue then others
Comes on a daily shadow, some things that are bound to annoy

For heaven's sake I wanted them to go away, these sorrows with pain
Was there chanting woes that followed my everyday life
Every misfortune had floored me, a time to be fed up
Such a brimful of cunning fancies, such was a reason to refrain
My possessions were styled for a poor man's money
A household known to be utterly quaint a pity without rhyme or reason
Them tales of woe that followed my life were simply always askew
Being bade to have a sense of humour, jokers warded off
Those pitiful follies from the past with no milk and honey

With all mights power, held my head up just for a while
At the starting of a day had soared on wings of hope then declined
Forever words of doubt peered at life's dawn, flawed forever
A person needs statistics to tell a story, it's the best style
Forever breaking down the bonds that had restrained me
The dawn from yesterday stands still while binding up my hurts
Had looked at the matters that concerned in yesterdays place
Was an unhallowed place with realism that will forever be

318

BOUGHT SKATES AT SAMS

Every Christmas us three boys would get skates at Sam's Place
These were brown second hand skates new laces and all
Sam sharpened the skates before we left his town shop
He sold hockey sticks along with pucks in his shop space
The skates from the Christmas before were used as trade in's
There was two places to skate at the dam or on the pond
At the Mill's place was a pond that froze over in December
In December to January is when our rink skating begins

This man Sam had everything under the sun in his place
In the summer we could buy baseballs at the shop
We bought bats for soft ball playing only from him
The hard ball bats Nick Nickol made from hickory was the case
If the skates got dull Sam would sharpen them for free
He was a great old man telling us stories when he was a boy
One day he gave us liners for the skates to keep our feet warm
Seems every month Sam was a great man to go to see

In the summer we went to buy fishing gear at this store
He always told us about the big fish that got away
The lures that he gave us were great they caught many fish
On the weekend we would have to go to Sam's once more
During those times you could go spearing fish at night
At the shop he had hip boots to fit us all nice green ones
From off the wall he sold us spears and gas lanterns
The catfish creek for spearing fish was the nightly sight

ABSENT FOOTSTEPS

A door closing forever, never to open finding no one there
To think of a long ago voice that's left absent footsteps
AN offering night wind wants to send lost time back to us
Did remember people within these walls real moments to spare
So glad when they were earthbound now only shadows greet
me
All empty now in silence them old corridors, having souls lost in
time
They have ascended to paradise only images in picture
memories
Only loneliness with the lost of friends of a world, nothing to see

No one resides there after the last closing of the door
Comes aimeful journey's that begin in life times then lost
Our world is not a place of absolute from the beginning
Only left thoughts of old days while walking alone once more
Now have only pictures of the old folks as we turn back the
pages
Wanted to bring back them faces to talk of great things
Them old portraits a forever posing smile are so silent
Have pursued every days feelings left on old time stages

Bygone moments thinking about it as so many times before
That yesterdays bouquet of hearts went sentimentally away
One's mind has been rummaging into past existence again
How could one reassemble creations just once more
New one's to love put into existence as old fade away
Each phase lest we forget there's pictures to remind us
Them days of some passing on, coldness dwells as we say
goodbye
In videos yesterday silence like a ghost is brought into play

LOVES LOOPS

A hundred million people can be loved at the same time
One's conscience is meekly seeking cues for love potions
We simply ought to have a sense of humour to laugh a while
In our church to commit adultery is a hideous kind of crime
Here upon those happy days our minds will not very much
The warmest corners are for passion that we all should share
Let's count each individual blessing in our kind of belief
Some new comers that are religionly shouting cultures it's a
crutch

Getting back to old times our civil duties we had to do
Among the pathways of righteous everyone followed the rule
Let stay as before morally justifiable type of clan
Only half of the world is at peace like me and you
Not all of us want to be someone's valentine in a civil life
Some one comes to ruin our golden grounds where peace is
True humans are filled with compassion with joyful days
Who in God's world needs to carry a gun or a big knife

Turning back the pages to the old world religion was good
The saying was to love thy neighbor as you love yourself
That face of love is never demure by losing it's style
Where have all true Canadians gone would join them if I could
Into today known life has lost it's haloed featured one's
Our world we so much loved is paved with to many other words
Here we are in the world of nod instead of a world of God
We live in a world of discrepancy's of so many off tones

ARCHAIC INSTINCTS

There is people with little history who have fallen on hells dirty
stones
No such things as a social gathering anymore it's
dumbfounded
With these new phones no talking, the room is in a hush
So many people staring into them out of this world phones
As we walk from old streets nothing makes any sense anymore
Looking at converted people there's so many sighs come from
me
Wholesome things are left alone to die a slow death of sorts
No normal telephone ringing it's hupped up music not like
before

When comes to break a leg to get things done it's butt set
These archaic instincts are long forgotten in the past
Not the old familiar work a day God send us Sunday
It's not what you earn in a lifetime it's what you get
During days of yore with times before that sense was the word
Sometimes old day ideas were wildly unreasonable deludes
Forever being routine chores at a barn day and night
Those tales about country being great for sure is absurd

While hunting among the artifacts found panties with lace
Must have been before I was born had never seen this
When playing at the Tordoff house these were in an old trunk
These people had all kinds of old time clothing at their place
As for my family we seemed to be always moving elsewhere
Every time we moved on down the road clothes were left
behind
Even our sleighs, toboggans and wagons were left behind
Where memories came back with clothes we could not
compare

THE DAUNTING FUTURE

Had parents that disheartened them yonker teens years
From childhood have been degraded never to happen again
When fifteen was sent to a farm to work, but a mother
collected my pay
Slept in a hay loft working twenty hours a day till morning sun
appears
The fact of this condition will evade any investment scheme on
the spot
That sense of humour if you ask me to participate will not be
there
Have dominating thoughts know exactly what this man has to
do
No one will ever find out how much money in the bank I have
got

Any dogma doctrine will receive no help from me a promise
This man who wore rags on his back with holes in his shoes no
way
One thinks their dealing with a humorous person of ill repute
Having a known dower of inheritance, any proceedings
awaiting demise
There is no intentions on my part to furnish money on an
invested deal
So many people will envy me for being well off for those days
ahead
Here the fact of proceedings in time a priority being all mine
Never again will anyone suck personal money from me that's
how I feel

The fact is that everybody is only a good weather friend today
Everybody now sounds like an echo chamber come invest your money
When off to Brighton will dispose of any persons investment plans
So humbly people pull the wool as false faced smiles take place
The consequences of being taken makes a person twice as shy
During pester times will walk then drive away out of sight
Have been taught not to trust anyone, always in it for themselves
For every dawn day there is somebody comes to rip off you can't deny

The list of consequences is a mile long for that bad omen trade
Such a farce for reality in so many ways cheating the clientele
So becoming life's moochers as a whole they crave doing wrong
Have worked, leached off of by the others, saved some money I made
On behalf of these coming better days for a man, feel gone inside
Our value in everyone's day changes with age not much you can do
My aim is to collect all my royalties from books that I write
Knowing I am an honest person gives me a great deal of pride

JUDGED FALSE MODESTY

Better to be concerned than nurtured by false words
Informants for matters be front and centre for each day
Must observe the fact being used than vary the outcome for it
Seems everybody has heard of these person identified as the
nerds
It's evitable that all instances are figuring out people sessions
Best to devote some time to parables commending goodwill
Be logical decide to use the right approach for the remedy
Using good sense instances intended for greater lessons

It's tomorrows outcome that determines the right answers
Should save a carbon copy when things are good, right and
true
The unity in life comes through kindness, how mighty is it
Lets not initiate a remedy without dignity for good members
Indeed us partakers according to fact pursue with honour
All disgrace with no value is a burden in a whole span of life
The dutiful one's are the source of merit to all be rewarded
To remain wise is essential for our unity in a delighted hour

Will have to pardon us for having a conscience it's part of life
The footstool is the becoming soft doing others rotten jobs
That degree of passion fulfilled always by a loving heart
There is others just and true beyond one's imagination belief
Be plausible in favour of the world at large to remember your
name
Consider in being an example for others in all good faith times
Where do our bad descendants get their wrong ideas from
Eventually comes merited consequences, are part of worldly
fame

All should fulfill their duties, not be irresponsible people kind
Out there the oppressors upset the normal function of life
Best abound in good works to accomplish a rightful goal
The worthy part reveals a mans stature with good thoughts in mind
Our fulfillment for everything done proper means a great deal
Have a divine generation of kindred people in our midst
Sometimes wretches out there with modesty for misery times
With full hearted joy never bastard afflicted we are for real

INAUTHENTIC CHARACTERS

My thoughts like dew spilt out onto another new morn
Our life is like a book puts every moment on display
With phony people they are inclined to exaggerate
The overstatement glorifies something later one would scorn
One's expectations followed up from the past with aversion
These deceitful kind giving tacit consent for conspiring
Along with three sons with discourtesy stemming from the her
That proper order of relatives has come to confusion

Having three striplings bound by a malice person
This maledict person has implied other people are the problem
The world does not need hate that makes matters worse
That journey through friendship should be good not worsen
Good friends are hard to find and hard for one to lose
There's a hunky dory part in our corner of the world
As for their part is to misapply the meaning of our love
When it comes to reviewing reality we can not chose

Maybe remain pessimistic like Murphy's law now
When ever is going to happen it will happen later
So be it her exercising control through alienation
With regret one must decline it's not worth a childish row
In every family there is the blissful one, no reality sense
All through my youth the black sheep what's the difference
now
Wholly moments were never forgotten from boy to man
The trinities have a wall built around them for a line of defense

THE RED HEADED TEACH

Each morning Mrs. Prouse went by our home
She had a heavy foot on the gas traveling at eighty clicks
All you could see was a flaming red haired lady whizzing by
Down the three mile stretch of road she would come
That Dodge coup going like hell with the pedal to the metal
She moved in a dust cloud all the way to Sparta village
Seen her when she left the main highway, dust across the fields
Would take almost and hour for these dust clouds to settle

Arriving at the secondary school at the Sparta place
A red headed French teacher standing high above her desk
She was seven feet tall wearing size twelve shoes
At ten every morning a French class we had to face
The next approach after lunch was algebra sessions
Sometimes I was wishing I was the unknown factor
About four steps to the back of the room she was beside my desk
This women in two hours taught three math lessons

Mrs. McContire was in the next room for lab test
Doing tests with beakers, test tubes and flasks
Such a room had a sulfur smell all day long
Her Bill could do no wrong he was considered her very best
She planned all the Christmas concerts giving people parts
My part was making a picture for the front of a planagram
It consist of human pyramids along with drama rolls
A girl Shirley came up front to tell when each episodes starts

OUR OWN BUSTER

The suck of the family not that smart as let on to be
All them privileges only for Buster, thought best of the bunch
Forever a mom was ornery towards the second oldest son
The Buster saved his money for himself, for him everything was
free
At his graduation was rewarded with a brand new CCM bike
But the day for my gradation received not one single iota then
The only noble person everyone knew was Buster having praise
Others burdened by obligations, none of the rest a mother did
like

Here on this memory lane the awful vibes really gets to a man
As for everyone else to get a bike, they worked to buy one
For the remaining six children they were not important enough
Such unfairness in these realms of time, what a rotten plan
So much lack of sense in this old world of memories that passed
by
All the wondering of how proper family life would really be for
others
There was never any short fall of saying why can't Buster do
work
Might as well ask a silly question do pigs really truly can fly

The prodigious of the sons passed from high school a sixty
average
Their lesser awarded boy passed out of grade twelve with
honours
We were all bad kids except Buster a mom's pride and joy
Her chosen one coddled, while the mistreatment an outrage
Every circumstance was the same, having despair sharing the
stress
To be ever mindful myself, forgotten by many through time
Whatever was just was not there which my conscience dreads
In regards to humility the conceited one ruled more or less

Was put to a farm the degraded son, scrounging money from me
The pilfering mother took every cent leaving me in only rags
Being her underdog all along, my day finally arrived to be gone
Went to a place called Sparta feeling free as ever could be
Became a hired hand on a turkey ranch, friendly people there
Now another episode this mom sent her coddled son down for my pay
Mr. Nicholson said to the intruder brother leave this ranch place
What belonged to this guy they wanted to take it without a care

ONCE UPON A DOOR STEP

At a father's country house children happy there
So much fun they had being entirely scot free
They had there German Sheppard dog with them everywhere
A trout stream to fish in every Saturday nothing to compare
The cement doorstop was three rounding tears high place
Here my children sat waiting for Dad to come home
Such a wonderful way for a father's life really to be
Here was a wife who gave me all kinds of hardships and times
to face

Was never the one to complain always tried to be fair
Had worked so hard to build a family home in the country
No one even offered to help me build my house in Plainfield
All the family did for the whole time of building was to stare
In two years time everything was set to move right in
Had no driveway came by the field way to my lot there
Then had to buy furniture once in a while to get started
Was my first marriage a whole new life here to begin

When it was time to come home from work the next day
My brother Bill drove stakes across the field thoroughfare
He claimed this was his property no trespassing here
In order to get to my place had to find another way
Where the stakes were across stopped the car this place
Anything from the car had to be lugged into the house
Was jealous be cause I had built a house and he did not
He claimed anything inside the stakes his private space

331

On the weekend I built a foot bridge across the trout stream
Drove beside my father's barn then came home this way
Nothing was built on my brother's land only stakes for the spot
To think this son built a house before him it did seem
All through life the elder boy always came first no other
He is the only one that counts it will have come to be
You should have not built there it's over stepping the rules
Give the oldest any rewards suggested by our mother

OUR MUSIC TEACHERS

Miss Gymer was our music teacher in public school
She taught us every good boy does fine and f-a-c-e
These were the notes for the musical scale for to play
By the treble cleft was the timing beat musical rule
In those public school days the piano was by the front wall
Had a stool that screwed up or down to fit the person
The first song everybody played was "Here we go Luby Lue"
Every Friday afternoon Miss Gymer came to call

On the weekends us boys went to practice at Garrods's home
There was a really old pump organ at Bob Garrods house
We were able to play a lot of songs that Gymer had taught us
My sister Margaret played by ear some days she would come
Once in a while me and my brother Bill went to Effie's place
Harold and Effie Nickoles treated us as if we were theirs
Effie Nickoles also gave us two boys acoustic guitar lessons
The harmony guitars me and Bill had came without a case

After our family had moved away Effie Nickoles died
She was in her forties when Alzheimer's took her life
As for Miss Gymer no one knew where she had went
To get in touch with her for some we had tried
The old Coles school we went to was renovated for a home
Max Fish had lived in the old school house for a while
He lived near the school you could hear him whistling everyday
These boys and girls we went to school with found only some

AT PENURY PLACES

One's body stands lonely wanting a choice of change
Having lack of money it's like loneliness will keep on singing
All moments become symbolical echoing their forever refrain
The mind remembers old days of poverty being not so strange
Each reality thing is like wet soil that clogging a drain
A while had closed eyes seen a dancing place somewhere
When coming out of this sleep just another drab day to face
Before was infatuated by a hope realm, but left with refrain

On past another day where a lonely countryside awaits dawn
Here back in my old time place with it's raggedy past
So many parleys to think about on a long ago roadway
Once in a lifetime forget about yesterday let it be gone
While day dreaming thought hungry cats were mewing at me
Telling someone it's chore time in a long ago Bergville
On each side of daylight with a life leading to nowhere
Thinking about these penury places so much confound to see

To remember winter scenes ice burdened pines back there
Had smelt the scent of dying vegetation in late September
That mind place of crickets morning voice in the basement
With no end to night owl cries with morning doves call to
compare
All my journeys thoughts similar with so much trauma then
A life time of pitch, shovel and holler giddy up whoa
The smell of pig manure drifting on a summer breeze
Still have some pictures in black and white when life began

TURNED MY CRANK

Became a Catholic Knight honoured by a church by my place
Must donate to a house of worship it's the rightful thing to do
For partaking in the service for some time received four plaques
How grateful we all are for your desire to devote your time with grace
Shall always remember here members truly raise brand new hope
The peace of mind we give you it's all given entirely for good will
We humbly expect you to do the minutes of each meeting for us
When all is said and done we are brothers with rules should cope

Having a good image of expecting to serve when ever called upon
You must do all biddings in order receive your wall certificate
Here we have the most wonderful group of do-gooders always
It's been part of the churches inheritance since Knights had begun
Here is the fountain in life that's been granted for everyone to share
Will confirm our rights of unity in hopes we are heard who ever
All together to practice the virtues of family life as a unit here
Above all must except our duty to fulfill such revere willed with care

Must be a source of the Knights to obligate your time if needed
Such a person as a hands on man to go fix it when we ask you
Soon they transform you as part of free of charge maintenance crew
Do whatever pleases the Knights raise your hand, the meeting proceeded
There is no partiality when you have been sworn in we are majority
Be it said, abound to the purpose, eager to the source it's our best game
What is customary your proned to do except it you signed your name
After ten years of being true blue, you get a badge for top seniority

That honour is yours as long as membership fees are paid
With a feather hat in my midst saying you must show up again
So sorry to say it's best to forsake you have to leave it will have to be
Was standing by his right hand proclaiming my goodbyes was then made
To remedy it all, chose a waywardness forever a sincere downfall
You must attend always be faithful to the church even though truth sets me free
Now is my liberty time out they send a bill in the mail for some fees
Even though I have called it quits, every Thursday be at the meeting was the call

WAS A FELICIFIC FELLOW

The joy gone from my house was a whole world died here
That sound of sheer silence gets to you alone at night
Was immeasurable hope for life's dreams waiting to come true
We endured hard times with our unity of greatness sincere
Once more our hearts as believers fulfillment was always there
Our merits of faith had no doubts helping to proceed onwards
Did foreshadow each bad moment with out best of intentions
So much loving kindness always found a place with lots of care

Our cares of the world had a secluded corner was the case
With good parables, edged us on to create such a great life
There was my lane of life where I walked with thoughts daily
Had accomplished the best purpose in life in our loving space
Must choose a purpose, then through patience you can get
there
The happiness part made a firm foundation that lasted long
Did leave out the times for interpretations of who's bad or good
As for our friends we had confidence in with them none can
compare

Once more in the hearts of believers our fulfillment remains
Had stuck to a rightful path, the one that is straight and narrow
To be left all alone with merits only faith moves me onward
Now being in the dead of winter only my body, it complains
With confidence am willing to discuss my thoughts out loud
Shall renew this man's image by trying to be happy once again
Let forever gladness find it's place in my mind and heart
In remembrance of a wife's hard work a man indeed to be
proud

Each dawn of a new day the adventure of mystery is out there
Wondering if finding another mate is right, with anguished thoughts
For despite the fondness living life goes, on grieved as you are
Out in the public have wretched ones those you must beware
Want another lasting time some how, just to be happy again
Best to purpose your old wisdom in these days to be right now
Unable to confirm there is hope in days to come it appears
Was married three times now this man is alive, why complain

A HOUSE NEAR THE RIVER

As I walk along the Moira river was bent yellow grass
All pathways lead up from the river to my house
The river was calm so early in the morn nare a breeze
A rising sun at daylight had finally made the fog pass
Seen the Indian fence that bordered our bush land
Was a cedar fence running from the river to the highway
This stretch of land my father bought in nineteen fifty four
There was stones piled under the bottom rail thrown there by
hand

Had build my first home here about a quarter mile from rivers
edge
Our dad had plans to build a split-stone house but never did
Everyone's intentions for their piece of land never turned out
Witched for water on my property then made a well
My brother sold his land on the west side by the creek ledge
At the front of my house was a trout stream gurgling away
So strange in a dream there was another house behind mine
But could only enter it in a nightmare a beautiful place
Maybe there will actually be a house build there someday

Across the front of my real house was thirty rose plants
They were of many colours climbing along the fence
The fence I had built from three inch round cedar rails
On the front side of this rustic fence it gradually slants
The way my yard is sloped my basement will not flood
An arbor seven feet high makes a passageway to the stream
Now snapping turtles cannot come into my yards there's a high
wall
At the edge of the trout stream it's banked with rocks and mud

DIVINE ATTRIBUTES RELIEF

The art of worldly wisdom is brilliance owned by masters
There is a halo of gold given to heavens chosen few
A man's best faith should be rooted in stone until journeys end
Sooner or later our spirits rise into blue angel pastures
Some songs not sung aloud keeping the joy to ourselves
Then comes the plaint of earth's reactions of utterance galore
Wanting to ambush merging shadows having quiet change
So much innocents in a wondering landscape to delve

Who has a beautiful life that blossoms every day
To many pieces in our life's wheel not understanding fully
The forgetting of some bygone wrath will become a blessing
Want to turn the corner of time with new episodes on their way
Have to stop a resuming echo make a new plain to play on
Every day cannot be like an excited person falling in love
So much transcend of emptiness waiting to be filled
Most days like a full moon when the suns beam is gone

Some people say this is a God forsaken world today
Are we out of the style of a former period of time
The past has it become a relic to remote for us
Will religion foreshadow us forever or how long will it stay
Have fear of God have fear of the devil a two sided thing
For each of us there's something peculiar to our character
Would be better if we said great minds think alike
How much inspiration can a few holy words out loud bring

CHALKBOARD BRUSHES

An old schoolhouse with blackboards on every wall
Every days lessons a fingernail would scratch along
It put shivers up ones back every time this happened
Then when a teacher went to brush off a mistake I recall
The fingernails on both sides of the brush would rub
Once in a long time the chalk would get small enough for shivers
Was able to find a long piece of chalk to use on the board
If I went to the black board would never use a chalk nub

Our class took turns going outside to clean chalk brushes
You would clap one brush against the other to clean
Was glad it was only once in a while for this chore
Some days were hard to clean brushes with wind gushes
Cleaning the blackboards off, from lessons took forever
First you had to brush everything off the board then wash it
To reach the top of the blackboard you needed a chair
Sometimes the brushes did not get cleaned in bad weather

Students took turns at everything that had to be done
In winter months the fire was stoked every half hour
The school was heated by a huge furnace was number one
No one drove us to school in those days we walked all the way
Having high snow banks was no excuse to stay at home
Nobody was lazy we were self reliant never renege
For going to school was winter and summer long in our day

THE WRINGER WASHER

In the kitchen was a wringer washer long ago
Beside the washer was two set tubs for rinsing
The only way to dry the cloths was on a pulley line
On the pulley line cloths were hung there at twenty below
Our underwear would freeze as stiff as a board
Was a wire cable stretching a hundred feet to a pole
After every wash hung out the cable had to be tightened
In those days a wringer washer is all one could afford

All the water warmed in reservoir of the cook stove
The water was hauled from a well some ways away
For water to be warm enough took most of the morning
Was Dreft laundry detergent with a colour of mauve
Back then Javex bleach smelt up the whole room
To wash clothes in those times was a whole day affair
Every full load the washing machine water was changed
Filled the washing machine then push clothes up and down
with a corn broom

The wash water was drained onto a gravel laneway
After every load this where the dirty water went
Also both set tubs were changed during each wash
This was an every Saturday episode of hauling water day
Our pulleys line were good for the high snow banks there
One could stand on the porch to reel the cloths one hundred
feet
People today do not know hardships of them long ago times
With a family of nine people needed lots of clothesline to spare

CLAIR RUSSES AUCTION

There's times unnamed still waiting down the way
Every afternoon Clair's wife would be calling him
Here's how it goes Clair, Clair, Clair in a high voice
Then she would ring the bell two times each day
These people had special ducks that flew above trees
The red ducks went to other farmers field to feed
He had fat ducks but he never had to feed them
Such farmers smutched what each person there sees

The man Clair Russ leased property to people then
When people grew beans at night he stole bushels
It they grew turnips he took turnips here and there
There were some accusing him time and time again
One day Clair's brother sold a load of hay to a guy
After buying the load of hay found a false centre
A box was built on the wagon rack then hay added
His brother was confronted about it, no one forced you to buy

Down the road about two years later he had an auction sale
He went around other farmers places stealing things
Our garden cultivator was stolen from our garage
All the things for his sale was locked up like a jail
On the auction day I went to see what this man had
Right away seen my cultivator there for twenty dollars
If you take any of my auction stuff I'll call the police here
How could someone like this man get away with fraud

OUR INDIAN SUITS

Went to a North American Indian house along ways back
These Indians made clothes plus other things they sold
The house windows had no glass just hides to cover them
Back on the other side of a bush not even a railway track
Their homes seemed so cold to us in the dead of winter there
A lady sat in a self made chair making moccasins
One of her daughters was making deer skin jackets
These people wore only light clothing they did not care

Our father bought me and Bill an Indian outfit
The men with their sons where out killing deer this day
We watched these women making frilled trousers and Jackets
Also there was fancy frills on sleeves to be knit
So much work went into making outfits to sell
These Indian inheritance was Ojibway we were told
In a shed by the house many deer hides hanging there
Everything that was made was authentic you could tell

How could humans live in such a freezing cold place
To get to their dwelling only a foot path lead there
At the main road a sign read Indians three miles in
All bush living Indians were a very hearty race
They did not go to school because of the clothes they wore
People would call them savages because they were not the
same
Me and Bill had these suits for a long time, then were lost along
the way
Nobody in this day of age lives like that anymore

PLANTERS PEANUT MAN

The first house in Denfield south of the store
Us three Brennan boys went there to visit a friend
Their father was a planters peanut sales person
In the front room was bags full of peanuts the hall had more
Our friend gave us four bags each to eat at home
Had never seen so many peanut bags in all my life
Still wonder to this day why would someone have all these
Even beside the dresser in the bedroom there was some

One day the house was for sale such a nice place
My father managed to buy this property very cheap
There was a house, a barn, a chicken house and pig pen
Being beside a store having black balls and popcorn was the case
On the south side of the house was a good sized garden plot
On the north side of this property was a very large lane way
All around the house was a flag stone walk way
A steal of a deal with a barn full of hay is what we got

About three months past when Dad brought two horses here
One horse's name was Picadilly the other was Carliol
The horse Carliol was a palomino with a blonde tail, blonde mane
We could not go near this horse because his kicking was severe
But Picadilly was a quiet horse she loved being around us
She was liked by everyone in our family, wanting us near
Picadilly was with the family until she got old and was put down
When we fed her apples or carrots she always made a fuss

DREAMING OUT LOUD

On the edge of impossible days my form was sitting there
For a whole lifetime man has reasons that clutches his heart
Either thinking about an adventure or really doing it
To reincarnate old songs for something to do but who'd care
Every song has an end but contains good thoughts for a while
Daytime infatuations are more amusing each time they come
Always being touched by existence hoping for the best
Those ponderous heads of characters intend to make me smile

Walking and talking must be with the Lord nobody's there
Maybe people think that I am a glib, nothing understood
For the old days my mind thinks no one should have any pity
Despite everything life was familiar no one to care
There is no comparison from the old to the new concept
Here was events everyone did it was a must to survive
Long ago it was all routine saying the farmer drew another load
away
As in these days it's not in the mattress were money's kept

How great it was to leave that place of no consideration
Here a story plot tells of many unfolding dire events
Was hard to get passed the halfway mark when I did
A childhood life of many messed up unblessed complication
An old fool said it's all love in peace and war for all
So glad those days are far behind for crying out loud
In my case no one modified the day they were all the same
Had predetermine my life at eighteen this man did recall

LEGENDARY JOURNEYS

The echoes refrain that came from yesterday sad domain
Behind my heels lay those years moving from place to place
Out in these country dwelling loneliness come calling each day
Being the only difference between each country place was
more pain
Was a poor man's blunders of being a cheaper place to be
When we lived in Denfield an Union Jack flapped in the wind
You were a prisoner in your own home in the winter time
Here the snow banks where as far and high as eye could see

Another village we lived close to was Sparta place
At this countryside plows plowed the roads in winter
We did not need a horse and cutter to get around each day
The only thing not so good was a three mile trek we had to
face
When me and Bill started high school walked three miles there
Had to peddle a bike six miles each weekday then
In the old days we still had to pack a lunch for high school
During the first year Bill had a whizzer it was not fare

Next the family moved to Plainfield bought a farm here
Our father allotted us two acres to build a house on
My house was built in the sixties a nice place there
The land given to me a son just one that was sincere
Had my home until seventy five then moved to Belleville place
On College street was a house I renovated the next year
Every plan soon faded and died in the midst of it all
Soon after came splits-ville then there was divorce to face

THE NEW YORK CENTRAL

In the steam engine days of the nineteen hundreds
That New York Central train a mighty powerful machine
When the train was coming seems there wasn't any end
The iron lady had traveled down many a rail beds
My father worked on these trains for a short while
Could hear the shuttling of the driving wheels coming
A big black smoke stake puffing smoke into the sky
Us children could hear our father's train whistle for a mile

On off school days we watched our Dad coming there
He would blow the whistle extra times for us guys
As he crossed the level crossing a big leather mitt waving
These steam engines with the huffing puffing nothing could
compare
During the time these trains went through farming countryside
Across the front of these trains was a cow catcher
Instead of an animal getting killed it brushed it off
Every engineer who ran each train done this with pride

Remembered riding in a passenger train starting out
Up into the train you would go with your ticket in hand
A conductor passed through punching everyone's tickets
A conductor when all was aboard he would then shout
He would pick up the step stool saying all aboard now
In the old days there was to much snow for a snowplow
Our teacher walked along the edge of the railway tracks
The only way our teacher got to school was after the train did
plow

ISAAC PIERSON PLACE

This man lived in a pine grove with two homes the same
He had a barn where cows had lived there sometime before
On the property there was not any wells dug at all
By the orchard there was two springs, out of the ground water came
The old man drank the water from the rain barrel beside the shed
In the barrels mosquito larva call wigglers swam around
His clothes smelt like sweat as if he never bathed at all
Isaac Pierson was a man over ninety, he was never wed

When we seen this old man coming along we would hide
Where he could not see us we listened to him talking to himself
He would be talking about all kinds of farming deeds
We did not want to face him which might hurt his pride
One day while crossing Harold Nickoles field he fell down
With our help he came to our house where he was patched up
He ate supper at our house this time thank us very much
While at our house ask our father could he drive him into town

Isaac Pierson died the next year with no will at all
For taxes Max Fish took over his place for cheap
The apples from the big orchard here was used for cider
Our family collected dead branches from here for wood I recall
These apples were harvested for about four years in a row
Max Fish bulldozed the trees to clear the land
He cultivated it then planted corn for years to come
Then both old homes were falling down they had to go

ILLINGSWORTH AIROPLANE

At my home in Denfield next to Russ Bowman's store
Our father along with me and Bill were working in the garden
All of a sudden out of a clear blue sky a plane swoops down
The pilot did a couple of loops the he swooped once more
We said to our father who is that crazy fool up there
Dad said it's Illingsworth the stunt pilot showing off again
This piper plane was a noisy craft sometimes it backfired
He would shut the motor off then free fall without a care

Back again he came free falling then start the motor again
The plane came close to our chimney then back up to the sky
So much noise from the motor during that climb upward
Such a performance keep us looking at Illingsworth's plane
Then he put his hand out of the cockpit waving goodbye
He had done all the death defying stunts for the village people
Everyone applauded up and down our street for this man
We kept watching until he disappeared into the Western sky

Our father explained that Illingsworth was low on gasoline
He must be going back to the airport now to refuel
Today sitting on my hunches still think about Illingsworth
This was the first performance us villagers had ever seen
The next time we seen Illingsworth's plane was at the fair
These other stuntman never seen such a thing before
He came across the tarmac flying upside down
Even at the Western Exhibition no other planes could compare

UNDERHILLES HILLS

With brand new toboggans the three went hill searching
Me, Tom and Bill my brothers wanted better hills
Walking miles through hilly areas trying every one
The best of all hills we had great plans of reaching
At last we came to Underhill's farm off the main road
These hills were like mountains heading across open fields
Mr. Underhill was in his laneway with his bobsleigh
When Mr. Underhill's daughter came, love for Bill was the
episode

Every ten feet down the slope was a goat path there
We found the toboggan ride was flying and landing thing
So glad when we all got to the bottom are asses were sore
In the open field so many big rocks gave us a scare
Had to lean then swerve, managed to miss them all
This was fun but dangerous for the first time down
Us three boys were discouraged for a rough ride all the way
Before the day was over lots of snow began to fall

Now the goat paths were filled and big stones covered
The next ride down the slope was great even at dark
A moon came to show us the way, it now was a nice hill
By searching the countryside something wonderful we
discovered
That next day we told our friends what us guys found
This new fallen snow was now nicely packed for everyone
So many times we went to this place lots of people there
There came noted skiers from several towns all around

FOREVER CROSSED MY MIND

On a country gravel road a place so remote then
Found myself going daft nothing made much sense now
Was like an obstacle as rotten as yesterday that's gone
Here was the garden needing weeded but Lord knows when
Had just washed the manure off my boots at noon
Who wants anything to do with a smelly farm boy
Better to feed the livestock first no dust flying around
The chore time now would go with the milk pail soon

They always say practice what you preach always
Telling or complaining does not cut it in a bumpkin world
Ask for a watch for some kind of reward, but it was no
Sometimes would not wave to a neighbor had good and bad
days
To call me skipper infuriate me felt like punching someone
Whether it be wild or domesticated hated all animals
When you became a nursemaid for them, gives one reason
The belittled part was pointed towards a black sheep son

Seen a beautiful crop of mushrooms gave them a kick
Then smelt the manure in the air, wanted to run away
Forever crossed my mind to focus on a better life
Some days felt like galloping the cows with a stick
Remember your heritage that's what our grandfathers said
The sons today do not want to follow their kinfolk
It's not like long ago it's freedom of speech so they say
In those war years depended on farmers for us to be fed

PONDERING TIMES

Anewed days of deep thoughts with a lot of contention
Have come to a old dull part of a man's life right now
Life comes to weighing pros and cons matters mentally
To be carefully thought out have the best answers to mention
There is sensitivity in an elders heart with all the hurt
No one is trustworthy always waiting for what they get
When truth comes around then there is honour also
A wish for family longevity duration with an anguish heart

By abiding with good thoughts will manage to pull through
For some they will reject me, let's offer them the worse
In regarding people so many of them are noted hypocrites
To have courage, tasks are difficult, but one knows what to do
Best not stay miserable, be concerned it's part of having
peace
Anybody else of human creation know how passion works
Being contrary is a conduct not tolerated among friends
With unity comes peace lets make it work that's my advice

Those who are deceitful best remove them from my space
The important part for matters have a pleasant manner
There is consideration with agreeing your conscience knows
Everyone's concerning mind will understand about being nice
Comes peoples suggestions applying to the old man scene
So much consideration goes to the state of immediate family
During quiet times think about our care free days long ago
In need of accomplishing the real purpose, don't be mean

Without money life has no price we would be all the same
Our money is here forever, must find ways of how to get it
Forever dawning is new wonders in life it's hard to keep up
The lucky one's are granted them reverent elements to fame
Moreover make an effort to phone for each one's birthday
In this great world there is strangers, being friends not met
Here in one another's dwelling place best we get along
With eagerness for the norm, be this the only true way

SOME MORE TYPIFIED

Them typified characters a real demention in fame
The qualities for life are aforesaid from our old times
Have plotted my words on their landing spot for good grace
Such a home on debonair street inside there is not the same
Often our humanity inherits nature of things mindfully
That confidence game we know who we really are now
Best to catalog our fame to embody what all came about
What we have derived at cannot be taken away rightfully

As for the ups and downs of long ago good luck came through
From commonsense generally found out we were great
On the paths of wonder was our parts to play for awhile
Seen the bricabrac of our best displays of what we do
Was intentional to flip pages back to yesterday dawn
Did emerge to dabble in what we do best for a lifetime
As for using whence term it's fitting to our personal self
Them prefigures of who we are in writing never to be gone

Have regarded commonsense, brings good events to follow
Furthermore occure values comes for what we had done
There is no pretense it's the way we are for all times
A man believes in practicing principles, with his knowhow
Being somebody with skilled talent for a creation made
That world behind me did catch up with me on this day
Better to belong with the loving side of better styled intentions
Does not matter how many books written or what is paid

Here is my valentine with heartfelt thoughts of you
One's destiny did leave it's mark for a year and a day
Now comes some statistical moment of past dates in mind
Let's all belong to the loving side styled all brand new
By all the same token are appointed to a task that differs
In every figure of speech there is a message indeed
Will try to integrate more vanity for more attention now
These people with insights into life become the winners

TOOK THE TRAIN

My thoughts for the world should this person take a train
Would add a piece of mind to utterance of good faith
Took the train from Belleville to Toronto on a special day
After completing grade thirteen a Loyalist was a gain
Had gained a passing mark of eighty-five and more
With these marks was expected into George Brown
This college trained me to be a forth to third class engineer
After passing with honours out of here opened a door

My first really good job was with McCain for my career
At McCain Foods got my steam time for third class
Being a third class engineer got a big raise in pay
Having utterance of good faith there's nothing to fear
Then was able to get a refrigeration license in a while
Now you're an A-one student with an honours degree
Had passed out from a class of gas fitter twos
Now when I leave on any train it makes me smile

The train took me away from a drap Belleville place
Sent me on a journey of no return for ever more
Have passed by them days for my black sheep times
Must we say a man bound for glory is the case
Comes that old saying you cannot keep a good man down
You can pinch me if you want, no need I'm doing very well
Using honesty gets a man where he has to get too
Was glad when I left Belleville a two horse town

LIFE''S EVILS

A minister Harvey Nicholson said do not marry this one
He took me to one side telling me not to wed Brenda
She will be promiscuous for all the days you live together
There will be no pity from me if you marry this son of a gun
Forever you will have this evil to pull you down in life
You are too good of a guy for the likes of her with a demons
soul
A minister must have some way of knowing a bad person
But I did not listen, took her to be my lawfully wedded wife

How right Harvey was this woman was just that
Call it a who do she do all of the above consequences
The list is a mile long from then until now there's no end
To bad to be naïve was unable to smell that she was a rat
But my mother said marry this woman she will be good for you
Seems me being the black sheep, was another curse on me
We got married by the justice of the peace at city hall
During those times it was up in the air as to what to do

All the time while being a mother of five children she was not
true
These affairs she was caught in the act but still lied to me
Was so much bad with her stealing, cheating and lying
To get a divorce was the only thing for us two to do
With the help of a children's aide worker came to my place
Her along with a children's aide man kidnapped the children
In them days there was not much a father could really say
The way things happened to get her way was a disgrace

FLABBERGASTED ONE

To find a reason to gripe flabbergasts most of us
Keep your conscience clear during this realm of such woe
As for the twinkling of triumph it is no longer there
Is there still people having sincerity of heart that don't fuss
With some love is not welcomely laid it needs nurturing now
Always seek hope it's a mystery minder for all of us
No best heeded words for some of them now it's dementia
When you say that you love the whole family they say wow

My portion is me deprived from complete sharing in lives
Best sound off these compassionates that's in mind
In a household nothing nurtured to please, but could be
Thoughts of Joy vanish that day when no friendship arrives
For any of the circumstances waiting is forever it seems
Have been so worthy of these moments then comes one more
day
In my loneliness place came sounds of a midnight train
Through it all happiness mostly comes in nighttime dreams

My thoughts are not your thoughts nor born in likeness
Without faith people get off the beaten path so much
Not so gracious when willpower turns weary after while
That downhearted feeling spent in a room of darkness
For the count of sorrowed moments paced the hall once more
Here close by me whispering is shadowed thoughts again
Been secluded in circumstances confided by no one
Being deranged somewhat, comes spiteful infatuation galore

Only songsters greeting me from the trees at dawn
My portion of life is mostly behind closed white doors
Them meekly thoughts in darkness as I doze off
Does compassion find a new home when all else is gone
The windows sunlight is only for me when it arrives
Still there is sincerity left in an old heart tomorrow again
What flabbergast me is there anybody now who cares
Best utter words of good faith lets see what derives

OLD STICK IN THE MUDS

Our pilgrimage brought us here through hard times
Advice to be willed in favour of elder ones long ago
The firm faith remains forever with it's infinite goodness
Must go to church on Sunday while the bell chimes
Here the conformed image of long ago being called folklore
Have assumed it was right what was formed long ago
There is confidence an old inheritance never to be finished
Our world is divided by dissension not like it was before

Use old fashioned rub shoulders once in a while to talk
Where is there a remedy out of mortality for a change
Did become ceaseless to progress, but remain hardhearted
Need of mutual respect amongst old members of the flock
Once in a while we stick our heads out of the dark ages look
around
Beyond all telling's will remain until the last man is down
Had bestowed on the population syncope words forever
Best be visible among minorities while being downtown

Also obedience went out the door to match the time
Someone foreshadowed that approached in a blemished way
Not all people can be raised up apart from the rest to rejoice
Today we cannot buy anything with a thin silver dime
Our homeland is for everybody, some persevere bad deeds
The author of life has been found worthy for changing things
Be optimistical for the outcome, there is culture terms
In the forecast brink for humanity be lucky if it succeeds

Must change times to match yonker images it seems
The futures old space will be lost as urchins of time
That coming generation is upending old host of humdrum
The harmony for life now is beyond our wildest dreams
In accordance to specter life is headed for damnation place
Our faith cannot remain forever, as of known, infinite goodness
There is only memory to enrich old standards forever
As for the deviant structures to life it's a complete disgrace

UNITED CHURCHES GONE

The church was some place to go on each Sunday
As for me being a sleeping time after a hard weeks work
During the old days my family became Protestants for good
Our minister would do the sermon then a pianist would play
Many people in a choir sang the Jesus songs for awhile
There was a Sunday school class right at ten in the morn
Each person had a special small books to recite bible stories
When we finished the class we put these books in a file

In Plainfield the church that baptized us was torn down
The minister Mr. Kersy organized a rink for a hockey team
He even helped to freeze the rink in the cold of winter
To play against other teams was Plainfield was renown
Was a place for conscious passion of devoted friends
Our lives then had a extended onamonapia it seemed
From grandfather to childhood visions came everlasting
That image for them days had so many glorious trends

When the church goes the people end up going to
That's exactly what happened everywhere in the country
Must be a condition of the times people stopped believing
Our history from the old days no longer lives we are told what to
do
The only church that stands strong if Catholic they are not
smited
Cultures have come to our place of birth to change the rules
It's a shame for battles fought for freedom condemned today
Maybe someday we will put our foot down for it to be righted

A FUD TIME

Them smells of new mown hay in far back days
An orchard full of fragrant apple blossoms blowing
These blossoms came in full bloom then blew away
Was a child with nothing to gain in those times nobody pays
You went to do work for somebody they came to help you
We were just short of being desolate in yore times
An old world with shovels, axes and pitchforks all around
So much fate aimed down the road nothing to renew

These moments where like squeezing toothpaste nothing
coming out
Waiting for them desperate moments of hope not there
Some days sitting at the end of a long path away from farm
smells
Our address was country number so and so for the rural route
Not reluctant in going tomorrow picking apples row on row
Was awe that ruled weekends after school was harvest time
Had to go out in the hot dry out field to shook up grain
Them old time riggers for thrashings us boys had to go

True to Canada on Remembrance Day held the Union Jack for
an hour
From eleven to twelve o'clock everyone stood in silence
A long wide belt slapping and flapping stopped up now
To run the thrashing machine the ten twenty had lots of power
First you hear a slow hum then away the thrasher went again
Went from farm to farm in those days for all fall seasons
In our fathers time people grew field upon field of oats
Even with blistered hands old guys did not once complain

NO PRIDE EPISODES

Even though as a young boy was severe moments to face
Went to school just the same suffering from trauma
My mother beat on me every chance I was alone
Deep in thought was to run away was the childhood case
One night we had company all the beds were taken
A bed for me was on the Morris chair with no blankets
Halfway through the night the fires went dead out
When I peed on the chair my body from the cold was shaken

Being almost four years old began crying with the cold
Out came my mother from her bedroom to see me
She grabbed a piece of cord wood, beating on my head
My father came rushing out "stop stop" she was told
The back of my head was a mass of blood running down
A towel was wrapped around my head to stop the bleeding
Being a very scared young boy thought that I would die
Then my Dad rush me to the hospital in our little town

It took twelve stitches to close the wound on my head
Not a soul was told about this episode back in the forties
So many times my mother's temper was out of control
The doctor told my Dad a couple more whacks I'd be dead
Another time the Tordoff boys talked to me and Bill
My mother came, pulling Vern Tordoff through barbed wire
She pulled him back and forth through the fence a long time
Our mother had a mental problem this son thinks so still

NO ONE PRAYED

The thing that taunts me was no one ever did pray
As for me found special prayers to say every night
Having much to say while kneeling beside my bed
It's a fulfillment for a heart to find peace each day
Most important for a person growing up is not to swear
Was so many people among us cursing half of the time
They thought of themselves as more aggressive doing this
Teenagers confide in bad things going as a pair

That tremulous voice speaks above all of the rest
But there has to be one in the family with consideration
To have pride no matter what's for my sake forever
Even though being surrounded by wrath had done my best
There was no affection among the lot as long as I live
In that backward old country place same old trot line
Seemed to have been a twist in the old time concept
To get something back one must first be able to give

For the moral sense malediction took its place
Better to look towards a new phase to stalk there
How can one go to sleep with a conscience to purge the soul
Was inauthentic confronting lives in the olden times case
The only thing the same today is a clock ticking away
Must stay noble like a clout by making better scenery
Had tried to form an association with a group of five
Such a waste of time having the same reaction as before
Even though each day got me down still a man must pray

A DILL PICKLE CROCK

In mid summer a special size cucumber was got
We had a big earthenware crock for making dill pickles
Ten gallons of pickles were made to last all winter
A brine made with vinegar plus dill added so nothing would rot
Every year pickles were made for this family of nine
The crock would sit down below by the southern basement
window
This crock had a thick oaken lid with a large rock on top
There was a bowl of pickles on the table every time we would
dine

So much remembered testing the brine before pickles added
If a potato floats on the brine then it's just right
We could not go to a store to buy dills in long ago days
To stop the condensed moister under the crock it was matted
The recipe came from our great grandfather days
Once in a while my father would sneak a pickle
In the neighborhood we gave pickles to a chosen few
Our family made the best pickles around everyone says

On the crock it said made by Mcneer in eighteen forty-two
Who knows how many people did pickles back then
Even the glazing on the crocks outside was partially gone
How many more years to go before somebody buys brand new
Nobody makes dill pickles ever they buy them at the store
Some people today are even to lazy to have a garden
There sweet pickles bread and butter pickles are in big
demand
My thoughts are that people do not like dills that much
anymore

SATURDAY NIGHT LILT

Nothing censored just a Saturday night get to do
Have flung dull times down by inviting friends here
These relatives are great friends to rejoice with
So many old tunes on guitar and accordion to lilt to
Such a flux of change from the same routine things
All of us looked forward to party time we cannot deny
Us folks will never bestride to a world of cronies ever
Having good sense of being along with all the joy it brings

Our rec room is an ideal spot for having everybody come
Have said fiddlesticks to boredom of a days run
Lets trump it up where delight plays the best part
In life most instigators want trouble, we are not like some
At Christmas have good wishes, please come visit all
We did enchant the rec room as many times as possible
For a while set laughter to the utmost with the folks
Hitherward we endorsed good times whooping I recall

All together it's been ten years for these occasions
When there's off times the rooms silence has a hush
Then comes them moments again to endorse everyone
Even our patio has had a few summer hilarious invasions
A celebration brought both kins one time to our backyard
We sang songs from the sixties to the eighties mostly
Nothing last forever but there's forever memories to fall onto
There was Allen, Bobby and Gary along with myself stared

TIN LIZZIES

From over them long ago hills came a tin lizzie car
A crank or two to start, then away she goes down the road
Every summer a hot trail to go on windows wide open
One gallon of gasoline was so cheap it would take you far
The old saying was two spools with an old tin can, away she ran
That model T colour black was typical away back then
The old putt putt had a wooden frame made from oak
For this Henry Ford he was the very first since era of autos
began

Then came a model A Ford more stylish from the rest
Had a oga oga horn to keep people out of it's pathway
Seems no time everyone was driving in class with one of these
Was a little bit faster car, know for sure it stood the test
Such an advancement had a starter to fire up the motor
Onto the road with it's harsh sound until putting faded a far
So many happy owners passing one another on down the road
With high wheels a great get away in winter for this putter

Soon coming along a brand new car the model B one
Being one of Henry Ford's better deeds for a neater car
The model B Ford had a rumble seat for only two people
Was great this outdoorsy seat trend that had just begun
To be made as a summer pleasure car for young lovers
Turning into a parking lot you signaled with your hand out
Straight up was a right turn straight out left down was stop
In those days lights were put on cars for nighttime drivers

LIFE'S FOLLY

Sometimes there is a place for conscious passion
Our lives have a kind of extended intuition to liberate us
My second wife after five years of marriage reformed
She told me who her family really was and the mission
They were Nazis during the second world war days
While the war was ending they came by ship to Canada
As pretend farmers were able to buy land in Forest Hill
For many years were able to fool people in many ways

Her husband of the time was a Nazi pilot of sorts
His mission was to put magnetic bombs under planes
These planes were the big Canadian bomber fleets
He would bring down as many as he could then give reports
Because of all his missions after the war it paid it's toll
On his farm in Forest Wood his wife found him dead
The man had died from a brain hemorrhage there
This pilot did not live very long after his German role

After being married to Ursula for eighteen years
This was the pilots former wife during that time
She was Ursula Brennan not Ursula buts check now
One day she was diagnosed with cancer, not good it appears
Two months down the road my wife did pass away
After the funeral her son Peter said to cremate her
He said next month he would pick the ashes up at my house
The son never came for over a year, but still claimed to come
These ashes in the urn were shipped special to him in a day

US REGULAR FOLKS

We are not the ones to change a beautiful day
Most times predictions come about having possible hope
On our horizon is friends being like strangers out there
As for us we are regular folks offering good will all the way
There are some friends like flowers short lived here
To have always been poised in a likeable fashion for all
Our goodwill is like counting sidewalk cracks it never ends
Forever there is no boundaries forever we are sincere

Apart from happy trodden paths, inside joy shines
With other peoples sorrow we feel towards them
One cannot mend an undetermined heart it waste time
Some kin the more we try some how their love reclines
They have closed their corridors where love should dwell
Even though we are old people we have care that lives
Came through life, seen it all, here's a man that really knows
Such people must have a problem that's absurd you can tell

To have faith is always included for our future days
Have to form goodness of heart with friends in life
Some people are a mishap generation out of work
Are a high hat race unable to understand good ways
The hetero is very ignorant in accordance's with other ones
Those people from the old school had principles how to act
Us grandfathers are not lost in time for the time being
How many people look for enemies when Dad has these sons

INSPIRED ECSTASY

Wanted to shape my day with some joy of heart
Have noticed how some things are altered in life
All my life looking for a place of everlasting love
For the most part innocents comes with evil to start
Our morning door opening brings life to reality once more
Will go out to meet people of a perplexed reasoning
Then returning home with wishes the day was better
To go to our nightly land of dreams we close the door

An ever influence of life is for goodly feelings again
If possible make amends to forgive then to forget
Would be best to pack your bags when friends sell you out
Must watch out for good weather friends, they are a pain
There was so many lessons learned from way back then
So many people with paper smiles that only last a while
The most gracious day was my birthday every year
As for this day would receive a brand new fountain pen

The only song people tried to sing was Happy Birthday
Sometimes folks would sing For He's A Jolly Good Fellow
How could anybody be a jolly good fellow in those times
A few times early some mornings I would run away
Came back late to see who had did the chores for me
Really it was not a one person job in a family farm life
Would get the beating of my life out on our back porch
My mother would say out loud "you know where you're to be"

LEWDNESS PERSONS

My intuition is to baffle nonsense forever
Please let me gladden this old world with more delight
Let compact the content using conscious human affection
Some people using new gizmos supposing to be clever
Forever that grand pride of importance to urge me
Would like to be a good Samaritan to inspire people
Those collaborators that are for me seek the truth
Should not go where all the misfits go it's a black hole you see

Hear a milk-sobs response when he listens what Mommy say
What Dad says grow up become a man you are old enough
Here's my best of wishes through days that are left
Come be a real human let's have a very nice day
Have only ministered hope to guide someone along
It's important to urge someone out of a dog's life in hell
Always confide in real hearts of good friends forever
Seems my sons all their life sang a sad old song

Want to leave old buggered times out of the picture
Let's not dictate solemnness anymore get on with life
Break a leg in order to get to where it's at right now
Best to change alienated people to a brand new future
Would be better to be daft belonging to an oddball place
From the grandfather role the Lord has not excluded me
Will the real grandfather please stand up to be counted
Seems so out of proportion to be belonging to a lewdness race

A CAT OR TWO

One night a cat came to our house asking to stay
Our home at this time was at Plainfield Ontario
The cat was an unspayed female about two years old
Should we welcome this cat a white and brown stray
A short time later the cat was gone Lord knows where
About two weeks later puss puss was back again
This cat was expecting, one could see at this time
In about a month she birthed just two cute pair

My sister Margaret noticed their front paws had ten toes
The mother cat must have mated with a bobcat
These kittens were pure white like driven snow
After a couple of weeks they followed my sister where ever she
goes
When they became full grown cats they climbed a tree
One day I walked under the tree both cats jumped on me
It was fun for them it was all in their day of play
This was their bobcat instincts everyone could see

They were not like ordinary cats they had a high pitched sound
The sound would scare the two dogs make them run
Every morning they were eating a rabbit freshly caught
These cats did not care for other cat food we had found
Both these cats disappeared one night gone forevermore
We knew for sure they had returned to a wild place
The mother cat was fixed having no kittens ever again
As for the mother cat she lay on a mat at the back door

AN AMIABLE FATHER

Down deep in my human heart my noble thoughts reside
Some create personal bias with bad action attitudes
The pointing out of love is a Dad's pact to fulfill
Lets delve in happy moments for the most part to confide
No one should bring sinful baggage to a good man's door
Best to rejoice it common to living for most days
Those attitudes deflect bad instructions for us all
Each life is not for creating trouble it's to explore

Being friends is not much of a task to ask as we proceed
Here is a father with a good heart behind love's gate
Will cast my lot amicable to all my kin forevermore
Have heard that prudent reply more like a bad deed
This day is not a solace pact treading behind us once more
Our friendships are not inviolate, only for certain people
My intentions are chaste, having good will in my heart
We have hopeful choices showered with goodness galore

Our conscience has reality speaking for itself each day
A resounding bell keeps waking my past as before
Get rid of all those that are like the days of yore
Have been frantic to send these menaces out of my way
My surpasses of merits leaves them as personal off beats
Being a man of the times shall close with my good grace
The church says we should pray for them, it's all we can do
Have been deceived long enough with their lies or cheats

THE MEMORARE CATEGORY

Seems like two worlds considering everything
What were previously learned facts as well as past experience
Come ridicule people in hidden places riling up the works
We become deceived as for the reasoning one could bring
One quest is to be off the victim list they put us on
Made for only the sake of argument that captions erased
In my prehistoric mentions have amended these faults
As for the menaces of society two wishes they are just gone

When these type of people raise that flag it's a false sign
They say please believe us even if we are a disgrace
Here you go this man has learned catch twenty-one long ago
Stay on your own black cloud nine you will be fine
My steadfast faith will keep me on the best side of life
Seems every year have to forward another phase with smut
Them good Samaritans of my kind say how precious is love
Forever they're out there stabbing the back with a knife

All of life's pathways behold are never ever the same
The point of view stressed watch out for deceit
Among a group is a pact if fulfilled for alienation time
Here us false folks are lets find another to take the blame
It's a very strange dude anticipating in cahoots there
Such romping's for the sake of being a galoot person
They are three son's of a who daddy watcha call it
Three's a company besides there's two makes a pair

TAUNTS IN LIFE

Comes a sudden taunt that pauses in my path once more
My everlasting thoughts come up every day right at dawn
For a time a landscape full of memories of my past
To think we are edified in knowing what's really in store
Once more comes a thought able whisper that taunts my heart
Being humble can be my guide for peace sake once again
There's not much freedom to wager a man soul sometimes
Comes the absents of old friends from a dead silence in part

Each picture memories in rooms that shadows us there
Have reaped that awful sense of sorrow once in a while
These taunts of every kind makes me feel down
From each lesson in life's place there's another time here
As if someone's name marks the spot in our past
How vacant that feeling of wonder who's next to go
The gladness of morn can turn to fate, before days end
What ever life has in store it has only little time to last

No one should bring sinful baggage to a good man's door
Come read the good book from Friday until Monday
During the course of it all comes absents of faith for some
Looking at religion from old days till now, some bad to the core
The very thing you think is right for you has been found to be
bad
These heads of church had been involved in awful things
To apologize does not cut it, being an inhuman act
When you check the war days things were so very sad

BEG YOUR PARDON

A caption from the realm's insults always
The content for conscious human affection is to care
Would inspiring them, get most to understand what's best
Texting defaces public union a real menace in it's ways
This era of life out from an old man's door is demure
That father of time has deceived our strident youth
It's like being in a house with no windows talking to the world
Each mind is contorted to a display hidden emotions for sure

We are not being refined we are declined with no thinking cap
It does it all for you, without gizmos we would be lost
Upon our world there's not face to face talks like before
These telephones, computers etc. makes landfilling crap
Better to do a resounding loud bell have people look up a
while
Beg your pardon do you have a moment away from your
phone
They go to laughing looking into their phone, otherwise no
To grin at someone in their phone it not a candid real smile

Are old ways really lost in time as gone forever more
Where does everyone go on their day off out to cell ville
With someone conversing they are told to be quite it's cell time
Here everyone sitting not talking with cell phones galore
All our wants are different in this world that's to be
Everyone has old as well as new opinions in which to share
We are not like the dog that kept the ox from eating
For us all it's suppose to be a peaceful free country you see

AVID PARENTS

A boy named skip a chore guy for many a year
While at my parents home cut wood all winter long
One day became tired of being the sucker doing this
Had threw in the towel being through I was sincere
Was sixteen now big enough to fight back to win
Not a child no more told to do it or else was not the case
Began to wonder who would cut the winter wood now
My life on another farm was about to really begin

That week was sent to Mr. Jefferson's farm to work was for real
The farm was in Trenton about twenty-five miles away
Sent me there with rags on my back, not a cent to my name
Had shoes with holes in the bottoms, slipping up and down at
the heel
In the daytime worked in the barn shoveling manure
everywhere
Was out plowing all night with lights on the tractor
A boy under the age of eighteen had no rights to deny them
Every month my parents came to get my paycheck there

Worked day and night by chance had a sleep in the mow
This work place was revenge against me refusing to cut wood
This farmer feed me one meal a day, ringing a bell to come
In summer lifted wheat bags into the seeder for him to sow
My feet were blistered was a thin as a rail, just grief to see
Could not understand being treated this way, the others not so
One day was eighteen took a months cheque ran away
Today own a house, have money had to set myself free

WHO DADDY VERSION

Some people spend all day staring into a gizmo texting
Then the question comes up a bout obese people
Seems a world all of their own in a silent room
They create their own death mission do it while driving
Having sound mind and body not sitting, doing other work
With every answer no one has to think with their wits
The old school portion of calculating has past it's era
Because they have found out now consider themselves a perk

For my reputation will stay with the old methods now
A man's money can be spend on more logical things
Here is me with natural pasture never peering down
Even though a fellow like me refuses but he still knows how
These electronic gadget people get rich off of some fools
When everyone gets into the trend it becomes a fade
Here we go with qualities of possession look I have one too
To look good in a crowd showing off then only vanity rules

This man tries to keep up with Jones, if his credit card talks
A must to pay as we get means there's nobody we owe
People want to borrow money from us, we never ask for none
The saying about some people money talk bull crap walks
That childhood money was taken, nobody now takes it away
from me
All my ambitions with education put me in standing today
Such whims in life are being with down to earth friends
No one shall put a sunder, todays happiness will ever be

WILD ONIONS

A special time in the spring when leeks do grow
To the bush with eleven quart baskets to gather leeks
This type of wild onion went good in egg salad sandwiches
These plants would sprout near where a stream did flow
After we had pulled six eleven quart baskets went home
Such nice salads were made from the tops of these
Was very good with home fries along with bacon and eggs
Next weekend to the bush for more leeks did roam

Could not understand a transplant in our garden died
But back in the fifties were able to grow Spanish onions
Took the wheelbarrow brought soil along to plant them
Using lots of manure to grow leeks again we tried
Seems they were a self nurtured plant picking their spot
A little bit of a leek went along way for home dishes
Wild animals did not eat leeks because it burnt their mouth
Where these wild onions grew was moss and tree root rot

When we were children there was oodles of leeks
Have gone to woods today there is nary a sign
Our environment must be in a dire situation today
Where ever you walk in the woods is dried up creeks
Any plant needs water to survive, but it depleted
To reforest our ravaged land it's a lot to late now
We have not been nature people like the old Indian ways
Nobody seems to understand in this planet what's needed

THE BRIDGE

I stood on the bridge at midnight
As the clocks were striking the hour
And the moon rose o'er the Belleville city
Behind the dark Church Street tower

For a heart seemingly was restless
Still a life being so full of care
So much burden of life laid upon me
Seemed greater than a man could bare

Whenever I crossed the Moir River
Such a bridge of cement had it's shadowed piers
An emotion of water heading into the bay
Comes the thoughts of those left years

To think how many times to come here
As long as the river of shadow flows
As long as the heart has passions
As long as a man's life has woes

So liked those waters rushing
Among them cemented piers
As a flood of thoughts came o'er me
That filled my eyes with many tears

How often oh how often
In long ago days gone by
I had stood on that bridge at midnight
A real sad place to go to cry

WINGS OF HOPE

Lets say hello to old gossip stuffed with grandeur years
Have those crumbling words of hope been redeemed again
To have followed the beat of one's desire overflows with hope
A part of truth from my heart carried on while yielding fears
Things are not always as right as rain waiting for a new day
In life this is where I am this is where I was in lost pages
A keen heart of a blind archer having missed the target
This man carried off wandering in depths of dismay

Was unable to find a pass key to a door enclosing good luck
Did travel those roads of life really that goes nowhere
Knowing there's true light of life beyond dreams it's at
Being old now slow wheels on the landscape to be stuck
We grasp the weight of time held forever in a heartbeat
Our dream's of hope become silenced a sad part in life
Again in that empty room comes whispering being to late
Now armed with a heavy heart, there's nothing to guide my feet

Evening soaked with sobs worldly memories fill my space
Some faith follows me bound to nowhere a sunset day goes
Comes again tomorrow for a grieving soul awaits again
The sun after dawn should maybe better this place
A grandfathers crumbling words for another spent time
Soon the sunset is perishable for us all lost to the world
So much peace with no dreams of hope to wait for
All doubts silenced into the darkness they will decline

WITHOUT FELICITY

As for our febrile fancy, some things are plain enough
There's a paltry day of being merry or optimistic
Always remaining with an apt expression leave it
For all that comes my way is refuse, wanting to stand tough
Some people on the kin side give you the worst kind of day
A bearer of abuse have pledged to put these people down
Such a sceptered race of odd people please don't cross my
path
So tired of being scorned as of now there will be hell to pay

Think me as being utterly quaint but just a casual air
My bliss is all used up many years down that road
Make your sessions text your days then stuff it
Make your paltry day in your own back yard I'm not there
Those forbidding trends are noxious for my faith
Otherwise pledge your marring hopes on a lost line
Fare thee well with your fardel of joys stay remote
Those who lie shall find their own accursed path

I was blind but now I see with such amazing grace
Such personality has strained my heart to just let go
If people do not act like adults it provokes me much
Now as a grandfather have some better logics to face
Must refrain from grief, had my fill from that life's story
Some people are actually born bores with smiles wiped from
them
If one wanders far enough you will find a few crackpots
When you have focused dynamic times there's no worry

FOLKS EMPATHY JEST

The old time saying such as doheckabvia per say
We become amused in events to arouse conditions of a
moment
A word deheckabvia can be labeled to almost anything
May history talk in your faces about the kit caboodle day
Our kin related things to the whole kit and caboodle origin
There is no products of choice with the whole kit and caboodle
Another way to say it is da whole kit and caboodle
When she talks about the whole kit and caboodle where to
begin

Here we are in an English speaking faithful world that's not over
When there's a predicament we say 'jumping Josafat'
Remembering all these jest people used back then
In those times people jumped from one self image to another
We have derived so many sophisticated words from ancient
places
Came to be use from jumping on the band wagon for say
Many English as well as German people brought it about
The beginning of it all from Bible times among the races

During boyhood years it was common to frequent these jest
Was wondering as to why people conversed like this
While visitors would eavesdrop if they were French
When someone says jump on it, being hurrying at it's best
Sort of a monumentaling language of sorts to rue the day
Another made up language was pig Latin not known to
strangers
Was great for the old crank phone party lines long ago
We altered the English language no one knew what we had to
say

PUFF BALLS IN FALL

To be that plenteous for puff balls no bounds out there
Went along an old Indian fence close by to the woods
Have awaited for this day in morn to gather puff balls
As you walked the fence line so many everywhere
A place where cedars flourished blue jays crying away
That shrill voice was insistent like say get out of here
Maybe it was their part of the world all of this time
Had filled four large hemp bags here on this nice day

We could only use one full bag the rest shared with others
The neighbors came to my car trunk for a couple of these
These puff balls taste good fried in Mazola oil a while
On the following morning fried them shared with my brothers
They taste so much like mushrooms when fried this way
Another method of cooking them is butter with pepper
Even with bacon and eggs a very nice early morning treat
Allowed other people to pick their own on another day

Some puff balls were left for a month or two
Every puff ball left behind turned to a yellow dust
Was told the dust was seeds to be scattered far
One day these dust balls disappeared when the wind blew
Year after year by the old fence was plenty more
They could not be transplanted only by the fence they grew
Those days gone builders came to build houses here
There was enough for everybody the same as before

MANY RESPITES

Many a misfortunes to have floored me
Nothing more fatiguing then ruddy misfortunes
Before a day ends it must have a beginning to wake to
By noon one could count each individual blessing to be
To what stage of a day is best to look for wishes
First you look out the window then go for more coffee
You are beside yourself cannot find very much to do
It's like the bowl you just go round and round like fishes

Pitiful follies lack theories from old times to new
With so much woe bent double spells brand new trouble
Have come thus far from a gray world of ill repute
Them horrible times of unrest finally a man out grew
Had indorsed now better times with glimmers of hope
Leaving behind the untruths forever to simmer
Such a whimsical duration badly frayed with strife
So much there with no manners at all one could not cope

In mind thoughts a haloed day is bound to come
Still the wrath of yesterday for shadows my thoughts
The unadorned proclaim there's judgment for us all
To want good things to happen need an encore on a drum
Using authentic words will not cover up by gone ways
So uncouthed with an unfound place in the society forever
Call verbal pin points massed just for starter days

A SEEDY REDE

Each life is devoted to purpose, the method of logic
Unlike others can be caught up in a beat of our own
Let beauty be undisclosed to justify ourselves
Every haloed day for sure claims a good verdict
Again that long ago gray world still simmers away
Thinking about how much time was wasted back then
Always wishing things would change by choice
But never challenged my impulsive heart that day

Should have went with my daunting moments for real
My wayward days where not sensible ever
In terms of sensible logic was optimistic in the long haul
Every part of farm life was noxious that's how I feel
As a whole they were a sceptered race of intellect one's
They were confounded forbearers with only lost hope
That act or fact of sudden devotion found a new life
The farms today are dying because of educated sons

Found myself going daft talking to peaceful eyes
They proclaimed me the centre of attraction them animals
Seemed each of them looked through you not at you
With these kinds of companions it's short lived then goodbyes
Have stood many times in an open doorway wanting to run
In spite of it all an open road past that doorway gone
Everyday cultivated a readiness for a hundred miles after
Had bib overalls with rubber boots a typical farmers son

MATURE MODEST FOLKS

The gusto of life's aspects are sate for some
But some formats have their geeks to contend with
While looking at the gist of it all be my self
There is not kin enacting in a fitful way like scum
Here we are mature modest folks with good thoughts
Nothing is more refined then modest folks like us
Must be greater things then woe to rule one's life
A resounding voice comes to our phone casting their lots

Let not that illustration rue the peace of a good life
Our demurs control every instant we will perform
These certain instances remain good in our peaceful place
Whence comes tomorrow we want to elevate this strife
Those grotto's are rare but do rant with attentive muse
Here we are in wonder staying modest people forever
Them eager words seem to fall on deaf ears now
Our courtesy should be an award, as for them it's of no use

A must to remember modest moments precious to us all
Pass this dilemma when comes our diligence joy
We only uphold those modest folks of our stature
As good people there's always budding moments people to
call
In hopes not like old times no bad scenes to contend with
Onward one goes avoiding calamities of our times
Give me strength to understand what makes people odd
As for a reason some kin folks being like this it's truly a myth

WAR TIME FOOD

Am a fud representative that lived in the war years
There was tokens with rations limiting our food supply
We had to appreciate it with ne'er an instance of complaint
Most people were able to afford pam, on every table it
appears
Then came mac and cheese loaf a sandwich mans meal
What amazes me is through our despair stayed healthy
Hard work must have been born in us from pilgrim fathers
On through our deliverance all family hardships were real

Being strong armed with might our triumph it brought
So gallantly we strived from that heartless enemy
In our house hold with sealers canned food to keep
Did everything in our power to survive while soldiers fought
The chocolate bar was a scarce commodity back then
Even sugar was in short supply, especially the brown
With pure of heart got through our miseries of old
Through praying with hope as a Canadian do what you can

Can remember there was no sliced bread in any store
Cereal plus oatmeal there was not much of it around
Through this time of struggle collected asparagus in the bush
We made homemade bread until flour was no more
There was leeks and watercress for salads and soups
At every meal everybody said "grace" that's not done
anymore
In this land of plenty who stops to thank our maker
Today it does not matter even no dress code for our troops

WHO PRAYS ANYMORE

Past on into the streets of time who prays
As we wander along roads our ancestor went down
Todays people do not think to thank for anything
The same roads the pilgrims struggled for in those days
That road is already made all you have to do is walk
Our push button world has made most of us obese
With head bent down looking into an iPod thing
Down that by way you go with free hands just to talk

In the church the young crowd don't even view the epistle
Here they sit or stand talking to one another there
The whole time conversing to one another during the sermon
As far as they are concerned do not care if it's a sermon or
ritual
By word of deed shall endeavor with hope always
From where does good merits come, should they know
Here the preteen stands eluding God's word once again
They must be thinking about invocations of muse days

No religious devotion, remaining a hypocrite there
Better not to be a moot of wonder it's questionable
The method of logic determines everyone's fate
Should one be daily in church where everyone is pious here
Man kind must be ardently devoted to purpose it's true
These are precious moments for an hour in this place
Only have every heart beat, every breath think words of praise
That great art of courtesy naturally it belongs to you

THAT CALGARY SIGN

Sand molding was done in aluminum star place
Worked as a molder way back in the fifties
Were told to start making a Calgary Stampede sign
The sign was one hundred feet high plus it needed space
Also it was one hundred feet wide, a huge thing
It took a whole year to mold, then complete the job
This being a bull and a horse large as it could be
With man plus machines this project took some doing

Took teamwork in the shop as well as away out there
The packing part for shipping was also a real big chore
Our sign was of many natural colours scenery and all
When the job was finished nothing else could compare
Besides molding used the crucible to melt the metal down
Did two jobs rushing to get everything done on time
Everyone made money on this outlay of good work
We all received bonuses when the cheques came around

Worked for Stan Carvarda for a several year span
Even clothesline pulleys were made by me here
A partner from Czechoslovakia brought die casting to use
There was die casting for three models was his plan
The Calgary sign brought more orders to our plant
As for me worked at night in the Morch building
So much business now having a night and day shift
People came from hard wares to buy was so much to recant

MY ARCHAIC KIN

For belonging to an earlier period Grampa farmed
His main occupation was a butcher all his life
The bad habit he had to be chewing tobacco then
Every one of his teeth in his mouth it had harmed
In the house was a spittoon making a twang when used
A cud container for his stuff was in his bib overall pocket
The clothes hanging up could be smelt from yards away
His whole life of chewing tobacco his body was abused

He was a horse farmer for many many a year
Such a mean grouch to humans and horses alike
Had a horse whip on every equipment he used there
So miserable seems he hated himself it did appear
This man cursed from day to night, ne'er a good word
It looks as though his ranting put people uneasy forever
A man that was known for bad deeds while cursing a neighbor
Seen him kill a cat one afternoon cause it had purred

This was my father's Dad they sent their son to an uncle's place
Because this grandfather beat on him every day
The uncle's wife made a big chocolate cake one morn
She gave my father some meat with vegetables was the case
Then she set the chocolate cake in front of my Dad
He finished up his meat with vegetables to get some cake
His aunt took the cake away saying I fancy you no like
As a boy my Dad was in tears from such people being bad

WHOLLY FROM THE PAST

That poised manner where you never go anywhere
Forever that pungent air that never went away
Whence to be ardently devoted to a purpose of discuss
The odes to the creek was a cow flap array there
Such a place stayed with old ideas having no hope
A place called Denfield was so far off the beaten path
Only one driveway that lead directly to the barn door
Still remember the hay loft with it's long brown rope

About twenty feet from the house was a pig sty
That pungent air was carried right to the kitchen door
Expecting a nice summer balmy breeze without smell
The wooden screen door was amassed with many a fly
How unpleasant can a day be with ostentatious formats
To retain something smart mentally it's not pitching hay
Being enthusiastic for sure it will not cut it
Every time we use the manure pile on out came the rats

Spent a few years waiting for someone to tell my future goal
Had so many ideas that became meaningless in the end
Only a flock of wild fowl seem to have a sense of direction
My mien at the future had a lot of misfit ideas all toll
Here being in the world of lads not much hope in the burgs
The previous owner must have been short, this basement was
low
The English people that owned the house before made some
brew
Our musty old basement always had lots of cider jugs

IN LIFE'S SILENCE

There's those oft times for all of us life is late
Here looking down that empty path that gets emptier
For some that earthly home is not needed as before
Them drifting clouds looking for a lost souls fate
A sighing wind crosses that lost path once more
Will hear a forever voice through the willows by a rippling
stream
Trees no more shall have to shade one from the sun
That earthly home not needed as in times before

My heart felt moments let me ponder through a dreamy night
Have left my pillow for you to dream on as of now
In the silence night waits one more time for morn
Them phones of life no longer answer at day light
No fear for warm hands during seasonal change ever
There's my kind of people that pray to the end of time
To be pardoned with peace in life's silence events
Every deed has been marked in good faith forever

Our gaunt world has reaped a common sense feeling
The hills echo with voices that keep calling my name
That eternal life has waters of reflecting images
Each momentary image for life enhancement is repelling
Had watched happy scenes in life turn to sad
Everyone's compassion should always be around
His powerful might will guide us through it all
Must keep up the sensations of trying to be glad

OLDEN GOLDEN DAYS

In that goodly portfolio there's treasured pages to hold
To stand in awe with the best part of our days gone
On hitherward to these graceful times we came unfolding
Once again fame will burst from it's somber state now old
For the time being was not trying to be an inferior kind
So well remembered that stone church it's bell that rang
Must be a reason for being cast in to a world with quaint places
Was like a chamber setting of desolation very hard to find

A family humbly born on a farming place so long ago
Still will never forget those nights of prayers said
Such a shock that change of face from young to old
Having left behind us our youth now solemn old did show
Forever aspects of long ago this life still sustains
Did come a long ways on a perpetual road of hope
For our old times this life needs some peace of mind
Gone not forgotten them by gone days with it toil and pains

Was like passing from a well worn road to a quiet nook
Here we satisfy ourselves being subdued to a decree
Almost facing momentary gloom no gusto in our life
Them olden golden days fined tuned now in the time it took
When one becomes a seer they can see ahead what's to be
done
Must be trow times for circumstances in which to perform
My logo humour rest on my moods of the time always
Even the prophets sake nobody rules a life equally
When you get old as me only walk because you cannot run

THAT EXTRAVAGANZA

Once in a while people want to be grandstanded again
One more time comes the sound of music in my space
In every respect make the best of times once in a while
That splendor of friends rejoicing will for ever more remain
Comes the waywardness foreshadowed by compassion days
So fulfilling was love songs even in the gramophone times
It's our divine nature to have heartfelt songs forever
With devotion we accomplish what set out to do as always

We abound with good feelings by having pleasures that day
All are welcome to come sing along when there is nothing to
do
Some people have an earthly realm of perseverance to do
things
An acoustic guitar hangs in the study for someone to play
Make an expected hour amid your busy day to enjoy things
Better to uphold happiness then be down in the dumps
The ramifications of a fore time is to make life happy
To parley with a song is more vibrant good tidings it brings

On the journey of life enjoy one another's glad moments once
more
Here is a home that has all the country songs ever written
Some are endowed with the reward to be able to sing
So much fulfillment in life with these love songs galore
With easy listening songs so much joy always comes here
Lets get gathered into a group to participate with good times
Sometimes a need for a feather in one's cap is very nice
When one mentions friends there has to be some sincere

So many dancing songs existed in days, now have gone by
Had the Heart boys playing songs in our teenage times
There was Lorne and Donny Meeks played guitars at halls
As for me and my brother Tom to play guitars we did try
A man would be inclined to say indeed you are welcome here
It's a forever honour for everyone to come to my home
Let's have a group, extravaganza play guitars until dawn
Now with our elder days the whole family should be near

WITH SILENT MIGHT

For my sake self esteem gets me where I am going
Have the patience of a Job with piety as well as affection
Eventually will become infatuated with only nice people
Shall approach the place where tomorrows peace I am
enjoying
Use moral courage to restrain that resentment with self control
According to me holding to truth words have always been
sincere
Let's mention that there is no one besides me to mistreat
Whatever is commendable shall keep on doing that's my goal

Some put themselves in the lamplight by forfeiting others
When there is manners in life where no wretches belong
While trouble brews that genuine desire has become
independent
What's been deprived from life the fault is all their mothers
Should understand the sincere part it what this man's all about
These forever going ons is that which surpasses all
understanding
Hope they will be envious of the father in time to come
In judgment the iniquity they have committed leave lots of
doubt

With compassion eliminated where can one go from there
Have a trustworthy side of life along with those imitators
Amid the uncertainties of so called people who do you trust
How come some are born with human likeness, some beware
The word that challenges an absolute day is just pursue
Being a father's indescribable future having deep knowledge
of things
Was envy people unable to inspire me, abstinence wanted well
Such a supreme advantage of knowing more of what to do

The most practical part of life is self confident part
If the father is convicted of something, what is it then
Them person using lies, best to hush them where they stand
Have never found out what's bothering them from the very
start
As cowards shall never shed light on that son ship thing
For my sake have established honour, but yours is disgrace
There is no one close to the father's heart in a humanly way
Forever hidden in the depths of misery no real hope to bring

ANYONE'S VALENTINE

Those school days the girl you liked received the best
All of loves fond words found in a heart shaped card
That grand moment of receiving a card saying you are mine
Also for a special reason valentines were sent to all the rest
Then there was other girls sending sentiments your way
So many times love comes in a mailed card from a far
During this month of February a special for special people
Them moments of long awaiting for such a day

It's a betiding world buying enough valentines for all
Such a card with a heart said what's best in two lines
With so much choice to pick from what could go wrong
Was so into sincerely for the times this guy does recall
There came hints of nostalgia for them long ago days
Remembered one little peck on the cheek it was so long ago
A small world so it was back at our country school then
Here the future still finds us holding on to heartfelt ways

An old day role call sending joy where it had to be
Can you believe someone liking girls before age ten
Even now if the past where to find us let's be sincere
Lasting forever love hearts carved in an old oak tree
In those days was only puppy love just a heart felt fling
Was a ride home on my bike cross bar then a kiss goodbye
To becoming my valentine forever the thought back then
A young boy thinking this girl with braids was everything

OUT OF SYNC

We now are the old one's many days did pass us by
Here we are standing apart from some opponents
The conclusion for our behalf applied unwanted
There is envenom forecasted with that alienated cry
That old time saying is we are good enough to be envied
Cannot imagine as good image folks confronted with grief
This out of sync portion with dubious mental quotes
A grandparents love so important unjustly denied

Such forbidding wrath manifested in a household
Non to swift is the function in relation to us anyway
Well the dystopia has no meaning to anything worth while
As beings they are completely out of their tree been told
Best son to daughter-in-law to become part of a civil people
Many good thoughts are deep rooted in my mind
Waiting for peace of mind to fulfill better days ahead
Are those who refuse to permit good emotions as a whole

Best to have no doubt or uneasiness among kin
Their act of instances are out of line, being flunky
For sure is an indication sign of being insecure there
Here my eager words surrendering good though, where to
begin
When guest get the feeling no welcome, you are betrayed
Having joy is much better then woe in family members
They made a spectacle of themselves grand scale
Them unordinary ways even from old times has stayed

AN OLD WELL

On a dewy morning as the horizon sun grows bright
A long ago place with only the rural scenery to view
Was a pallid day now thinking, all them years shadowed there
All gone that shadowy ancestral ire far out of sight
Lurking in a minds vision that well for drinking water
Some how my thoughts of yesterday emerged once more
A long haul slopping water trotting down a path to home
Bringing pail after pail of water for washing was a rotter

Our place of gloom with pastures with a dull sky
So many chattels rendered in a live long day
An urban place where poor children had to be born
Was all hard work, me being the unfortunate guy
All of that remorse seined up travelling down memory lane
When each morrow came with boredom made me yawn
The act of instances rendered left no time to frolic
Everything talked about from long ago was such a pain

Many times a day seen drawing water from an open well
Some days the pail of water had a mouse in it
We would dump out the mouse then fetch another
In the middle of summer the well went down to nil
Had to go to Harold Nickles' place a quarter mile away
Our water was brought in milk cans on a milk cart
Such a change from drinking dirty water to real clean water
These cans of water had to be hauled every single day

PARDIE OF YESTERDAY

As personal credence shall arouse moments of yesterday
Want to censor every query to it's very utmost
One should factor in respect it's part of daily life
The past shall be muted saying farewell for such a day
Such a prospect of impressions not of a nice place
That ranked lingers from old times without love
Out of an old world has been proclaimed that woe
Here's a man that's face the foe seemingly a bewildered race

Not every person seeks out to delight other ones
My life will always be captivated as Mr. Nice Guy
Treat me nice treat me good treat me like you really should
But it depends who's out there could be one of my sons
Wishing all the joy in the world but a kibosh ends it
These squelches are in every little town like it or not
There's a reputation to render for me being true to heart
Being my custom every afternoon to dream and sit

So many old time fretters for fathers were no fun
The Pardie follies as a manner of speaking are blunt
Be the man head of the home back then suited his fancy
Shall ornate with emphasis cursing got things done
Was the gusto of them times enacting a crude life
Talking about far yonder on an old dusty gravel road
Them coffers of yesterday with very little money to go round
In those times every farm boy owned a Jack knife

NOTEABLE TIMES

That children's circle of growing up
All those memorable words said
Such notable times of children's talk
Those by gone years with thoughts to recoup
Bud a walking up from Grandpa's field this day
With his little dog that he took everywhere
To recall thinking the dogs name was Tip
He was a boy of few words not much to say

One afternoon he arrived at our Plainfield place
Walked Bud around showing him afar fields
While viewing the land told me he will be a cop
The intentions was being an OPP was the case
His words was a goal for his life's career
Being an awarding job among a distinguished few
Those were noble words for it to all come true
Even though while hedging I knew he was sincere

Brother Tom seen Bud at Camp Borden one day
He was taking training for to play a cops role
Nothing could be so wonderful as the uniform he wore
There was lot's of truth in what Bud had to say
Had a lot of gumption that really was to behold
Not a place of fun and games it's a reality part
Without any question he was a great friend to all
I did tell part of the story but there's much more to be told

WEEKENDERS

On weekends have found people that while away the time
Such a short duration waiting for the time to start
There the old fishing hole awaits all this long week
The old creek scene in days of yore was so sublime
A clue of hope rest on Weekends with good fortune there
Them ventures path to go hunting in mid afternoon
Having spent most of the day with a sun filled sky
To wander wooded paths where game birds I did scare

Still undaunted have come to resist the hot noonday sun
As for the Weekenders there's a poor mans friend indeed
We are sons of misfortune money wishes with endeavors
When you are young it's a portion not a blessed rich one
Will be only a poor worthless part of life to inherit
Here was another daddy belonging to the very same race
What else can a Weekender do but do ordinary things
Onward our freedoms go forth when we can really spare it

A poor man's day of work a day God send Sunday
In the shades of a darkened hall family pictures hide
So perhaps for all it's related to a down beat race
On Weekenders time will go hunting on a Monday
This Saturday several fellers played cards for a spell
That poor man is still waiting for ponderous periods to fame
To have effectual callings no splurges to a final goal
We work all the weekdays for wages not anymore to tell

THOSE ASPECTS OF DURESS

One afternoon while working at Maurice's place
My job was a sub contractor for Maurice Rollins
The police came to the job site to arrest me
When I ask what was the charge no answer was the case
They transported me to Napanee prison on this day
With no judge or jury nor a charge, was wondering the reason
This cell reeked with urine making me sick all the time
Their jailer told me to be quiet sit in my cell with nothing to say

When meal time came around porridge with maggots was fed
There was an open toilet to do number one and number two
A pail on a hook you filled with water to flush the toilet
At the far end of my cell had a cement slab for a bed
The cell had no lights so you went to bed before dark came
Was a guard at daybreak ran his billy across the bars for wake
up
So much wonder as to way an innocent man was here
Could not wait to get out of jail, find someone for the blame

Spent four months in Napanee prison, no cause for it
When time was up here could not afford a lawyer yet
Wrote letters to City Hall's judges with not one reply
No one wanted to pardon the wrong doing or admit
Wanted consideration for being incarcerated without fault
No one came forward for forgiveness for their mistake
Where are all the rules of conduct when they are really needed
Their moral principles should tell them it was an insult

SOME CANNY MINDS

In this bestriding world some have inklings to deceive
Not so genuine as they make themselves to be
Seems they are rendezvousing with ways to cheat people
They think people are dadders being completely naïve
So avid in their ways with ideas generally are bad
These are dubious affairs obvious the cheating kind
My intentions are to parley with hints of distrust
Best be evasive about making a commitment, be a nerd

That one man's destiny is to indorse his real intentions
Will always come to a pious moment to assess life
In a solemn manner good people let modesty rule
The trow time of circumstances teaches it's lessons
If it's not by word or deed it's full of misdemeanors then
Some wait for last will testimony not for love but for money
Was them instances that they seen that denial came
To be a laudable custom choosing the right woman or man

The trite moment came for manipulating old folks
Here comes the old sob story of not being the chosen
Within a heart seems to whisper be aware of things
The predictions beckon me to be aware of culprits
Their art of scamming not paying workers is the case
My endeavors reach out to truthful people every time
Having being lead to false belief wanting it excepted
 To such a degree or extent I am the man who owns the place

AN OLD BUCKSAW

So many old methods of logic we have to do
To keep the home fires burning had lots of wood to cut
The old bucksaw with elbow grease filled the demand
During the course of events there was so much hullabaloo
Wood placed in a saw horse as the bucksaw cuts away
Chunks of stove wood after stove wood piled there
A lot of wood cut every day to keep our house warm
Had to keep cutting wood after school every day

Every limb of wood came from Isaac Pierce's place
Here in the old apple orchard was lots of fuel
The dried apple wood burnt very well for sure
There was cedar cut in lengths for starting fires just in case
Being whole hearty there's bygones being rehearsed
Keeping the house warm was an essential challenge for me
Others enjoyed the day while I did all the sawing of wood
Again unfair issues should be censored or cursed

So much coddling goes on during the coarse of events
That peril in life will lay claim to a scanty rebut
Them same tones of urge to keeping up supply and demand
That old bucksaw had no idle times making wood contents
Was an old fashion way on an old fashion day
Onward we went to hue more trees to warm our place
Nary a day goes by my father's hauling loads of wood
Only one child had time to work others had time to play

HEMP ROPE SWING

The rede behind the manner in which children live
A real good dad makes hemp rope swings for them
Here children swing for hours enjoy themselves always
What makes your family happy is the little things you give
This simple poles with rope love is in the making of it
A good image lies within one's heart a need to take part
Good faith begins that journey of hope for us all
These swings, teeter totters and sandboxes are it I admit

On down the pathway's of good grace presented here
The sate of a father is the way a home should be
Comes the gist to guide us with real sessions quo
Such up in the air we go flying again, a little bit of a scare
Seems I have left behind me youth days of a family now
Such a perpetual road my youth then the youth of my children
My father pushing me high on a swing next my youngsters
On weekends it's not all fun and games there's grass to mow

In the family portfolio there's treasured pages there
That backyard a real amusement place back then
A sin and a shame today my old house everything gone
Where these playthings was a gravel laneway here
My old home elderly people own this country place
The house is run down as if life had left forever
An only indication memento it was there the bird feeder
Was a desolate place full of weeds everywhere was the case

A FERRET BOX

What shall an eye behold in scenes from long ago
Will always remember the hard times we did have
On a Saturday afternoon with a ferret in a box
We walked through the fields with a hunting dog did go
The dog would chase a rabbit until it went into a hole
As soon as this would happen our ferret went in
Our ferret forced the rabbit out the other end
Each time we captured a rabbit soon four in toll

These cottontail rabbits were very good to eat
This was our meat through the hard times then
The stewpot was filled to the brim in those days
Was a help when we ran out of other kinds of meat
Also the tanned fur was good to make winter mitts
For good luck all of us had a rabbits foot key chain
He the dog had all the rabbit head for his great feast
Our old hunting dog got his rewards as on the floor he sits

That white ferret for his commitment also was fed
The ball of white fluff was a regular nice pet
He would curl around someone's neck then go to sleep
As soon as the ferret was put in his pen got a rabbit head
The ferret every Saturday was frisky could not wait to go
In the box he went then the box had straps to my back
One day our buddy the ferret was very sick then died
Like all the other pets we made a cross by the fence row

THEM KISMET CHATTELS

By word or deed through life get something in return
Came out of despair of hardships now triumph comes
During the clangor of it all hope came to be there
Those doing bad deeds, obnoxious ones in hell will burn
Only as a couple us have carried out our earthly plan
Them demis are at stage three hence getting there dues
Befall the surfeit of the past swindle ends here
In years gone by her mission was rip off who they can

Amid the sighs come time to reprieve what's ours
First of foremost this squab will get what's coming
An act of goodness we will be awarded some time
Nothing is more refined the modest folks like flowers
For every crossroad of life there's attitudes to face
As for some people being scammers without any respect
Such as our endorsement muted those to the utmost
Life's a conquest like snubbing foes is the case

While looking into the great eye's of wonder is misfits
A wise intention is to avoid them forever more
Out there is crouched scammers waiting to spring on prey
Have scanned my emotions using all of my wits
Came a long way on a perpetual road for peace of mind
During each trow time of circumstances got through it
In old times inconsiderate foes had no regard for others
Nothing is justified in dealing with the rebuked kind

ETERNAL TIES

Telling such a story reaching into yesterdays kind
Being part of travelled gravel roads of long ago
Lets make the images to fill that old picture
Here a yonker one with only fishing on his mind
A can of worms in his side pocket with his fishing pole
At early morn is when the fish bite assumed by all
The collie dogs hair was full of burrs from head to foot
Walking along at early dawn, alone not ne'er a soul

Here sun up reborn to start another beautiful day
So much logic to getting down to the fishing hole
Maybe catch a whopper to make a day worth while
Would be nice to boast about the one that got away
For every generation from youth to old memory paths
It's like a night time landscape disappearing until morn
Thought times set in solemn hours parleying there
In the silence of blatant moments focus on rathes

Unable to be able to restore all of them old dreams
This humanistic mar overwhelms every aspect
To retrace foot step treads they are not the same now
Maybe bleep out an old pathway try to arouse old times
Come out of your house wearing a fedora type hat
That long ago concept would make people look twice
Had to say to others it's me doing once upon a time
Was acting out my old demis, trying to be modest for that

RACY ODES

Those pathways in the distance came a long ways
So many potions to contend with as we go
Looking at dusty pictures with a mind set there
We are all on a solitary journey of hope from old days
A foggy morning reminds me of a young heart of suspense
As of now it taunts me undaunting from long ago
Came haunted whisperings in my ear old jeopardy
From a particular time of abuse still makes me tense

So much in the past came blatant moments whiles
My pillow has held many a bad dreams right from youth
These ado's go head long into a night time landscape
With hope had visionaries of many folks with smiles
Waiting for happy modest one's in a peaceful place
That nice side of life where the world would be fine
Have censored my past to the utmost of how it was
Giving out amorous words indorsing what I had to face

A young life of so many scenarios to go through
Everyday managed to rid crouched shadows of old times
Was moral courage has brought me thus far
Them entreating moments of goodwill did pursue
So many things come to mind more whole hearty then before
Must have been a reason for the cast of a lonely world
That perpetual road led me to elder days at long last
Had summoned my grateful heart finding love once more

A PASSAGE TO HOPE

Our hope is the most potent thing in life ever
Here we come unto tomorrows road with wonder
The silence of alone walking towards the sun
In solemn manner while jostling by a quiet river
That is like life sometimes we whisper sometimes loud
So much peace that had beckoned me here today
Was a solitary journey hearing nature for a change
A place to be inspired being a lone traveller without a crowd

On through the moments of the day taunted by my will
Being old now going on my own time to revive my senses
Had paused once in a while in thoughts of old friends passed on
This earth around me seemed out of motion so very still
With mind cessations to inspire the mysteries left there
Nobody to call out my name anymore like ghosts on the wind
When you call they say try your call again, number unknown
No one to sing songs with anymore really near and dear

Here is me with a powerful might guiding me on
An old heart here full of good thoughts untold
From there to here all those years passed no more
Waiting for an old friend to cross my path they've gone
When things finally got better a man is too old
A journey must have a beginning come to an end
We know that to the here after will be our final move
A man will sleep forever with no washed clothes to fold

HOPE RELIVES

Let hope relive from morning with a cheery onset
There's a social union where mercies are defined by us
Comes daily things to taunt you nine times out of ten
Most problems are answered by prayers, best not to forget
With a blessing gets us through each dreadful day
Every time the priest replies as we confess, it's undaunting for all
When goodness stands out hope comes soon, close behind
We cannot all be the chosen few no matter what we say

Somewhere a kind of memento of how many bad days we
had
Like another given chance come out of that squalid mess
Hardly enough room in the length of day to turn around
A wha week for awhile some ho ho that fate thing just to be
glad
Within frailty things, comes hope to win, one does recall
From this time forth pity does not make anything better
Such as an Adam clause do things proper or have
consequences
More or less one must define sin a choice of purity for all

The fact of hope is a feature to be justified each day
During torment of debts hope is the only reprieve for us
How drab life can be in the reality, we all come to know
Where mercy is defined there's a need for us to pray
With purity comes regard for happy precious times
Pay no attention to inconsiderate foes that put you down
There's the worst of days that taunt me especially winter
We are here to do our best until the last final endly claims

LIFES SO PRECIOUS

Let our days be fashioned where everyone's civil
Here we be as God grants each of us tomorrow
Forever a portion of life to be immeasurable
A time allotted for each of us is frivol
To suffer what was brought unto each to bear
Having mingled one thing with another in pure hope
Was times of doubt but more easier to try to console
There's nothing so obvious of all things in which to compare

An outreach to eternity forever he will stay
In a precious place where heavenly thresholds unfold
To be entranced by the spirit of this holy one
A host of chanting angels took him to a better place
Here within the realm of heaven so far away
All of God's angels, Bud surely they will love
Only good thoughts remain, knowing where he's gone
Such a wondrous holy light all around on his descent
The heavens light of true warmth so vast from above

After life is a dauntless journey for us all
That concept of eternity reaching into the sky
Have held steadfast faith in the most Godly one
A believer, it was the plan for these utmost to recall
On that someday soon we will get heaven's command
Hosts of angels come to take us to another place
For sure in reality his goodness of heart lives
Some new found place in the here after is where we will stand

BENIGN ONE'S

To always be a friend let love be tomorrows pulse
My memory takes good thoughts everywhere with me
Being good natured requires much love of the heart
The hype of it all coming down to forgiveness, what else
For peace is measured in silence on my very own time
Most dull moments, whisper somber tones not to be heard
Then shall cast the first joyful sounds, other's then will follow
Our self esteem once in a while will not cost a dime

Even though someone is beautiful they are not perfect
After all a benign style should rule the best of days
All should have an open mind without personal bias intact
These great ideas are a sensual thing, we have come to
expect
Wear a smile for your umbrella, being a worth while thing
Have looked at pictures everyone puts on a fake smile
When viewing worldly people per day, they are not happy
These photos are created with a smile that is more inviting

Each mornings smile caters to us having a better day ahead
In every life a little rain must fall. Face it for a while
There's always ways when faith is on our best side
Let's dismiss the odds of prophetic one's great minds have said
Given powers over life's love, would be divine for all
Every morning outside the door emotions run askew
Days will serve their ends and with whatever faith may do
We all do what we have to do, just let the pieces fall

SO AWESOME

Comes the timeless feedback before we are aged
How must we free our lives from most earthly cares
To have perform miracles would have to be a different rank
Will bring back roses again comprehending a time to be
enraged
Those written prayers control all the goodness that brought
Have been given my conscience for a good direction to follow
Something that last is nice to do, with a righteous touch
How can any man explain the concept of all thought

We fail to set our goals because of what we dread
Most times will not have any use for peoples reasoning
There is no doubt when angered a reason to shout
Every day, repeat a greeting "good night" before going to bed
Our secrets we whisper remaining secretive forever
Here before my weary eyes stands another long night
In sleepy times we will go into another dimension
Be somewhat lacking in style one's being over clever

These parents are our pilots to make us fly right
Have always blushed when caught in a little white lie
We know childhood years were not exactly perfect
Even while an earnest plea of goodness is in sight
All should adopt a better discipline by using our charm
Had looked on childhood years there's nothing perfect
What we mostly regret is the ungiving of true facts
Everyone needs respect never to bring about any harm

MODESTY INDEED

While some memories tread back to yesterday
Do not regret bad friends they are best gone
Hate sucks the life out of well being every time
Two faced foes are not worth the time of day
Come live in my world with good thoughts for everyone
On ringing my doorbell I am not home for belligerent people
When one door closes another opens with rid or to be
A good deed pattern cut from the right stuff is how it's done

Whiling away love a void remains in it's place
Good fortune finds you late having pain no gain
Also one never misses what they never have
Just call me Mr. Kind mind I'll answer that is the case
Come to bear with me truth is my best answer
Best to tell the way it is do not fudge an answer
In the here after one cannot change that curse in life
When one lies it's comes back to bite you like cancer

The old saying is blood is thicker than water is the case
Would like to sleep through it all when trouble brews
Those bad omen ones plague one's mind indeed
Best not to be a worry pot put joy in it's place
Worry finds life everyday without searching out there
A good life's plan is to challenge things for the best
My worst part is lost in time end of a bad story
Today now elders have found people that really care

GIRL FRIENDS

Two young brothers with girl friends was the rage
We were courting girls whenever we got a chance then
My girlfriend was Donna Bowman next door
The brother Bill's girlfriend was Phyllis Roberts, he's seven years
of age
These girls where courted inside the church privies
Having the thrill of it all kissing while hiding out
Them privies had two seats where we held hands
Me and Bill wore a tam with a suit we called skivvies

Walking to school with the girls an every day thing
Our parents were never told it was our secret
We bought crackly nut popcorn to share with the girls
Inside the crackly nut pop corn box was a golden ring
The ring was given to the girls pretending to be engaged
A couple of real Casanovas in a very young world
The thrill was beyond our wildest dreams for so long
In our thoughts if the parents found they would be enraged

After we moved away these girls where forgotten about
Had later found out was only puppy love not real
Still at age ten we never thought about any girls
We became more involved in the baseball, who to strike out
The vigor of sports in readiness for a once a year field day
Our Coles school were hard to beat winning every year
Nick Nichole made us illegal bats driving a ball out of sight
No one else touched our bats every time we did play

DAYS ASUNDER

There comes matrimony for dramatic times ever after
How sweetly comes a time of love to sooth one's soul
Them whispering where like bad breath in the wind
Unable to change my feelings in heartfelt moments of laughter
Have been above my pillows of bad dreams for a while
An old time saying if a woman receives a ruby it's gladness
Every dream of wonderful land last a short beautiful time
Want to see kind faces in everyone with a pleasant smile

So much distance divides us in this ambitious world
Unable to be modest in this era of old times reborn
Within my space comes friends from all sides with love
These are traditions like old sweaters being repearled
Comes scenes of solemn hours every day to parley with
Let's not hast hope it will come along on it's very own
Them days of penance as well as days of prayer seem to help
These ados go head long as blatant moments of myth

A touch of beauty is helpful in getting a good reply
Having good looks is only skin deep we still need to strive
My thoughts recall them barefoot summers as a boy
Having watch moon beams climb steady out from a nightly sky
When silent times came by still hear voices from afar
From young to old a divergence of feeling haunts my soul
Them first rays of sunshine from youth until weary days of old
But still to come along is good or bad in this humanistic mar

MAESTRO UNCLES

Every Saturday night during the summer days
Our uncles Wib, Wally and Ed played instruments
My uncle Wib played the mandolin, a real pro
Then uncle Wally the acoustic guitar he plays
There was uncle Ed that played the Hawaiian strings
Can still remember the song ghost riders in the sky
The way they played it sounded like hoof beats
Here sitting my thoughts of all the joys it brings

Another great oldie was the "Tennessee Waltz" tune
While they played you dreamed about dancing then
Once in awhile Wally played alone, Gene Autrey songs
These songs were "Back in the Saddle Again" to croon
Then came some Irish songs like "Tura Tura Light"
So old is the song "You Are My Sunshine", but still nice
A real old one was "Vagabon Dreamer" a very sad one
We finally played out all of the songs by midnight

There was always the next Saturday to come about
We always wanted my uncle Art to come play the fiddle
He played "How far is Heaven" and "Golden Slippers"
For some reason he was always to busy to come out
They had a band called 'The Pine Toppers' in their town
Was a huge family of fourteen children just some played
Their father played the tuba in the Salvation Army band
Sometimes my uncle Art played the fiddle at a hoe down

A KITE

Us guys made many a kite but none would fly
My brother Tom did run like hell down a hill for lift
But when it was suppose to fly the kite nosedived
To make it sour into the heavens we really did try
We tried attaching more silk stockings on the tail
The cawing of near by crows seems they were laughing at us
Our kite looked the same as the neighbours was
No matter what we did the flying part did fail

One day we decided to go to Harold Nicholes' place
As soon as he seen the kite he knew the problem
He said each side must not be the same size
One half of the kite must be two inches was the case
This way were told it will tilt into the wind angle
Our kites now had souring ability to climb high
Such a relief seeing the kite sour on upward
The kite went up as high as the string with no tangle

That curse was gone, now it was deemed to fly
Made even higher kites going were eagles sour
Now there was no fault with the craft it went up
There was also balanced tail weight in which to apply
We found things for flight had to be made a special way
Harold Nicholes waved to us from a far giving a V sign
This man was like a father to us showing us lots
Here we were out fly kites almost every Saturday

WIND IN THE WILLOWS

Here looking out todays window to a far off place
Them windy willows keep calling to me in long ago
The old fishing hole called Catfish Creek in thought
Out of personal bias them forbearers in a young space
Down a dusty road at daybreak times hard to forget
My old trusty line and reel getting ready for a bite
A lunch was stuffed in my bib overalls pocket
Under my favourite willow all day fishing I would set

Had a pegged line to keep each fish on that I caught
Such a nice place to be on a warm summer afternoon
Once in a while the willows sent a nice breeze through
Here a young boy fishing using a lesson my father taught
The willows seem to welcome me every Saturday
Would like to go back to walked down this same path
A path lined with golden rods in the fall of the year
Before I leave this world would like to go back some day

It's possible that old black iron bridge is still there
Maybe go down to the creek side skip some stones
Then throw a big stone in the water for bullfrogs to jump
Was such a boy back then living without a care
My favourite hat was the bring 'em back alive one
Was an outdoorsy child with a dark brown tan
In dreams young life keeps calling out to me
Them long ago days doing everything under the sun

A RED MANTILLA

By night comes girls red mantilla ruling the way
Behold in those days an attire of red garment travelling along
To be modeled to be envious for the best attraction
Being a shrewd contributor of attraction day to day
Such women's ambitions to be eyed by men back then
Among the flirty women here you will see her
For olden days the red mantilla with bright red lipstick
Here or elsewhere these women seek whoever they can

An old tradition seemed to work so long ago
These days was to fetch a rich man if they could
Was obvious it brought fond friends this ago time
In an old care free world flirting was all they know
Such a persuasive kind of woman to catch a man
That red mantilla surely found their husband
Those fond memories was how women played on men
With no education being a housewife was the plan

Todays world is not a naïve place for the male
The education part rules the day for smart ones
These smart men do not parley with red mantillas
Our men of this time laugh at an old time tale
Have cast old tradition along the way side
This new era would condemn the scenes of old
That bright red lipstick is not used for a new trend
There's not such simple lives now we have more pride

SAP BUCKETS

Tapped ten maple trees along the fence line
With my hand drill it was a lot of hard work
A brace and bit was the tool used to drill holes
Every bucket to catch the sap was all mine
There was ten spiels driven into these trees
Was in February drilling and tapping took place
The sap was gathered during morning and night
Some maples were bigger with spiels in threes

Every Saturday the kitchen table had many flapjacks
Each weekend was worth waiting for such a treat
There was no thanks just was a good Samaritan type
A morning table had four piles of flapjacks ten to a stack
Had a good flapjack recipe the mix has lots of lumps
Was put down with the saying thank our Lord for trees
My remark was to thank the tree and me for your sake
It's better to give than to receive then stay chumps

As for giving there to many people, greedy ones
So much work went into making syrup for all
The sap was hauled to the old kitchen cook stove
A big vat was constantly filled one of my concerns
This kitchen stove had to be stoked once in a while
For the sap runs it made five gallons of syrup
Our house at Sparta for every year made maple syrup
When the job was finished it took down the woodpile

A COUNTRY DOORYARD

An old frame house setting far back from the road
Here a big white gate met the fence at laneways end
Every morning just outside the door a tabby cat greets me
Was early the dew was still on the grass that's unmowed
Had to brush cobwebs from my face under the arbor gate
A few steps more an old pear tree with pears to eat
We grew citron a kind of watermelon that's good to can
The garden was in need of attention in a weedy state

Our house was rented from the Hippleas out there
Us boys had to walk three miles to school each day
On going to and from school two German shepherds came out
We had to carry a bit stick for protection from that pair
Made us hate school because we were always tired
Was a bell free that rang out loud right at nine AM
Outside privies were common for those times
An old rusty tin roof it's painting time had expired

Was an old house we lived in that creaked when a wind blew
The front veranda had already rotted all away
A laneway that had grass in the centre out to the gate
Everything about this house needed replacing brand new
Could not go out the front door the veranda's not good
For milk we had to go to Hipplea's farm for some
At middle of summer the well went dry a truck came to fill
Many mice came inside this house that's made from wood

PHANTOM THOUGHTS

Each day of life it's cares we let be known
Forever hold the fond memories in our heart
With so much goodness wrapped into a lifetime
Left such a golden diary in ones life to be shown
Our lives have a possible dream we all walk through
Those lost ones are like memorial statues there
Now all these open roads have their lonely fields
The whiles we live soon we become alone it's true

As we walk in life's sunshine the darkness is there
So many attention dreams comes to remind us
Forever blessed lives then forgotten the haloed yields
Here leaving a phantom landscape in a realm to beware
This is the plodding of lost dreams in dark corridors
Out of life's hope a whole world of ours gone forever
Still we hold onto mountains upon mountains of memories
Along a timely distance to be lost ones, comes for tellers

The book of times never closes it's like seasons
There is one thing for sure we came from lonely to smile
Most of all comes those seasons remembered not forgot
Being best never to be forgotten we have our reasons
Out of life's memories a whole world for us did wheel
An every so often thought has it's many perceptions
Within a household a golden diary delving the pass
One must and foremost hold on to memories I feel

WE ARE THE WORLD

So much difference in stature everyone one of us
A true Catholic will pray to find new peace of mind
While enhancing our future comes them overwhelming roles
Our hearts often have tawdry needs making a fuss
We are tethered by life's woes when money is lean
No matter what tomorrows ideas are, the results very
By altering some facts brings more content, becoming lax
Out of these days needed to find some more esteem

Have seen self conceit, those thinking they are God's gift of
man
Once in a while our lives are construed by demure things
Based on real situations have learned to forget and forgive
So happy for a morning sun, it begins an all new plan
Often times doing what we dread, but it has to be done
Here in memories a store room with shelves full of remorse
It's told that's the reason we keep things of sorrow hidden
With untruth there can be guilt with everything under the sun

All of us need to be awaken from demented dreams
Some weeks are shrouded by parameters of discontent
Always accept old age with humor it's a better style
There's love that presents commitment, always best it seems
That worshipping part is always better before we reside
On one of those days most find new hope abounding with joy
Forget about demise let it be of no concern in elder years
Be thankful for our health along with a whole lot of pride

HERE'S MY CANDLES

Have lit up candles for my great love sake
Some keeps blowing them out every chance here
They do not understand friendship only hate
To happiness they must light so little time to take
Come out of them crouched shadows see the light
Through the ages life is precious so make it loveable
One's logic is important for visionaries of lives
How good tomorrow would be out in plain sight

In making friends they will stand by you forever
A stranger is a friend you have never met before
Should not curse commonsense it liberates life
So daunted is hate we need love it will endeavor
Let's brush old curtains aside lighten up this place
Our conscience best lead us to a good feeling part
Every life requires a great deal of love, for good mind feelings
For patience it's ingrained, courage is one's self heart
Here's a lot of friendship it only needs a place to start

When giving gifts of love the notion was already there
Deep down in my heart my good graces are forever
All my good blessings are being pledged from within
Among the dado's still the presence of an old rocking chair
To be infatuated by a rustic rocking chair so still
Many grandchildren were rock to sleep in the afternoon
Wishing to count all the candles on their cake each time
Wanting to see a child hurrying upstairs at free will

ETERNAL TIES

Was in life so many stories going away back then
Not at any time was it precious or loveable
Better to paint thoughts as they were long ago
Making logic a visionary of the times from age ten
No need for pity to inspire good feelings it's not the call
Them confound days of yore confirmed at birth
How good tomorrow will be depends on who's sincere
One's life is like being confined behind a brick wall

Be better not to educated anyone just be a farming son
The haunt of life is how to get away from it all
A no wit pitchfork man working in fields of time
To be fourteen to be brought back every time you make a run
At age eighteen one if free to go choose your own life
Will not cruse commonsense it's time to be liberated now
To be a course changing on a good fortune type place
By age twenty two had a house along with a wife

When looking upon each phase let's change the mind set
Old times like edging night skies bring on the darkness
Every day a gaunt world to face in them old times
Let windows of life bring more daylight without fret
Adept ourselves for decisions to on step the wiser ways
You're welcome at my house, but leave sinful baggage behind
Must think it's odd to drench all good days with prayers
It will help reluctance to come here one of these days

MY AMOROUS WORDS

May some of my comfort be held in tether today
Always to indorse love for all hearts in my mind
Being on the nice side of life make the world be fine
Be kind wear good will on your sleeve, no hear say
Each mom to have happy faces, no nostalgia guff
Have breached my thought with farewell to yesterday
Once in a while breath sentimental sighs that it's over
Now off times of better days make life more kind
That old dull world of woe now is gone so far away

For every crossroad there still attitudes in mind
Here is one man having a hint of loving respect
As for my personal credence will arouse the rejoicing part
Once in a while lavish thoughts known as expected kind
Them snuggle episodes give you a feeling it's family
Our past as well as present unite here nothing will change
We are them old saintly one's that stood the fates of time
Have gallantly arranged our life to be friends willingly

Did remain pure of heart from the trodden dust we came
By word or deed we have endeavored through it all
During the clamor of strife hopes sake is there
Best be strong armed, cause might you hold no blame
From out of a place of despair so much triumph it brings
Must have true hearts in the course of our events
There's no issue to remote challenge it as before
Every family stride together with all good intention things

MODEST PASTIMES

Long ago times forever waiting for days of calm
In todays world best stay modest while others go bad
Without any interruptions for conniptions that's my role
Then comes monitory wondering looking at my palm
Most days want a door to slap my butt on the way out
The best answers to protocol be sincere it's better
Have given weekend moments a time for to vent
A man from a hard fisted place will always have doubt

There is judgment marks greatness, quakes the day
Again in my twilight of love have a whole lot of time
My modesty prompts me to inspire each individual
Life is not star spangled it's a gaunt world not for say
In histories says our world life after is eternal
Our hope is only desperation for our free will
Each life time is the fundamental inanimate
More or less our death is our final wholly farewell

A long journey from young to fud life but it's here
Onward we all must go now comes precious moments
Is it an illusion time gone so fast for our destiny
The scene of ballgames played having glory there
Still here a resounding voice from a far "batter up"
So many fitful moments wanting old to be young
The eager words only comes to surrender who I am
These elements of precious time finally will just stop

THE TEDIOUS DAYS

Sometimes are choices of amusement to enhance a day
Had spent most of my time looking at the old pictures
There was some people existent others were gone
Whether in life or death having forever roles to play
Have showered the moments with tears of regret
Here comes each notion treasuring long ago times
All of my moments defined thinking about folks
Had so many uplifting songs to sentimental to forget

At this particular time my heart ponders in sadness
So much life to adore to blossom then for death
All that striving for merit wondering the real reason
Was so many avenues in life then just for gladness
Today had a chance for my restless moments to vent
In a lonely room had parleyed here since the morn
My bygone relatives have littered history as heroes
Between the twain or the other much love has been sent

Another day of seeking elder embers per room
A redeeming part version seeing who's around or gone
All of them hardships planted in our old time place
This day resting on my shoulders is the old time gloom
Thinking ever yonder of journeys indulges of snow
A Dad in winter getting us where we had to be
Us children snuggled with blankets in a cutter traveling
That voice resounding from back then with giddy up go

UNDER MY ROOF

An old house with oil lamps smelling all the while
Among the vanished furniture a rocking chair there
So much wonder in this building of old by gone years
Within the rabble of long ago such remote style
Half painted walls of lathe board a spectral somber of ah
Seen elder dusty pictures here browned with age
In an eager moment found mold behind the sink
Seem the furniture was hand carved by the name I saw

Midnight comes stirred like a spiritual member there
When a grandfather clocked bonged enough to wake dead
This clock also a handmade structure from a maple board
My place of the hour stilled had paused for a bonging affair
Here was my poised moment counting all of the chimes
Was idly sitting in an old rocking chair rocking slowly
Without rhyme or reason sat for hours imagining
Had contrived this night for peace of mind in oft times

An old life is pointless we have done our part
Left here with a calm mind no logic to anything
In a tense arena to tired to do a days work
Must be a better world beyond a chair place to start
There's knowing what's ahead you yawn about some deed
All the while your conscience is inspired greatly
Now confined by age only walking in a short space
The government pension each month is all you need

DEMURES OF LIFE

Such a heart felt moment with lots of despair
Those cruel time messengers now came along
The scenes of two stepsons not worth a rotten shingle
Have sat in wonder why are they with no care
While soul searching need to cast them out of my life
Her boy does not deserve to be part of our will
On one hand declared he hates his mother's husband
One son said I do not want to be your son to my wife

Them numerable haunts have left my mind wondering
Must be someone commanding her son actions now
He has no earthly passion for me or his mother
A business the son with his wife they are blundering
Best to leave a silent part for it all wash our hands
My wife Jeanette's son knows his mother has terminal cancer
This man does not belong in a place where there's love
We have people for the will loving back that's where it stands

Each day hurries onward not a whole lot of time left
My wife has four to five months left which to live
One cannot rest when there's manipulative people around
These inner emotions are disgusted with this pest
Being genuine is a concept that grows on good kin
Deep down in the heart is tomorrows grace forever
Our compassion is our pilot guiding us through life
Here's my space only wanting nice people to come on in

OKEY-DOKEY DAYS

Hoping everything is meaningful only a day away
When things are okay would say okey-dokey in old times
Everything in us should be great always end of story
Then comes the monitory wondering what best to say
Even during them delicate decisions best think a while
The point to stay modest let the rest do what they want
We can change ourselves but we cannot change others
Come you can do it think of something happy to smile

I am the earthly passion supporter each day
Always standing here to be scoffed but it's real
Then twilight comes before my rounds are done
My life is full of good deeds not a burden in any way
Best we search for a glad day it's now late in life
Now tell my visions in a wish that will really come true
On the highway of love we must all travel there
Have had enough of them long ago days of the strife

Even when life taunts us we are never to old to cry
Behind each memory in mind is glad and sad times
The kismet of life comes to us all in a later date
It's nice to be good friends but bliss to say goodbye
That matter of wonder the living ever needing love
My act of courtesy being indorsed every time
Seems this man's emotion are defined very attentive
But words can be outspoken when push comes to shove

COLOURED STONES

Down those roads of gravel to our one room school
When it rained the coloured gravel stones would show
Our honey pail lunch boxes were great to hold stones
Us boys would sell the stones to people with a fish bowl
Most village folks had goldfish numbering four
The fish bowl sat on the windowsill at the sunny side
There was lots of pocket change from stone sales
When we sold them a few stones they always wanted more

The pocket money we made bought crackly nut popcorn
Inside each crackly nut box was a golden ring
Our girl friends ended up with the golden finger ring
With this gift could walk the girls to school every morn
Us guys Bill and me were all the rage for them olden days
These rings were a symbol of friendship for two years
This went on until our family moved to Yarmouth centre
The gathering of coloured stones for us really pays

Russ Bowman came to making many sales back then
Other boys copied us by picking up stones to sell
These crackly nut popcorns sold like hot cakes
So many thoughts of memory lane with puppy love moochin
Out of that forgotten life the future was up ahead
Only have become a remembered place in time so long ago
Those lines of life have been crossed no going back ever
Have never looked back found a real love instead

OIL CAN SHOES

Harry Tilberries garage gave us boys empty oil can
We made oil can shoes by bending the middle down
The cans then fit tight around the sole of our shoes
On down the sidewalk us with these cans ran
These tin shoes made a lot of noise with every step
A Sunday time it was not allowed for the sake of peace
Within our thoughts amusement was our only goal
Very soon this became an all youth session to prep

Boys will be boys the more noise we made the better it was
Down the sidewalk we went clickty clackity all the way
Here was an old fashion day finding something to do with cans
Our idea became a fad all children were doing this
Back to the garage for more cans when a hole wore through
Being country boys at heart we were the rough and tumble
We the boys always came up with something out of the
question
A lot of children came to our place, there was things to do

We also set up races with can shoes ready to go
The winners got cats eye marbles for a prize
Had to run from the church to the general store
Us guys put on a completely noisy clattering show
There was people standing on porches clapping away
It was a good way to spend a Saturday afternoon
That era passed because oil later was sold in bottles
That old expression break a leg getting things to do each day

THE BLUE HERON

One day Tom my brother brought a Blue Heron home
He told us the bird had been caught in a muskrat trap
The birds leg was injured and needed medical attention
With splintered leg along with clipped wings he could not roam
This Heron was put in with the chickens to stay
Here with a long beak with lanky legs looked out of place
He seemed to enjoy his new home eating grain there
No one could touch his chicken family he protected each day

That Blue Heron was king of the pad you found out
Do not turn your back on him he would spear your butt
Other times came running after you with his beak
He was a nasty bird to deal with there was no doubt
When the chickens went to roost he went there too
A hen went on the nest to lay an egg he tried also
His neck and legs were to long disabling him to go
The nickname given to this ugly bird was Mr. Blue

Each morning the roaster crowed he tried too
He would scratch for worms like the chickens do
So many things he learned from the hens there
Some time later he would come when called Mr. Blue
One day we let him out of the chickens pen
The bird went down to the creek for fish then returned
His food consist of a variety from that day forth
He would go away for a few days but returned now and then

FRIENDS FOREVER

Have sat alone moments, reposed each thought
Old scenes that seem to rest midway of oft times
It taunts me like to whispering in ear forever
An old weary heart so much happiness it has brought
Having friends are like beautiful flowers in our days
We do not need vanity to flatter only noble honour
Our odes lead us to the splendor of wonderful things
In need of pleasant hopes readily forecasted in many ways

Them gates of once upon a time are still open
Comes that onward stride of intent for one's love
Our errands are in good faith always everlasting
Let's paint a nice picture with all hate being gone
Them memories are like the sunset always reborn
So daunted is friendship to be plied to life
Deep down in my heart is genuine things forever
Such blessing from the book of faith it was torn

The conquest is easy there's more of the same
Did look in memories store room to see who's there
Being not remembered is like a song that's been unsung
Must go hither or go back from the place I came
Should one cope with things or just be in our thought
Without rhyme or reason comes these trumped moments
We are like composers leaving our good words forever
These days of replaced joy in an old heart is sought

MY ORBS

Many a time have had orbs swirling my head
These heavenly spheres being not ordinary things
Have been told it's a sign of being a holy saint
With this symbol comes a powerful time to be said
This halo has many colours like a spectrum there
During the turning of a ring of coloured light force field
The coming of these started in the year two thousand
When this is just above me there's nothing to compare

Every time there is an orb forming it's a stand still
Must this be a foresight coming from a far
Within the orb prisms of multi colours flowing
The trace mode last for twenty minutes to fulfill
My almighty soul seems to have heavenly vision
A creation of some sort brought by angels above
Such a phase comes unexpectedly out of nowhere
Within the realm beyond clouds there's some decision

Someday that code of silence will tell it's meaning
The quietude resides about the myth of it all
A for bye special time is not optimistic in the least
In the remarkable moment all radiance is turning
Maybe a time will come to parley with Gabriel
Would be able to have a moment for some answers
Along that avenue of pondering will hear it all
That fact of consequences has a fact of goodwill

THEM REMEMBERED FEW

In a long ago village remember Sam a post office man
He was always in good spirits had stories to tell
Them boyhood stories of making paper snappers
A special way you folded the paper like a fan
The hand motion catching a wind made a sound
Then he put a coat button on a double string
It was rave among my classmates at school
This button made a humming noise going around

At home after showing our father this string thing
He showed us how to cut our fingers off trick
The string would go in around your fingers then pull
Now the string had to pull off without a finger sting
Then there was using this string to cut your neck off
Sometimes like this seems to stay with you a lifetime
In life there's always those people that ridicule all
There's always them few boys or girls of intentions to scoff

In the back of Russ Bowman's store a pot stove
During the winter people came to sit around here
There was one man in particular show card tricks
Once in a while he revealed of how to make the move
My father at home showed how water came from a penny to
me
Was great fun learning these great feats of magic
These moments of splendor never leave my thoughts
Them boyhood times there was plenty of tricks to see

PEDAL PUSHING DAYS

On a bike I poised once in a while down a country road
Seems my thoughts were on the old fishing hole
Past some water filled ditches of tadpoles there
The fresh mowed hay smell lingered a lasting episode
A brush cut boy on an old country road peddling away
That sudden irk of the wild push did help me
Here following me man's best friend with wagging tail
My collie dog his coat was filled with burrs all day

On the way home pick up mail on a concession mail box
Had checked the time on my Timex wind up watch
It was five thirty time to do chores at the barn
Before supper to off my boots and my smelly sox
Pump water on my feet with cast steel soap washed there
Such was an ending pedaling day had stretched to yawn
Now quietude lets me think where to pedal tomorrow
With a sigh or two it will be bed time very soon
At rest in wonder where that whole day had gone

The STP bike took me down many a country road
To the store to get a few things we could not grow
These were fond days having a bike someplace to go
Them weekends gone fishing these were wills of hope mode
Then came those farewell days to biking it had to go
My brother Bill and me bought a car to get us around
A model A Ford called a Tin Lizzy took us everywhere
In high school having a car we were nice to know

HERE'S MY CROSS

Them emotions of life are in loving folks forever
Have heaped up great moments of a lifetime
We must not abandon love for true hearts
Only resentment is heartless pursued never
In memories store room it's held on to there
Here's my cross it's not the only one that counts in life
In conscience there's a thousand words to tell about
Sometimes to follow you around should be loving care

Better to brush hate aside go to loves place
Them dearest joys are standing waiting for you
It will pledge blessings from within portions
Out from loving hearts there's still much more space
Each time is genuine it's a natural human soul
Here's my thoughts it could be yours who knows
Deep down mindset love is to-morrows grace forever
The hating part is not a pretty picture it pays a toll

Being not remembered through life is a song unsung
Most wholesome lanes to follow are all of good faith
Come serenading good thoughts nobody's left out
Best bad deeds left out there for that generation haunt it brung
Must set our years a pace let goodness rule every day
Come lend me your ears have only good things to tell
The jest uttered is my regular road I always travel
My compassion strides have brought me a long way

A LEGEND LIVES

That haunt of her footsteps comes to mind
Only yesterday she walked there telling me things
Amid my thoughts gates of time have not been closed off
Hence forth not in reality comes in it's sort of a demented kind
My perspectives are prophetic in a lot of despair ways
Seems there's never ending memories haunting me
Was only trite hope to thine or thee as being suggested
That everyday inspiration had no divine hope at all
The mission of many prayers had already come to be

Such a lady loved by all, forever reminiscing her love
Wish she could have lived longer but except it away
For the most part despair is what we wallow in
Always to be told she will be in good hands up above
My Jeanette had so much giving in her heart for all
The marriage years of wondrous moments armed with delight
Whenever someone brought bad deeds she overlooked it
If somebody lied these type of things was not her protocol

So many good thoughts are deep rooted in my mind
Her hope was in desperation until something worth while came
More endeavors in her grasp where not to be it seemed
This lady would rather give than receive she was this kind
In a solemn manner she would jostle through the day
Her intentions were inspired by goodness of heart
An image still in my mind of her telling me do it right
Was only a week ago that our maker took her away

MY LONELY ZONE

There shines that ruddy light from a street pole
After the twilight this beam opens up the darkness
The impulse of belonging leaves me in a lonely zone
That entrancement of these thought versions takes it's toll
In the wrath of my discontent comes clock sounds once more
Here in a man's room of lost ventures of a loving heart
Indeed comes gloom here it's sad she's not around
A vacant chair there to haunt me not like before

Was to my recollection she wished for a long life to be
At my lonely zone on silence has come to do this part
Had not wanted to interpret the sad chapter now
Them turned pages have narrow walls closing in on me
The scene today seen pondering no happiness to be found
Comes a paused world of indecision just wondering hope
So much hush in my sadness room with no one around

The darkness moments of widowerhood dreaded as can be
Forever thinking of belated times still possessing my heart
Those weary eyes unable to rest during perilous hours
Here on the street of my future only mystery to see
All my good words including deeds thrived just yesterday
Them winsome measures are hopeless perhaps now
That train of thought has heaviness as if doled out in dreams
Every endearment asks for attention every single day

NOBODY FOR ROSES

A bouquet of roses censoring my sentimental day
Now having only a beautiful moment left in my heart
Each birthday greeted with a genuine happy smile
My thoughts enhancing each precious word to say
As always was twelve perfect roses standing there
Such a gift a creation of a beautiful love potion
Had a treasured feeling of lasting romance forever
A token of our love awaiting in those great times of care

Have drenched the earth with prayers every day
With some morality of help in concerned moments
In need of courage to get me through the hard part
The want of my wife to get better but she past away
Those blessing do not make sense being all for nothing
A summery of regret, even flowers make no sense
Have showered my moments without rhyme or reason
To look out on streets of time some staying some going

Everyday wishing she was here, but nobody for roses
Like an elusive dream nobody there for me anymore
Had a long look in memories store room on a hubbub
afternoon
Her birthday is on May seventeenth with no proposes
Forever to make myself ready to sway past yesterday
Still so many good thoughts stay deep rooted in my mind
Forever thoughts remain etched in my home space
Have tried so hard to amuse myself for a better day

WEDDING BELLS

To remember the weddings my heart days of love
A life excels on times together making ends meet
Them inward thoughts rise or fall dividing up times
So many ventures recalling the first one push or shove
Comes serenading of thoughts in raising a family
When looking upon each episode a bad one the first
With all them misdemeanors was best make a change
Have no love for a two timing woman, my kids I love dearly

My thoughts are intermixed, cluttered by bad perception
After divorce came about disheartened by her disgrace
Now looking for happy endorsement to a brand new life
On todays time censored my will of the best intention
My lady died with cancer after being married eighteen years
In this woman found great virtue then a sad farewell
Something to be endured this unbelievable concept of life
That day could not help myself shed a lot of tears

In need of good feelings to form new found hope
The only earnest plea of commonsense is to just pray
Within the space of a year found a new girlfriend
Along with all my sorrowful times was able to cope
Out of a place of darkness life did blossom once more
We have been a great happy couple for twenty-one year
The book of life ended up with death in April 12/14
On through momentary gloom this man had to face
Had to travel down a hard luck road when sadness did appear

ALL ALONE AGAIN

To keep tomorrow still secure as can be
Have considered matters prematurely for now
Hard to say about my kept style it's time for a change
Would like to leave it in shadows like a fallen tree
Should one push away daydreams a vision to be gone
A wish to keep to-morrows dawn waiting in repose
The old world was loved now death took it away
An elder man is not soothed with sweetness as one

Them old days with happy hours now only sad
If I had an untamed heart would run away
Must be a reason for being cast into the world alone
But there is still a goodly portfolio pages to be had
Having past a phase still going forward for each day
For the sake of loneliness comes a familiar look
There's my yearning heart in the course of events
Comes those trumped questions of what next to say

Whole heartedly there's choices to rehearse for me
So many things come to mind in weighing life's fetters
The saying stand by me when you're not strong but who
Here is so much remembrance to quake life to be
Old scenes in thought vision my wife standing there
On down the hallway remote as it was a day before
Much comes out of a moment in reminiscing old times
Can still see her calling me from atop that stair

MY ABODE

Here is a farming mirage where someone really lives
A place of harsh stamina images of growing up there
Was a countryside of summer open fields winter drifts
Such a place where everyone takes no one really gives
There was no joy in it only monotony hard work events
Everything stayed drab from the beginning each day
Heard swamp frogs every night croaking up till dawn
Have proclaimed myself a middle person full of comments

These tense arenas of work fields had hardships going on
Morning till night trudged barren fields fetching cows
Seen the old plough horse grazing on his off days
If it wasn't for being a boy this guy would be gone
Recall a quick morning skirmish to breakfast for all
Come to mind the kitchen an aluminum coffee pot there
Also and old chipped teapot ready with tea for a few
Was a farmers almanac that everyone read to recall

My family abode being so desolate, the middle of nowhere
A fob of sorts with no intentions for the future
Many foods grown from ground with daily weeding
Our landscape of spiders to bugs nothing could compare
Them weekends chore of crushing eggshells for grit
A whooping crane flew over our house every afternoon
The crane told us that time chickens had to be fed
Here evenings at a run down farm house was lonely I admit

NEEDED GOODLY GRACE

Have looked down to pray to liberate my day
Alone my strength still reaches with heaviness of heart
Forever solitude greets me while reaching for love
Such things as love a very delicate one would say
As of now practical feelings impacted by fate
My hope has left grey pictures of sad feelings
In an old world we are not sure of anything in time
Here is a man needing someone to love in a lonely state

Again alone sitting in a journey of memories as before
So many lost dreams to contend with impacting me
A wish for a day of general joy for a weary heart
By times old moments appear in mind once more
Them good times marks the place where I like to be
Most afternoons cowering over lost love again
We are mere folks wandering through life awhile
No young spirit anymore only a limping poise to see

Wanting pathways to vary with other thoughts in mind
Must go to a solitary journey of hope this day
What's coming our way sometimes is not inspiration
Being a lost spirit elements that's lightly reclined
Seeking the good parts with a sweet "Amen" needed
Have thoughts of coming out of dark corners claimed for old
In constant hope of good things is where the future finds me
To atone my goodwill to the church one must proceed

PRISTINE TIMES

Fill our coffers with joy to perform best of all
Make this earth an eternal theme of goodwill
Let them be patriots when we find them out there
Be an eager beaver censure life to stand up tall
Out of the good chasms of human life a future calls
Behold a matter of fact the living is always needing
There's time after having fun for bad moments to interrupt
In the parley of life s great things a little rain falls

Old must not fail in it's hospitable duties to cheer up
While looking into great eyes of wonder caused humor
There always sense of humor to help fill one's day
Sometimes a person of vile self has intentions to interrupt
Neither faith nor fortune deliberates this kind of thing
Them bigots are out there, must turn our other cheek
Such untolerated grammar seeps through day cracks
They litter our good world with the curse they bring

Life can be good there's plenty of magic our there
The face of morning should be gone before noon
Overcome the blues greet people in a joyful way
Be always eager to smile it brings sunshine and care
Because we are old we do not have to be miserable too
Let those miserable grandfathers be lost in time
My blessing to always be pledged for all from my heart
It was the trend of old times with hating that's true

AN OLD PASTIME

Most of my abilities was fixing what was needed
On a rainy day would sit in the garage carving axe handles
It took four hours using broken glass to shape handles
The next day fitted two handles in axe heads then cleated
Them days there was no happiness for dogs and children
In those pristine times things where not up to par
Each prospect took time to make with no power tools
To make something was a lengthy task away back then

At night could hear mice pitter pattering about
My theory was to trap these varmints where they ran
Took a tall glass milk bottle fill it half full of water
Put a ramp up to the top of this bottle for a route
In the morning had five drowned mice down inside
From night to night got rid of a lot of mice here
But these critters multiply soon there will be more
So much coping in earnest showed that I tried

During the summer months made trailers from car parts
Using the wheels along with a drive shaft housing
Here was a trailer tongue with chassis to mount to
A strong box from wood planks for the load it carts
Every trailer made was painted dark green then
Each one of them was sold for fifty dollars cash
The rabble days of long ago was hard to make a buck
Through the years with fathers help managed to make ten

THE COOKS DAY OFF

Between four thirty and five went to a dining place
For my wife Jeanette as well as me to Swiss Chalet
Since we bought the house in the year two thousand was here
Such precious times now gone forever was the case
Life becomes like empty paper with more things to say
Them moments of heart filled times is no longer alive
Unknown the peril of life how long will it really be
Did miss my lady have been grieving every single day

We came a long ways with full devotion for one another
Here was our little corner of the world now left silent
Have gone through all those empty morns no love one there
A couples dreams now, lost hope nothing to talk over
On through time pausing so many moments sitting to cry
My old world is so dull now the courage is all gone
Most days are wretchful awaking here alone
Every afternoon is like stillness of stones to pass by

We always had our loving hands taking away the blues
So much caring in a household a short time ago
Them burning embers have gone forever, no more
In the closet is so many of my wife favourite shoes
This lifetime tale of love has been taken away
Our lives a beautiful idea filled with so much devotion
No more days of magic just doom or gloom for me
Amid my thoughts comes the longing every single day

MY EMPTY ROOMS

Every day comes the beating of such a lonely heart
Have just that ticking of clocks in each room
Some evening giving so much aversion to my thoughts
These halls with no footsteps has it's memory part
Such fond moments like sunlight in our bedroom
Those twenty two years come to mind many times
Always seeking lost paths is my ever longing thought
Only night shadows accompany me with my gloom

On this long trodden road misery has stood alone
With no rest have rendered another early morn
One life stands alone in yonder doorway forever
The episodes for tomorrow still more things to be sown
That book of love of life is only half written now
My corridors are all empty no early morn voice to hear
Must life be an illusion of here today gone tomorrow
Are we able to know the evitable, have no way to know

Comes forever restless days, the absence persist
Our life is like counting sidewalk cracks with an end
We have no intent of sorrow in life, your fortress can fall
Them prayers for goodness of heart you must insists
Here's my life with open doors for friends galore
A well worn path we will still frequent forever
The spirit of darkness is still with us all there
Was her way with people many times before

HEART AND SOUL

Since words were invented love takes over them all
Life is enthralled by wanted most solemn ideals
Our peace good will part comes before it's said or done
When mingling with work or rest both we install
Let engaged our heart and soul in everything we do
Make my day through wholesome lanes of life
Always try your best to shower moments with joy
To behold lend an open ear it's well worth listening to

Memory is like a summer sunset it will always be reborn
The conquest has incite roles with names on all them
For ever misdeed there should be a passion supporter there
A distinct speech is a gainsay theme right from the early morn
This concept started from the golden rapture with yonkers
Such insults exposed for sure is of an awful bad jest
In a land of bad friends wishing them out of my zone
With a good heart and soul, some people make you bonkers

Do not cry at my happy window go to a shadowy one
One needs to treat people moods in the right places
Maybe need more tokens of pleasant hope to flatter us
Them vain ones have no spot in my house be gone
Here a whole new set of rules transmuted elsewhere
The complex of it all is to stay in paradise lost
Be better to speak with peaceful people then assert myself
Must stay outside my circle or they can kiss my derrière

REMINISCING OLD TIMES

Them cold hard facts of life at first to face
A permissive wife wallowing in devious confound days
An out of sync of a proper person point of view
Here a man of good intentions she corrupted my place
Such damnation facts causing that unfolded hope
Without truth there's no guilt with loss of faith
Was that kind of dirt you cannot wash it off
These prophetic women one is unable which to cope

You cannot plea for commonsense it's a waste on my part
All the blessing in the world cannot change awful people
She cut her wrist several times in my bathroom
With a problem person you do not know where to start
One day jumpt off a bridge into icy waters of Moira river
The trucks came to rescue her as soon as possible
Had a troubled lady for sometime to come here
When they pulled the woman out she had a shiver

Words cannot describe what a husband went through
She copied a woman's signature forged a cheque
Stole gum or a chocolate bar when at a store place
Dress our children in snow suits walking without a clue
A sad state of affairs went on seems to eternity
With such bad principles a mother still kept each child
Here virtue was overlooked a misconduct ruling
How can there be an exception to omit this morality

HOITY TOITY DAYS

A commoners summer we happened to go there
Some trying to liberate themselves to hoity toity ways
We are a classy rank with a maid doing the work
How could anyone do such things with no money to spare
Will forever scoff the privileges I do declare
Here they sit as an attentive farce having their say
The old expression of pooping higher then your shirt
To bad us pilgrims had come to such a classy place
Me with my wife did a walk around seeing the display

Another time we were invited to a ritzy hotel place
The room service was called up to bring up some drinks
Her credit card came out right away to pay dues
These relatives where forbearers of a credit card case
We where so liberated in a primp and proper way
Nice to preen us in such an uppity perky fashion
Was trying to be fussy adapting to rich famous times
Us lot were trying to something we were not on this day

They were muted some time later to bad debt
The heart of the vain posh it tumbled down
No more world of credit cards to lurk about with
A saying flat on their keister that they now are set
How they tried to flatter us during hoity toity days
We are going to be millionaires she bragged to us
While pacing our kitchen floor recited this speak
Now comes poverty unable to afford hotel trays

LIFE MERRY-GO-ROUND

Many changes has thrown my life into chaos
So much wrangle on my horizon from day one
Have found no peace only churl with upset always
Always shining my shoes either for funerals or weddings
Did come extremely adaptable to making decisions
Them yesterdays to climb over trying to reach the future
The main theme of it all is blab people ideas
Maybe things will get lost in time is my intentions

Have come through three crossroads for life's sake
Did tumbled the rocky patches many a time before
Has not been a sentimental journey experience
There comes more oppositions with other roads to take
Keep nurturing sad goodbyes with it's woe predictions
These idle moments are compiled with no prospects in mind
Here sitting in a room as a castaway inhabitant
What has a man done to deserve all of these convictions

Take care people always tell you see you later
To advocate good will assumes everything is alright
The contrary part comes along when waiting for luck
In life's wide path of predictions luck does matter
One should take time to read an epitaph they suggest
When it comes to showing normal signs there's affection
There's a source we are always waiting for forever
So many thoughts crowd my day of what to do that's next best

GRAVELSTONE TIMES

On the roads of time remembrance dwells there
The atavism of pictures brings old memories back
From them times till now have been searching four leaf clovers
Them old lanes of life have invisible spirits forever
A landscape swept away by time for many heartbeats
There was war misdemeanors but we managed some how
Someone brushed the curtains aside creating a new scene
Here was a place for dreams just waiting when it starts

Had to say "Amen" to prayer time to get to long ago
Again my dreams head back to yesterday once more
In the midst of scenes saw Grampa with horses plowing
Beside him fields of hay ready to be put in store
An old farm dog, a true companion, was always there
Far off a car whizzing down a gravel road dust flying
We had to prosper through hard work no welfare back then
These days of push a button world this could not compare

Comes a morning that shrouds glens with church bell sounds
Here square back cars heading off down a gravel road
A family always wanting to acquaint themselves with God
Our resolute of will power was from dawn till dusk grounds
We held good blessing thanking our maker for it all
Was undaunted fortitude of pray together stay together
Those places in time of sweat to yield wasn't easy
An old saying back then together we stand together we fall

TORNADOES UNKNOWN

During my growing up years in Canada had no tornadoes
The skies had thunder and lightening with lots of rain
These storms with lighting set buildings on fire
Then came the invention of lightening rods episodes
Many trees were split down the centre by lightening
To remember at night to see streak lightening flashing about
Some clotheslines attached to a house lightening came inside
There was cattle being hit that lay while dying

When two thousand and seven came we had five tornadoes
First a thunderstorm erupts then a tornado follows
A funnel extends to earth with a forward motion then
After descending from clouds many miles across fields it goes
They are still ongoing today never knowing where
The thing that brings them about God only knows that
Suddenly the sky turned pitch black then no sound
One day on the four hundred highway this man was there

Now a days when you hear thunder watch out below
The saying is all hell will break loose very soon
We must understand the emergency response guidelines
Everyone must find a basement in which to go
In the Sioux Valley of First Nation had five homes gone
Our mother nature raised it's head in long ago times
When there is loss of life most when it touches down at dawn

HALFWAY TO HEAVEN

When comes the light of another day it has life's pace
On through them streets of time for our own sakes
Nothing could be better for days that lay ahead
Most times set apace by a healthy creative space
For every mind with commonsense values to do better
Some days filled with love, other days fill with awe
Then years set apace by how much money gets us going

Most wholesome lanes of life are bound with fate
One day was brought to hospital being very sick
Was diagnosed with hepatitis along with brain infection
The luck of the Irish was assumed it came to late
In a few days went into a coma with not much hope
Here was my body on the bed with me looking down
My body was at peace with a spirit being heaven bound
A day a doctors faith with life support which to cope

After a little over three months sat up in my bed
Some all mighty magic took place on a wonderful day
The parents dried their tears welcoming my return
My mother said God made it possible no to be dead
He must have had something special for you to do
My life had merged into writing books from that day
Since being a poet love has taken over presence of mind
Hope in prayers will always be there for me or you

SLIGHTLY BEFUDDLED

There is always a message according to Murphy's Law
Do not shoot the messenger his offerings are sincere
Them ruddy words stay away from our house applied to Dad
The frailty of these children growing up is what us two saw
While pondering, wondering what her grudge was all about
Did persue the passion part striving to make something work
Our right disposition had been dashed for some unknown
reason
Must one ask why the love for united friends be in doubt

Could someone send a message enclosed with that mystery
today
For crying out loud there must be shame for such awful deeds
Only holding some faith which otherwise was controlled by
deception
There is not justification to condemn a nice father this way
In accordance to it all what is the purpose of this intent
Having splendor of heart is part of this man, but immoral is them
So many false meanings handed down for marring the truth
Amidst the pleasant part of me, want a happy message to be
sent

Even part of unity has no remedy, as for elders good standing
Again meaning is overshadowed in dealing with two faced
aims
There is the old saying be damned if you do be damned if you
don't
Have tried with all my devotion with a lot of intent demanding
Here is those oppressors slightly befuddled like the new dawn
Seems forever daily comes that feeling some are nasty hosts
No one is trustworthy on the sibling side they tend to lie
The disappointed part is awkward, always a portion that's be
gone

While getting to the after thought two people can play that game

All bad tidings exist that's customary for each fact being told

Whenever sadism abounds indeed there will be great problems

Somebody will find many a sad story caused by that shame

Since long ago life has been contrary conduct part of an old role

As for the same purpose honest splendor will be getting it's dues

Have forever endurance of commonsense to help me on through

From the beginning of my childhood was a bad situation all toll

SYCOPHANCY MADAM

Lets meet a salient with her cronies arrogant as hell
Nary a smile on the grimace of submissive woe ever
This world with those who dwell there is some nasty kind
There is the netherworld surrounding such people in a spell
The whole caboodle are compelled to making false doubted
dues
Here is a coward hidden by a shadow plaguing a good man
A woman not withholding to the truth in an awful deviant way
Where in the world can a conceited household be with no
clues

Then comes a man with pure heart from an excellent city
Has a remedy to faithfully adhere to likeable friends forever
To gain stature in life must have awards always coming your
way
Do not need the madam's friends being dull, need ones more
witty
Being greatly disturbed for their sake out of touch with the
world
Have both word and deed pleasant, without vengeance of
sorts
As for some accuser nothing was wrong, she's not wanting it
that way
Here is a man that meets his obligations even now that he's old

Did accomplish my well off place in life where is yours
On my journey shared a common heart with whom I could
Comes some chosen thoughts of dignity, all with goodwill
Tried to fulfill good friendship, with nothing from her doors
You cannot please a sycophancy madam nasty hosts domain
Best to observe the day she put blemish for a families loving role
Must create things that are nice to the world it's part of Joy
Be bonded by faith a better path with hope again to regain

The joy of a household not to be intimidated it's a man's castle
As for me action speak louder than words, knowing where to go
Such partakers in wrath only have misfortune with no gain
No way of knowing why these screwballs created such a hassle
Should have understanding for a fellow man it's meant to be
Best to have a face happy to have family around for a while
How selfish people are keeping family all to themselves now
These elders to come visiting, all the growing children to see

ELUTED CHILDREN

A world that's forever full of cock and bull stories
From youth times storks brought babies to our house
So often the truth is absent while we were growing up
But if we told a lie it was off to our rooms memories
Such fables as Santa coming down the chimney night
If we stay awake he would not leave only toys here
Was a tangled web of parleys that made no sense
Being an eternal theme staged by parents was not right

Then go to search for eggs the Eater Bunny lays
As for conceptions to the rules rabbits do not lay eggs
Always pacifying a child with fairy tales back then
Must perform events to suit a child fancies everyone says
Our baby teeth came out at a certain age a sure thing
For every tooth the Tooth Fairy came much to our delight
A life that came to be was not filled with truth so long ago
Most stories came from Mother Goose the magic it did bring

From the lost coffers in time made nice childhood dreams
The grew up part made no sensible logic today
Was such a merry manner for the times we remember
Here had thoughts in a dado rocking chair it seems
As a child the rocking chair was my favourite space
See myself hurrying up the stairs Santa's on his way
A ghostly comer lit up by a Christmas tree long ago
Now only a spiritual world in my old age lonely place

LIFES PASTURES

As in a story we reach back to days of yore
Have left those pastures of lost meaning forever
Beyond these times found life precious moments of love
More so in memory like a summer sunset reborn once more
Was confound days whiled away forgotten forever
Being a man of good deeds after so many years declined
The numerable haunt so difficult through time
Did rendezvous in good faith so much to endeavor

Had that visionary hope things, take time with courage
Out of a place of darkness found answers that day
Best strive for merit the best legacy to be found
The twain of ideal moments on front most stage
Since words were invented love over takes them all
Without old time thinking have found were one belongs
Them eyes with wonder finally turned it around
My destiny of contentment was a true protocol

Shall no man put a sunder here forever
A hush left in hither place a man calls home
That common sense comes with peace of mind here
Comes diversion with loss of a love one to endeavor
Here the loneliness of quiet moments in empty rooms
Such unfond feelings of optimistic hope lies ahead
Shall ramble onward where every destiny takes me
The twist of life has been faced now with so many assumes

MY HELPMATE

With my soul mate gone no one inspires me today
In them old thoughts generally become fed up with
Spent some time circumventing plans to relax on
A poor old fool having no sceptered moments per say
At these times peace of mind was disturbed by fate
All are bruised spirit episodes with no merit now
Them wings of hope are grounded without notions in stone
From the book of life have paused with courage of late

The social lapse needs a reason for soul searching
This is not a pure serene world only gold diggers there
That lingo of exasperation brings on sighing forever
Maybe confide with theories it's the best teaching
Having a different stanza beware of guest more
Best to trump the friends idea do not be a goodly fool
My potions are genuine pledged from faith always
Could be a villain that comes walking through your door

In the evening hush here ticking of clocks there
All thoughts are heaped up for some new adventure
Them dreamt abysses of magic unfound at morn
The logic part is important gets on with reality here
To be told lend an ear only some speeches mean well
Comes envious one's that imagine their future dreams
Here's where a guardian angel comes in handy some day
Are those fondling with your tolerance any one can tell

ONE'S HEAVY HEART

Those visions of remembrance passed on here
For every milestone there's memories within
Many recollections come to mind in this room
Our wayward times of wishes where so dear
One's image ponders in my everyday thought
Often times want yesterday to repeat itself
There's those unfinished wishes were left behind
To build up great hopes suddenly sadness is brought

Another day of growing old brought by the dawn
Them built up hopes that can take one day to fall
Have them leisure hours now always drift to yesterday
One year very much alive then the next year gone
My concerned esteem, now only vivid hope here
A reason for intent is hard to cope with each day
Did count my blessing having so many friends around
Need patterns of goodwill with our beliefs sincere

Will always have memories captivated in my mind
Each daily effort of choice to foresee a coming day
For a whole life time my best graces were foremost
All my thoughts remember spent paths, the loving kind
Our life is a moving platform to step onward then cease
We had understanding a true body of hope with care
Those sad days tears did fall, but managed to rise above
With self courage trials have put myself now at ease

SUMMER GLADES

About joyful moments it's connected to blue summer skies
Them evoked commotions they contribute to nice warm days
The figurative language of shorts or bikinis on display
A storm is about to brew again every time a seagull cries
Today a sun awaiting inside a stormy afternoon to drench earth
This rain lays heavy on nature for some time, finally the sun
Seems those times of natures eternal purpose of change
Suddenly a beautiful sound of birds chirping with new birth

This is how it happened in them old days that's gone by
Comes lurid details of life's work being destroyed
The world today one has more minuses then it has plus
In todays world one never knows what comes from the sky
Every year has an event situation of loss of loved ones
Them conditions of life are unstable in these times
We all struggle for our dreams enclosed with love
There those heart filled times then comes them sad emotions

All those joy times to woe circumstances out there
Out of them haunted chasms of life the future calls
Comes so much aversion to contend with in growing old
From young now to old being like fruit tree's demanded to bear
Them children now having children in a world not so good
Such an all new pattern in life not much grace to it all
Again sunrise inhabitants on just one beautiful day
The awe justifies the means would change it if I could

SUNDOWN BRING THE DAWN

The dawns of a lifetime paces our day
Our thoughts with memories do come about
We would all like to be righteous but there's sin
What concerns a life is done in a very special way
Being asleep the dawn comes for us to wake
For happiness it will not follow you every single moment
You cannot sleep all day in order not to face regret
At night we pray then in the morning for our name sake

A cast of weeks you play many roles of discontent
Where in this world does anyone get off doing wrong
Here under the sun comes a stranger not to trust I recall
Be good to everyone as if you were a friend being sent
The saying goes that a stranger is a friend you never met
Seems the robins are crying for rain is their big wish
Was sparrows in the cedars twittered from early morn
When we have a beautiful summer day not wanting the sun to
set

Have gone past bird songs of day waiting for hooters of night
Where owls stay during the day time Lord only knows
These night hawks search hills or meadows where food is found
Had still been able to hear goose honks, the sun is sunk from
sight
A yonder orange moon ascends southeast of the town
Soon comes another dream in a different land of nod
Will be off to bed soon again as we wait for the dawn
All the street lights are on now everyone's blinds are down

THE CRIK

One's life is like raking leaves back the wind blows
Here we were in yonker days the creek we called "crik"
There yonder it lies where all the bull frogs are
On pass our place then Lord only knows where it goes
So many tales to tell beside this little crik place
A fishing day by the bridge Bill cast caught Tom's mouth
Was a lot of episodes being curtailed each day
The hills by the crik was us youngsters playing space

The crik even fed water into a pond for swimming
A place where friends join us on a hot summer afternoon
This pasture was our playground for many a thing
We made a cross board with an old rim called rimming
With the cross board we ran pushing the rim ahead
An old tire was a toy also rolling it down these hills
The old tubes from these tires with air floated on the pond
Was four guys in a row down the hill over the crik we sped

Heaped up these great moments with lots of able fun
A child searching for adventures flew kites off the hills
Here was a place where we had lots of potions at the crik
In these times so much reality with friends had begun
Our lives is where freedom leans that our future needs
Let us always walk together as peaceful friend in a world
In mind can still hear them cheerful hello's of back then
Even today my pleasant heart moments still proceeds

BOYFRIEND DAYS

Even though we were married twenty one year
My wife Jeanette told everyone he is my boyfriend
They would ask why do you wear two wedding rings
It's just to show that we are permanently sincere
Then again George married me twice to prove it
Once Protestant the next time Catholic taking vows
Since the occurrences nothing would divide us two
Every song of love fitted into our lives I do admit

The sentiment of exception with tendencies here
In our outlines of good dreams greatness never ends
She was my keepsake to be in my whole life forever
Where ever we went everyday a couple near and dear
Strong hope lingers where reality dwells no other
Sunday before eight off to church a true fact then
A love is precious with potions of great joy days
That happy couple with a mind set of faith in one another

Have told her this man will not fail you in any way
Here is my gentle voice questing a heart full of joy
A magic touch for everyday at it's very best it seems
At night as well as morning we both had time to pray
The gentle door seem always ajar welcoming friends in
Such a lady would drench the earth with prayers daily
She was ready to parley the day before the birds sang
Every morning right at six when her morn would begin

OUR BEING PART

Was such an empty morn without a love one there
Only her idleness in that chair of unforgotten memories
An old man's heart burdened by the loss pondering forever
That unknown peril in life of how long we will be here
On them highways of the world we have traveled together
Every Sunday her urgent moments of off to church
Had little time to mark that place now lost in time
She was my rock for all times of logic, being no other

Having twilight shadows now ever surrounding me
Here in the living room smiling pictures of memories
A room of much silence to contend with drying tears
Such a sad face in dreams of lost hope shall always be
Many emotional days will come when alone here
So mighty was the future now sadly it is all gone
Here I am aging alone in time no more goodness to see
So much compassion created, our world did disappear

In our little corner of the world worked hard to survive
To be known life has it's forever changing episodes
We must except things reality has placed on us
Them wonderful moments of heart filled times no longer alive
Will always have friends to help bear the grief of it all
We planted a good life as we watched it grow together
In that time of a million plans now suddenly has stalled
As for the end someone has to reap sorrow I recall

SUGAR BEET HARVEST

Each part of life has legends we cannot get around
In life's challenge there's a whole lot of things to face
Our abilities were overwhelmed sometimes, farming
Most of our destinies are some what thither was found
Was so much muddle in our daily task caused a yawn
Sometimes my father would dish out unhallowed words
To unnerve my thoughts looked for some place to ponder
As a boy them old hard times are not forgotten but it's gone

One day other father decided to go cash cropping
When he found the Dutch people made enough money for a
farm
They grew twenty acres of sugar beets to sell them
Our father thought we could do this for profiting
These nations were put into play early one Saturday
The planting seem to take forever that May morn
Such a father with son's errands a back breaking chore
With a field of growing sugar beets there's no time for play

Still recollect the day these plants started to grow
Had hoed the small plants for a while it looked great
Our father's insights had hope for a little while
Then the weeds came up also row upon each row
Every weed was higher than the beet at the end of May
We sickled the weeds each time they grew tall to rid them
Was no money to buy a farm here where reality dwells
The crop was a failure no profit on that harvest day

SLUGGER McDOWELL

The bully of the school yard he was eight years old
A boy of six was me when Slugger called my bluff
He could boss everyone else but he tried me for size
An Irish fellow like me was small but knock him cold
With coons eyes he got up off of the ground to walk away
You had better make peace with George or consequences
That dude of the times in nineteen forty eight made peace
A vain man's heart gaunt, getting unraveled by woe that day

When someone challenged me gave them a funny face
Came the end to that impious bully of them old times
Had to put the schoolyard in order forever it seemed
Best not to fool with someone from the Irish race
A big peaceful villain rarely crossed my path each day
Such a mindset for those olden days to now relive
Everyone looked up to me as their protector of the time
An overgrown coward lost for words with nothing to say

The scenario's of growing up was a challenge to do
So many times look back on life enhancing my thoughts
Nobody hurts my brothers or sister watch out for me
You will be suffering todays grace mostly black and blue
Treat all moments of goodwill with courage always
That old time destiny had it's adventures of sorts
Even Andy Devine was afraid to come out of his house
Every time he did there was a dispute in those days

GENERAL TWADDLE

In those days after lunch the mother read tealeaves
Have no idea where these words of fortune came from
With all those pitiful follies optimism brought hope
Had to invent good moments for that sadness it relieves
Better to be like peace trees then unravel woe
Outside our circles of love there's always villains here
Let's assume magic for children where there is no bad
A visionary with it gentle winding path with where it's nice to go

Oft times in the muddle of daily tasks imagination comes
Spend times searching my memento shelves for long ago
My thoughts pictured them bicycle days on a gravel road
Them brothers and sisters altogether a family of chums
A lunch pail slung on the handle bars bound for home
Had rendered a moment at school of going into class
That loud belfry bell sounding for miles away back then
It tells us if you are not at school hurry it's class time

Was a spectant shiver of scratching nails on slate
While brushing the blackboard it's bound to happen
A pointer for the blackboard was a attention tool
One must pay respect to the teachers wishes or get fate
Today have inspired my conscience for old times sake
Was the crank telephone left in a shadowy old house
Them comrades of old did party line for the last time
Comes them moments to be edified for memories intake

LIFE'S CINCHES

There is no doubt dignity will recognize the good people
Must live in a manner worthy to attain the best returns
Our moral courage will eventually get us through life
It's hard to reform the world just look after your castle
Whatever you choose do not make the same mistake twice
Keep a clear conscience endure the signs of the times
That concern which surpasses all understanding is deception
An earnest endeavor of daily conduct is try to be nice

Those great many uncertainties of the world cannot be fixed
There is unfair considerations for elder people from their kin
No one comes to comfort them in sadness or cheer for the
loneliness
Here among the worldly advices never believe what is said
So many instigators trying to say take equity out today
We cannot benefit from this participation it's a money grab
Most people taken advantage of their humble heart then
The good sense part is nurture family unity, the best way

When old leave some intended things until tomorrow
Best reject whatever is contrary it will amount to nothing
In as much we would like to find joy concerning others
With patience we hope for the best having no sorrow
Some people are important not confessing every concern
Would like to give you every thought, word and deed of the
day
If some has justified the purpose then reveal the reason
Everyone presses forward there is many more things to learn

We all want the most confident hope for life's guidance
Will have to pursue reality to get a genuine answer
The mentioned portions of circumstances was some charity
Each ancestor always poor in the long ago remembrance
When you do not owe anything, money seekers come around
Many days become acquainted with unending woes
Without consideration was a transgressor no manners at all
My loving wife was just put under that cold cold ground

THE HUGGER MUGGER SON'S

By whose will can we restore everything to normal again
These children were proud of their conceit with a huffish mom
Whatever is true, whatever is honourable is a good choice
Become impatient speaking to miserable peoples woe to
sustain
There was no one besides me with a sincere heart on that day
My conscience dreads liars full of conceit, would prefer others
A father has pondered untrue words with no answers
Never any help for reprieve with their low down ways

Will forever hold that fervent of hope while time passes
What can you expect with a Ma counselor alienating siblings
With a concerned mind am reaching out for an understanding
Have hope for those who sit in dark sad type of places
The purpose of the happenings makes no sense anymore
In earlier life needed more hearts of believers in me
Which things are more important to seek judgment or kindness
Tried guidance to conquer despair in their lost world before

Once hypocrites are found disregard them someone said
Amid the uncertainties of life must urge justified guidance
Many convincing proofs does not arouse peoples attention
Some have forgotten how to be happy, being indeed dread
Seems some follow the paths of unexplained aversion
When there is understanding, comes hope beyond all telling
One does not know what it's like to be betrayed in life
How do we encourage down hearted people in a sincere
illusion

When can some one start making them a new worthy life
As for my sake that growing up generation has been blemished
My son was like an urchin unable to face his company
They totally disgraced us visiting them me and my wife
Give me strength for a difficult task of disoriented people
A mother that's benevolent will get what's coming to her
On only one's accord cannot bring any change need unity
Have given friendship my best shot but now I feel unable

ONCE IN A BLUE MOON

There is those shadow wisps of imagination in mind
Once in a long while intertwined interest you must hear
With each portion of life we deal with comes common destiny
Have come to use the word possible it's commitment is more
kind
Sometimes you cannot wait to tell good news by telephone
Have wonderful people for encouragement are when down
hearted
So long the distance of tomorrow twenty four hours sun to sun
Without my mate comes sighs to deep for words in nights alone

Each one's life is a parable that's on a journey of good faith
Must chose a good birthday message for a happy day
Working for Home Depot Sunday is a day of rest sometimes
Best be conformed to a good image justify it in part for us both
Sometimes needs more than faith and hope it's a catch twenty
two
I am convinced the house needs cleaning, here is an old
person
One of those mornings at daybreak will shake out them mats
If you change your mind about going to the beach tell them
it's you

Have always loved hourglasses there is no daylight saving time
Whatever is honourable give it your best shot to be worthy
First and foremost intending to finish yesterdays job before noon
No ambition to wind up the eight day clock to let it chime
On days off did relive the remembrance staring at the wall
Did convince myself have to conduct life in the same fashion
Keep telling myself I am doing good keeps my moral up now
My interpretation is two more years of work did recall

Just wish this man had a hidden mystery like my siblings do
The wayward with all it's woes does bewilder this man
Here is a troubled heart that ponders until sleep comes
If they have a change of heart let me know before life is
through
Above all should once in a blue moon try making family peace
It's their circumstances there is nothing I can do to help them
Forever hearing common misconceptions with all of its pitfalls
My wish is that they would be nice enough to come to my
place

OFFENSIVE FOLLIES

Our bonding of unity this is a source of upstanding people
Along the paths of time someone killed friendship to be
It's truly not right to cohabit with a man an unlegal wife
There is no mysteries to commonsense it for sure is truthful
So fulfilled is the alienation of siblings, assuming my fate
The awe filled memory of being cast down with disorderly
affections
It's a mystery how can human morality receive any honour
Only good thoughts to ponder in my heart knowing it's to late

Did approach siblings with pure of heart to be left in disgust
When people become galoots you cannot inspire them at all
Among deviant host compassion reeks with images of rudeness
Her blemished insight is a citified bound monger of must
With my words of truth have a more understanding what is right
Knowing vengeance reaps sorrow leaving a bad reminder
behind
Her pursuing of follies, craving deeds to hinder life's harmony
Having integrity to be a good man is a manner of good insight

On my journey of goodwill perseverance gets me on through
By living in a right manner there is nothing to regret in the end
An attentive father according to others had did nothing wrong
Have devoutly gathered on this day loving thoughts for all of
you
The goodness will shine through for this man's deeds forever
Seems someone did stop the messenger according to the kin
Almost a whole generation of mystery caught in a time squelch
To accomplish a plan of dogma just one family member to
sever

When the mere darkness has dawned it will awaken the facts
With those feelings to harm have accomplished forever bad vibes
Such authority was continuous from an oppressors voice
In growing up time respect was converted to being greedy acts
It only takes one bad host to make a difference today
With alienation it's bound a family to their selfish nature
So much anguish in former times children were acceptive then
The father none existent part, she managed it to be this way

LIFE'S PRECIOUS MOMENTS

To strive for the possible to always find a way
For whole hours have stood thinking about moments
The absence is not forgotten this fate lingers on
Hope to find happiness in my wanderings some day
Still remember her weeping asking God to let her live
There is so much care for a time that's gone tomorrow
Them many a picture contain all those wonderful times
All those good deeds with each merit it had to give

To purpose an interpretation of hope for better days
While onward comes to mind loves journey never ends
Shall stand alone just waiting for renewed times
There's always a remedy to life in many ways
A lot of months have reaped sorrow even in dreams
Much bitterness came during the silence of night
Here there is no peace to fill my heart as before
We cannot find life's other part for our world it seems

So wondrous having friends to raise one's spirits once more
Need help for getting through the broken heart tearful eyes
Here forever things hurry onward never to surrender
Having nothing else to sooth the spirit as in times before
Walking the floor each night counting footsteps that's how it
goes
A man can only live by things that are real with faith
All them heart captured thoughts with only sad feelings
Them nights of lonely moments has so many woes

HAVE REAPED SORROW

When explained my loss brings on tears
The memory of an old man responds again with sadness
This bond holds on to me with all of it's might each day
Them together adventures for all of them twenty one years
Was no magic to raise life's spirit as it happened before
For each day it had a meaning during those together times
Here was like a man awakening from a bad dream now
A single venture has no meaning only loneliness galore

Forever will despise them moments having played an awful part
They shall get their bitters on another far yonder place
Had come to make friends as relatives being smite on that day
Not so long or rough is life when you got the best of kin from the start
The heartless became my invisible people vanished from my sight
Will always come to see a pleasant day at wanderings of good faith
Shall only parley through welcome door steps in time
That heart's right hand of friendship will be alright

Something during the mist of morning turned my thoughts to yesterday
Had been so great to look forward to us chatting walking along
Also the splendor of a couple watching a beautiful sunset
To have become lost forever on that alone farewell day
Would like to have heard a loud church bell break the silence
Must remember the past while expecting our utmost future
In memory of loving heart that's reassured more than words
With proudness I shall say a nice prayer in her remembrance

FOREVER NOSTALGIA

At age five lived in the village of Denfield North of London
Looked favorably to going to the store for some jawbreakers
In those days there was no bubble gum, just minted gum sticks
My brother Bill was going to school then he was the oldest son
We always had pigs as well as cows housed in a hip roof barn
Besides that we had two horses, one Carlyol the other
Piccadilly
Piccadilly was a chestnut coloured horse, precious to the family
The horse Piccadilly was a real pet for all us children back then

Our pet pulled the cutter through the snow during winter
We had to travel by sleigh from Denfield to London for supplies
The village store man Russel Bowman always had bread for us
This boy like going there because he liked his daughter
In spite of it all with hardships the merchants were very nice
Sam Freeburn the post office man threw big pennies for us to
find
Them pennies we found saved them up in wooden match
boxes
Still remember the church bell ringing, during the day rang
twice

Somehow did remember our reverend, he wore a round top
hat
His name was Timothy to my recollection, a very nice man
All willing hands had to work to survive back in those days
The drive to church in the back seat is where my mother sat
The church had men's and women's outside privies with
wooden seats
So many colourful windows all around the whole church area
Still remember special books for children in this lower place
In the church basement is a place where everyone meets

At last summer the maple tree branch is ready for chin-up
Them gravel roads with dust clouds blowing across fields
Did not mind going to the store for crackle nuts with rings inside
Also bought Dreft for the washings a once a month trip
Was an old iron cook stove with reservoirs to heat wash water
An outside hand pump was where all the water came from
Each Saturday was wash day many gallows of water hauled
Note the only reason Bill went to church is to see someone's
daughter

CLIPPITY CLOPPING

Those days will always remember Piccadilly our horse
When we moved from Denfield to Yarmouth Centre she came
Anytime someone went to the barn she wanted attention first
We would have to bring a carrot for her it's a must of course
She was a loveable horse, she was by the fence after school
During growing up years was so much enjoyment from her
The family realized Piccadilly was getting old, soon to be gone
After supper we had to do our homework the golden rule

One morning hear the horse crying out from barn stall
Our faithful friend was down trying to get back up again
When Dad came home he said we cannot leave her in this
pain
The bone man was the only person around that we could call
Us children cried almost the whole day our friend was gone
About a year later our family moved to a place called Sparta
Here the rent was only fifteen dollars a month, good deal
All of us were still grieving no cutter rides ever from now on

The only person that had horses was Jack Somerville now
It was a team of black horses rambunctious as hell
These horses were difficult to keep in the pasture field
No matter the height of the fence they escaped anyhow
Seems every time this team came to our place to be greeted
We would have an apple for them when they had arrived
Mr. Somersville came for them with a whip making them
nervous
My father said it was such a cruel way animals were treated

Some days me and my brother Bill went to Heather Fishes'
place
She gave us riding lessons on her horse western style
We were told if anybody fell off to get right back on again
Max Fish took us boys for a waffle day at his mom's was the
case
Every other summer Saturday we went to his mother's home
This man was an early morning whistler, heard him from school
Us two brothers where his hired men when Max needed
someone
This person had a German Sheppard dog that always had to
come

ONCE WAS CHADA

Here on 1166 Chada Avenue loneliness could not survive
Seen it all, done it all with commonsense remember it all
The future is not an option it's out there waiting for me
By my earnest endeavor will be a daily conduct to derive
A problem well stated is a problem every single day solved
If at first you don't succeed redefine some more success
The best vision is insight, then make a grand first step
Being a member of good standing forever being loved

Here on Chada came a relative not having a spark of decency
A clear conscience of this makes a good reason for bad
memory
Those being compulsive leads to an unpleasant situation
To wish to share one's divinity with personal nice generosity
Let's bring our peace into the hearts of all with no despair
Method in my madness is in the heat of every moment
Every thought word and deed of my life has truthful honour
Must sell the place get on down the road to somewhere

Sometimes beneath enthusiastic days comes unfaithful one's
Those who love only money lose it eventually to the world
As for family along with friends want unending happiness
From the depths of my heart hope to obtain joy of friends
In a special way triumph all things, they are precious now
Be ready to serve others as you would have them serve you
There is always a message to listen to with labour of love
For those who are contrary they have no clue anyhow

Here is a man always determined to make things better
Seems for ever kindred mistreating family circumstances
All true seekers are welcome it's a matter for new friends
Must foreshadow benevolence best lose it for ever
Some will one day pose the truth to merit better understanding
Like a Samaritan shall accomplish that which I purpose
The wayward home is waiting to start my life a new
When all hope prevails will be settled there some morning

BEST OF BOTH WORLDS

While we need to manifest best thoughts to create a plan
One must govern all things in harmony with words and action
There is greed that estranges us from one another
The rich reward favours integrity with perseverance when we
can
Let's be heirs to the happy ever place, add it to our fame
Our home place foundation is a man's castle of great dignity
Best have realities of adoration rejoice in one's presence
Great patrons reaffirm their passion always leaving out shame

Where will humankind find guidance when all other has failed
Having patience of waiting for another day something else is
done
Must present in our midst a good image to unite each day
For love in life you have a valentine that should be mailed
Kindness surpasses all understanding on our life's journey
To run the race of our present life confirm it in good faith
The partiality part has no claim to fame, delighted by none
There was a hindering part brought about by someone's
jealousy

Best to grant encouragement for harmony then rejoice after
Under one roof can talk about memories of the long lost past
Was those dedicated with complete sincerity for a life time
A remedy found in mortality itself should be presented forever
Using forgiveness alone compassion can always unite us
Are some saddened by the certainty they going to die
With a sincere heart humbly commend condolences given
Best be more eagerly intent to change these with no fuss

The sources for life is fashioned with friendship to care
All those holdings to the truth make better being s in the world
Through gifts of merit for life is the respectful thing
Have mutual respect it's part of decency that we share
An acceptable fact that through participation we gain
Our honour must always walk with us on journeys of life
The dissension and discord sometimes we will over come
As for both worlds try to accomplish what you plan

ONLY THE TICK TOCK

From the rising sun to it's setting we had one another
There was our hope to enjoy the fullness of everyday
She had many friends to call from this world out there
To always accompany her, we done everything together
Here tick tock a member reminder she is gone forever
So many days filled with wonder, pondering away as before
Nothing to fulfill such friendships we had shared unending
As the clock ticks away, so many memories in the night hour

While living honourably can undertake good judgment always
As for a brood of vipers they just mope in the town of node
Am not a mute person to know if good people do sing with joy
There is abiding folks that have never ceasing happy ways
During the signs of the times them good images to remember
Here is a man without instrument words it's from the heart
Shall always confide in others that have ever lasting faith
We all derived from pilgrims to become a world member

On cloudy days she would say sun come out with two eyes out
To care with trust, looking forward to longevity was our plan
Having love with no end to be bestowed on good people
forever
With inspired words, unity friends create a good family no
doubt
Must have perseverance for days ahead to remain focused
In days coming wish to drive away from old darkness of vice
Along new paths in time will have to search out my destinies
Here in the midst of things a reminder the good times have
ended

There is no one anymore to walk with me on life's journey
Alone with only thoughts seeking things lost in time again
Those tearing eyes never cease through her loss most days
Having a fatherly faith, sustaining good merits every day
Need dedication for the life to come, which to remedy things
As a devoted person am a believer, a worker striver makes it
The people to fulfill friendship should have no ending
How wonderful life would be, we all need the joy it brings

OUR FAMILY BAMBOOZLER

A member that had duped his aunt out of lots of money
The aunt ask me for guidance for this kind of affair
She had ask him to pay back the money in so many words
Such a lowly thing to do was promise then renege is so phony
One must merit what they promise, always live with the truth
Being the author of the story seek to sanctify what's best
There is no honour among thieves because of their immortal
ways
In regards to the truth have a message that's full of wrath

All circumstances show no determination to pay the piper
It's amazing that the request is not being taken care of
Will have to regard some people of having malice no intent
Was for sure not a sharer of family affairs but a taker
Every time this man speaks to me he is benevolent as can be
These people on his wife's side have a deceitful nature always
Somebody who is not trustworthy, concerns his kin to why
Our lawyer has subdued leans on assets we will get to see

Have chosen this to get the aunt's money back on a court day
For not paying back the money owed to his mom, he is off the
will
If some needs charity there is places to go for that
Must live your life in a manner that's worthy to the world
someway
What is expected their conscience dreads is do a lawful thing
Cannot understand why they are miserable they owe us the
money
My portion is directed towards imitators alienating others
According to his age ability he could work but he does nothing

The consideration for an old person is not there only bad vibes
These transgressors that take people, they must be stopped
An agreement is like an oath to faithfully do the right thing
How can anyone live like this based on nothing else but fibs
That entrusting message was sent, evidently is a refusing part
Have summed up the word confirming these kind of people
Here was a generous lady the lender, this belongs to her
My father taught me if someone's word is no good, it's bad start

BOUND FOR CHANGE

Was a vile past that long ago had no real meaning
Being completely exasperated that wasting of time
To wish for buttons or whistles to control motives
That life of sordid characters of manure cleaning
Here was me ready to create better ideas always
Went on striving more seriously ready for a change
Looking forward to better ways to make a living
A feeling that pestered my thoughts for old days

Them bad fancies from chasms of yesterday now gone
So many years spent regretting what went on each day
Where there's no love there's no use just morbid
Really wanted change for each day that did dawn
All of my life wanting to be on Easy Street for say
Wanting to make a happy endorsement to my life
That past forever with many sighs in need of relief
One's life should have some comfort with thanks or pay

The personal meaning held in tether for many a year
Not even a hint of respect only impressions of woe
Forever censored my intentions to the very utmost
Did say farewell to it all went back to school for a career
Onward hued by reluctance found my life's place
Had been summoned from a shadow past forever
All the wealth standing in immortal bloom was there
Was now an heir of that so long a intentional race

SOUND OF WOLVES

In Mudcat Lane being a wilderness in them old days
From this place during darkness wolves howl there
These animals litter history from pioneer times
Here a haven setting of hills with streams along the ways
Most nights they parley with other wolves from afar
A foray of deer and rabbit skeletons everywhere
When the moon comes up spine chilling howls unfold
Then hill top chanting comes beyond the swampy mar

The wolves retreat has scary haunt every night
They walk in tree shadows not easily seen
Their obscure night lets them hunt without showing
Them general inspirations are tuned to a night time sight
Each must perform their skills surround for the kill
In these dismal suburbs danger lurks everywhere
A lonely desolate place with an ungraded gravel road
Along this perpetual swamp road is many a hill

While going hitherward there's lot of mosquito there
Best you wear heavy clothes in such a haven
Where so ever a day finds me it would not be here
Once was enough to last me a life time, was hard to bear
But nostalgia hinted my inward thoughts once more
Four lone wolves crossed in front of me checking me out
Had personal reasons to blast off my shotgun
In a hurry with fright the disappearing of all four

GRAVELY DOUBT

Another day to venture forth hoping for the best
The morals of right or wrong are so perplexed
Once in a while hold a solemn chant to clear my wits
Sometimes we crave decency to be different from the rest
Are we old fools from an abstract school of the past
Ipod phones are pathetic with people always looking down
Such a feeble fancy of texting a real whim of sorts
Seems like a plot for humanity how many years will this last

Leaves that old days features with a forever frown
Life today seems to be an urge of some psychics prediction
Have counted each individual blessing with a lot of doubt
Children for this day of age could be born always looking down
From the fud world found ipod people are quaint to be around
While in a room the format rules nobody talks always texting
Who's who in a world of solemn chant no converse at all
No one communicates verbally people sitting with no sound

At times worldly life is voiding talk only sending words
Another days closure without conversing the youth
So misfortunate whence this new era raised it's head
Even each unit the ringing phone has dismal music chords
By times am in a state discontent with no sign of relief
The abide part we used so long ago when morals came to be
Where does one get positive thinking with no gizmo in the way
All this ballyhoo will come to an end someday is my belief

DUBIOUS LAUREATE

Must one take a new direction with a better out look
Have always had a mark of honourable distinction
Through many years a lying woman changed all that
New ideas drift into one's mind to enhance a good book
To solemnly swear it's like a revolving door it will hit her one day
There is many strange episodes in relation to her residence
The Osh side Brennan family are those peculiar ones
Here is a brooding kind of strange people everything they
portray

Has been like trying to haul down a forever stormy day
This brooding puts shame in my heart with regret
All of a lifetime patience of ours was fully stretched
Meet with dissatisfaction in trying with good things to say
Them times of the child illusion now is impossible to change
Our name Brennan is an upstanding name demerited by them
With future times try to reveal compassion some how
A brain washing strategy was plotted for this derange

In the bible it says do unto others as you would have them do
to you
It's better to give then receive to make us proud
Let history accelerate to a better level for the future
Better to turn to another page be willing to start anew
The dubious laureate, evade these ways from now on
One good though will follow the road of hope tomorrow
Wish there was many ways to hold friendship together
For that appalling part of life for families just be gone

TOTTLED ONWARD

All that wisdom racked up from years gone by
Was endowed with thoughts while tottling onward
With years passed have become crouched and haggard
More weak but stay noble, although with pain I sigh
To go strolling in daylight or dark whatever suits me the best
Many early morn landscapes have trudged along with me
Such old working day missions a purpose obliged to
Some days needless adventure, it was better to rest

How much of time has past recalled from long ago
Seems my old school mates are still in the shadows that pass
Being here standing gazing out a gloomy doorway
That fiery spirit of yesterday has lost it's embers glow
Sometimes enshrined in a woeful moment that befalls us all
There was girls that played hyde and go seek until the bell rang
Here's where we were at a one room school playing anti I over
Wishing old friends had not past on they could come to call

All my old people gone, left watching squirrels running about
Watched a sunset burning the horizon sinking low
The darkness has left me in the land of shadows
A summer soon passing winter weather now will enroute
Them frail footsteps that throttle along holding me
During the brunt of those hard work days has played it's toll
Have many a thought of these days before going off to bed
Having mercy gets a senior through the day with more to see

OUR VIEW MASTER

Now the Viewmaster is claimed as a vintage one
We owned a model C in nineteen fifty two in Sparta
Ours had the reel where a side button moved it around
The best way to view the pictures by a window with sun
When the first Viewmaster was made it was not a toy
In the reel was Mickey and Minnie mouse characters
The things changed this was claimed a children thing
Received a Viewmaster for Christmas as a very young boy

Thanks to William Gruber every child had one of these
Did not seem that long ago, makes me feel old, this a vintage
Walt Disney characters were the main features then
Was films with characters that aimed for to please
When we moved from Sparta, Ontario to Plainfield it was gone
Once in a while at garage sales Viewmaster were seen
The only colour they came in was red plastic long ago
In the nineteen eighties imaging made them a brown brawn

Such a long recollections older children had showed us them
Back as far as nineteen thirty nine were at a world fair
Some second hand Viewmasters were dated for then
There were other copy cats doing the sepia tones in black film
The Viewmaster stuff other companies caught on later
A patent back in my childhood days meant something not now
No one knows what's vintage or something that looks like it
From long ago until now there comes an antique imitator

COVERT IN THE PINES

During the sixties had built a house in a Plainfield place
The South side of my home was bordered by a forest
A trout stream babbled along just past a cedar fence
Once in a while a timber wolf in the evening showed his face
There was several cottontail rabbits came up my lane
At night howling wolves along with barking foxes were heard
Here was a wilderness land for wayward hunters to come
All summer long mallard ducks on the river did remain

On Saturday morning I would head down Mudcat Lane
A few cottontail rabbits shuffled across the gravel road
Then muskrats were plunging into the creek there
By the cattail ditches there was many a waddling crane
Into the pines to look for partridge I would go
Here they were in these covert pines hard to see
Better to lay belly down under the pines to see them
Each time one partridge was shot it was put in my stow

Under the covert of the pines prowls many unknown
There was also a fox hunting game birds at the time
When he seen me with the gun he left here at once
The sound of the gunshot a great many partridge had flown
Also hitherward two raccoons rambled quickly along
Unnerved my gun being pointed past my devotional feet
Here a family of deer stayed behind the male protector
A buck deer came to greet me as if I did not really belong

SELF JUDGEMENT CHALLENGES

When love has no trust to explore you must recline
Those ones that judge men there's too many characters
Have been through the realms of kinfolk some rude
If my true compassions has a bad effect that's fine
Those regrets are inscribed for a long ago place
If this man were to write history it's not so divine
There was the excess dimmed by the effect always
An all life wish to change opportunities in my space

A rueful mystery whence made a claim for peace
Long after still comes that whisper of remembrance
Once again have been irked by kin with no effect
Will always be loyal to good friends others will cease
One thing for sure there is no need to ponder over disgrace
Well it's like men to boys, men are all grown up people
Life is like a bump in the road once you get over it, it's smooth
Nonsense rings true when you said do not come to my place

The old fashion saying try my way or there's the highway
There's a big sun shining out here it's for both of us
You can be an auger all day long that's not including me
Kiss my ass I'm Irish, can sing this song everyday
Shall never have personified means ever to the jerk again
Nothing can sway my tolerance of treat me bad as before
I'm not really a bad guy there's just some bad people out there
Any matter at hand my goodness of heart will reign

THAT MISSING ROSE IS FOR LONELINESS

That missing rose is for loneliness now
Have put an angel there to take it's place
So many loving thoughts come each lonely day
Those happy moments I shall remember somehow
My Jeanette is gone never to be forgotten
Must say so sorry for my promise not kept
It's not the way I really wanted it to be
Sometimes there is people so mean and rotten

Want you to forgive me from your place above
Have but one companion only in dreams at night
A familiar voice that calls George for a while
This man is still looking for hearts full of love
So many things for this old life hard to face
Then there's tomorrow that night voice gone away
Only in the night she is with me one more time
There is so much sadness along with that disgrace

The angel is not like a rose that dies and fades away
Wish life was like the sun had never left this earth
But beyond here there's that forsaken lost place
That angel that seeking you is around each day
Each night have my pillow to dream on again
Most people are self righteous no one else really counts
Just do what they want pushing people out of their way
Life can have sunshine then sometimes it will rain